HTML CD

An Internet Publishing Toolkit

For Windows®

VIVIAN NEOU

•

MIMI RECKER

Prentice Hall PTR

Upper Saddle River, New Jersey 07458

Library of Congress Cataloging-in-Publication Data

Neou, Vivian.

  HTML CD : an Internet publishing toolkit / Vivian Neou, Mimi Recker

    p. cm.

  "Windows version."

  Includes index.

  ISBN 0-13-232331-1

  1. Hypertext systems.   2. HTML (Document markup language).

I. Recker, Mimi.   II. Title.

QA76.76.H94N46 1996   95-32304

005.75—dc20   CIP

Editorial/Production Supervision: Lisa Iarkowski
Page Composition: Lisa Iarkowski and Ann Sullivan
Interior Design: Gail Cocker-Bogusz
Acquisitions Editor: Mary Franz
Manufacturing Manager: Alexis R. Heydt
Cover Design: Energy Energy Design

 © 1996 Prentice Hall PTR
Prentice-Hall, Inc.
A Simon & Schuster Company
Upper Saddle River, NJ 07458

Microsoft® Internet Assistant for Word for Windows®,
Copyright Microsoft Corporation, 1995. All rights reserved.

The publisher offers discounts on this book when ordered in bulk quantities.
For more information, contact:

  Corporate Sales Department
  PTR Prentice Hall
  One Lake Street
  Upper Saddle River, NJ 07458
  Phone: 800-382-3419
  FAX: 201-236-7141
  e-mail: corpsales@prenhall.com

Printed in the United States of America

10 9 8 7 6 5 4 3 2 1

ISBN 0-13-232331-1

Prentice-Hall International (UK) Limited, London
Prentice-Hall of Australia Pty. Limited, Sydney
Prentice-Hall of Canada, Inc., Toronto
Prentice-Hall Hispanoamericana S.A., Mexico
Prentice-Hall of India Private Limited, New Delhi
Prentice-Hall of Japan, Inc., Tokyo
Simon & Schuster Asia Pte. Ltd., Singapore
Editora Prentice-Hall do Brasil, Ltda., Rio de Janeiro

CONTENTS

The Future of HTML: HTML 3 and Netscape Extensions   123

Windows HTTP Server   189

ACKNOWLEDGMENTS

The authors both gratefully acknowledge the following people for granting permission to include their software with this book: Thomas Boutell (Mapedit), Mark Bracewell (PolyForm), Robert Denny (WHTTPD), Howard Harawitcz (HTML Assistant), Chris Hector (RTFTOHTM), and Leonardo Loureiro (LView Pro). We would also like to thank our readers: Christine Chase, Mark Lottor, Thomas Powell and Thomas Steihm. Their insights helped to make this book more useful and understandable. Our editor, Mary Franz, and our production supervisor, Lisa Iarkowski, kept the project on-track in spite of an unbelievably tight schedule.

Mimi Recker would like to thank Jim Pitkow for sharing his enthusiasm for and in-depth knowledge of the Web. She would also like to thank Neil and the Larsen's for their encouragement and support during the writing of this book.

Vivian would not have been able to write her portion of the book were it not for her husband, Ray Curiel, and his willingness to take care of the important things in life while she worked on this book. And of course thanks to "the important things in life," her kids, Tomas and Alejandro, for occasionally allowing her to write.

INTRODUCTION

When Thomas Jefferson first conceived of public libraries, he could not have imagined a world where people would have instant access to vast, globally distributed repositories of information. Today, the Internet is making this possibility a desktop reality. However, until recently much of the information on the Internet was difficult to locate and use. Fortunately, the World Wide Web and its browsers, such as Mosaic and Netscape, are leading the way in providing easy-to-use, seamless methods for navigating, and finding information on, the Internet.

The World Wide Web, commonly known as the Web, has made many gigabytes of digital data available to Internet users with a few mouse clicks. Data on the Web consists of documents. These documents, sometimes called Web pages, may contain text, images, video, audio, even executable programs. The Web is thus called a multimedia system. In addition, Web documents often have embedded cross-references or *links* to other Web documents. This automatic cross-linking of documents to other relevant documents is called hypertext. Because the Web links data presented in many media, it is called a hypermedia system.

For example, a document on the Web about tandem bicycles may include pictures of the author's bicycle, a recording of *A Bicycle Built for Two,* and some information about spoke tension in wheels. The author of the document may know of another document located somewhere on the Internet that has extensive information about bicycle wheels. Rather than quoting the other document or merely listing its location, the author of the tandem document makes a link to the document about wheels. Now, when reading the tandem document, the reader can click (or issue the appropriate command) on the link to view the wheel document.

Documents on the Web such as the one we just described are written in HyperText Markup Language (HTML). If you want to make your own documents available through the Web, you need to learn how to use this language. HTML conforms to the Standard Generalized Markup Language (SGML) standard, which is an international standard (ISO 8879) for defining structured document types and the markup languages used to represent those document types.

This book covers Version 2 of HTML since it is the most widely supported version at this time. HTML Version 3 is still under discussion, but some of the planned features for this version are so useful that browsers are already beginning to support them. Thus, although HTML 3 is still evolving, we have included information about those elements that are already in use. We also cover the Netscape extensions to HTML.

Who Needs HTML?

The most obvious use for HTML documents is to make information available on the Internet. The World Wide Web is the fastest growing Internet resource, and HTML is its "language." This book will provide guidance for your HTML project— whether you are writing an extensive document to advertise your company's products, or want to link some personal documents into the Web.

Even if you do not plan to publish documents on the Internet, HTML can still be useful. Documents written in HTML can be viewed on almost all computer platforms thanks to the vast number of WWW browsers available (both free and commercial versions) for almost every type of computer system. Thus, HTML is an excellent choice for authoring on-line manuals or company documents for in-house use.

What This Book Can Do for You

By the time you are done reading this book, you should be able to write sophisticated, snazzy-looking documents in HTML. You'll learn about all the basic formatting commands, as well as how to use links and forms. We'll also teach you how to add pictures and sound to your documents. We go beyond the plain mechanics of HTML document creation—we also show you how to organize and lay out your documents so that they look as good as possible.

But that's not all! We also show you how to convert existing documents into HTML. You will learn how to set up a Web server so that you can publish your HTML documents on the Web. Best of all, you will find the tools to do all of these things on the included CD—you don't need to get anything else to produce and publish HTML documents.

Conventions Used in This Book

When we refer to actions within browsers, we will say to "click" on the item. If you are not using a mouse with your browser (for example, if you are using a line-mode browser), you should use the command that is equivalent to "clicking" on an item with a mouse.

We use a couple of icons throughout the book to point out important information:

We use this *tips* icon to point out useful tips and tricks. You should pay close attention when you see this icon.

We use this *warning* icon to draw your attention to areas where you can get into trouble. Follow our advice to keep from drowning in the rapids!

In chapters where HTML elements are discussed, we close the chapters with a section called *The Good, the Bad and the Ugly.* In these sections you will find a summary of the design tips and warnings introduced in the corresponding chapter.

Contents of the CD

This book comes with a cornucopia of HTML tools. You will find everything you need to turn a Windows system into a complete HTML authoring and publishing system—even servers and connectivity tools that will enable you to publish your HTML documents on the Internet. Here's a summary of the things on the CD.

HTML Editors

- *HoTMetaL*: An HTML editor and verifier
- *HTML Assistant*: An HTML editor
- *Internet Assistant*: An HTML editor add-on for Microsoft Word

HTTP Server: WHTTP

A shareware Windows-based HTTP server. You can use this server to publish your HTML documents on the Internet. There is no cost if you use it on a personal basis, and a low registration fee if you wish to use it for commercial purposes.

NetManage's Internet Chameleon

You can use this package to connect your system to the Internet. It comes with WebSurfer, a Web browser that you can use to view your documents. You get a free 30-day evaluation period, and a $75 discount off the base price if you choose to use it beyond the evaluation period. Additional charges from service providers may apply.

HTML Toolbox

- ***LView Pro***: A shareware image-manipulation application. It can be used to convert images between different formats, get screen captures and resize images.
- ***MapEdit***: An application to create image maps for clickable images.
- ***RTFTOHTM***: A DOS application to convert RTF to HTML.
- ***PolyForm***: A shareware CGI forms-handling application that provides a central interface for writing and organizing your forms.

HTML Document Treasure Chest

One of the best ways to learn about HTML is to look at HTML documents. We've provided a "treasure chest" of HTML pages, including:

- Templates for personal home pages
- Sample business home page templates
- HTML element demonstration pages so you can see how different HTML elements look in different browsers
- Form templates (order forms and response forms)

- HTML document to download over 10 Windows Web browsers—including Mosaic, Netscape, Interlink and more
- Free icons and images

And much more!

We have incorporated real links to documents on the Internet in some of the documents. These links all worked at the time the documents were written. However, the Internet is constantly changing, and since documents often move or are deleted, we cannot guarantee that all of the links will work when you try them.

HTML CD Menu and Setup

HTML CD Setup makes it a snap to install the tools included on the CD, and our exclusive menu application provides an easy-to-use interface for accessing the tools.

What You Should Know

This book will teach you everything you need to know about HTML. Before starting this book you should already have a basic understanding of the Internet and World Wide Web. Although we will go over some basic Internet and Web applications in this book, you should get and read one of the general reference books on the Internet if you plan to do HTML publishing on the Internet.

However, you may just want to use HTML to develop in-house documentation or information manuals; for that, you should find everything you need in this book.

IN THIS CHAPTER, YOU WILL LEARN

- HOW TO INSTALL THE CONTENTS OF THE HTML CD
- HOW TO USE THE HTML CD MENU AND SETUP APPLICATIONS
- HOW TO USE THE HTML CD DOCUMENT TREASURE CHEST
- HOW TO CONNECT YOUR PC TO THE INTERNET WITH INTERNET CHAMELEON

USING THE CD

In this chapter we will explain how to install the contents of the HTML CD, and how to use the HTML CD Menu. You will also learn how to find the documents in the HTML Treasure Chest you wish to view. We will also explain how to use the trial version of Internet Chameleon to connect your PC to the Internet.

Installing the CD's Contents

The CD includes the HTML CD Menu, an interface that provides easy access to all of the HTML tools on the CD. To install it along with a number of the applications on the CD, either choose your CD-ROM drive in File Manager and click on SETUP.EXE or run SETUP.EXE from the Program Manager:

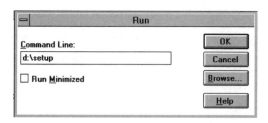

If your CD-ROM is not on drive D, be sure to replace "d:" in this example with the letter for your drive.

Setup can install LView Pro, Mapedit, RTFTOHTM, WHT-TPD, and the HTML Document Treasure Chest. After you start Setup, it will give you the option of either installing all of these applications or of choosing specific items:

If you want Setup to install everything, click on the button next to "Complete Installation." If you would prefer to have Setup only install specific applications, click on the button next to "Custom Installation." If you choose Custom Installation, you will be given another menu:

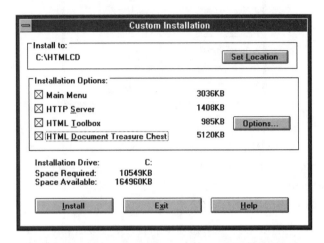

The default location used by Setup to install everything is C:\HTMLCD.

Setup provides an option to install applications in alternate locations. If you take this option and install your applications in non-standard locations, you will not be able to access them through the HTML CD Menu.

Next check the boxes for the items that you wish to install.

Installation Option	Description
Main Menu	HTML CD Menu
HTTP Server	WHTTPD
HTLML Toolbox	RTFTOHTM, Mapedit and LViewPro
HTML Document Treasure Chest	HTML Documents (note that you can use these directly from the CD if you prefer)

You can also install individual applications from the toolbox by clicking on the Options button next to the toolbox line:

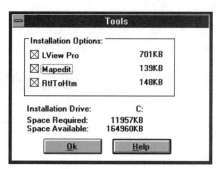

After you have made your choices, click the "Ok" button, and then the "Install" button in the Custom Installation window. Setup will then copy the items to your hard disk. You should see a screen similar to this one as it completes the installations:

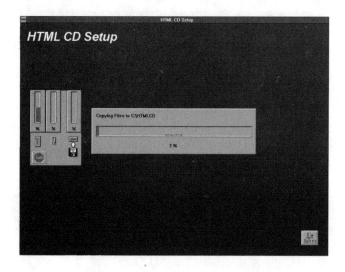

After it is done, it will create a new program group named HTML CD with an icon for the HTML CD Menu and another icon for Setup:

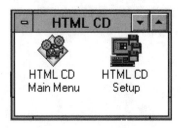

If you did not do a full installation, you can use the HTML CD Setup to install other applications at any time. Simply click on the Setup icon, and follow the procedure as for the initial installation. If the need arises, you can also use Setup to reinstall the applications.

Some of the applications on the CD (HoTMetaL, HTML Assistant, Internet Assistant and PolyForm) have their own installation programs and cannot be installed from HTML CD Setup. These applications must be installed from the File Manager or Program Manager before you can access them through the HTML CD Menu. Refer to the sections in the book on the applications you wish to use for detailed installation instructions. Remember—if you wish to use any of these applications from the HTML CD Menu, install them before trying to access them through Menu.

HTML CD Menu

The HTML CD Menu provides an easy-to-use interface to start the applications included on the CD. Once you have completed the installation, start the menu by clicking on the HTML CD Menu icon. It will display an introductory screen, and then proceed to the main menu:

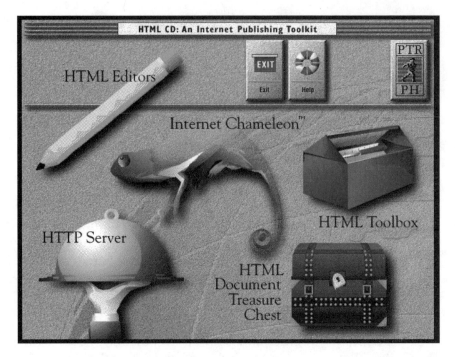

To start an application, simply click on the icon for the section you wish to use. You will find HoTMetaL, HTML Assistant and Internet Assistant under the HTML Editors icon. RTF-TOHTM, PolyForm, LViewPro and Mapedit are in the HTML Toolbox. Note that the Toolbox only provides an informational message about RTFTOHTM. Since RTFTOHTM is a DOS application, you will need to run it in a DOS window rather than from Menu.

Since Menu is a full screen application if you start more than one application you will not be able to see the window for anything besides the last application that you started. When you want to use other applications, you can switch by typing <ALT-TAB> (hold down the Alt key and hit the Tab key until you see the application you wish to run, and then release the Alt key).

Application Paths

In order to start an application, the HTML CD Menu must be able to find it. Using the default locations in Setup insures that Menu will work correctly. You can see a list of these locations by clicking on the help button in Menu. Next to the help display you will see a list of applications and the paths that Menu uses to find them:

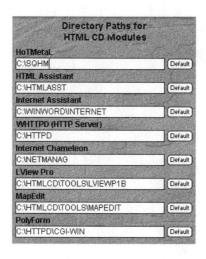

Menu will allow you to change an application's path, but the change will only last for a single session. Everything will work more smoothly if you stick to the default values.

Starting Applications

Starting applications from the Menu is simple. Just go to the section of the Menu where the application you wish to start is located and click on the icon for that application. You will find applications in the following locations:

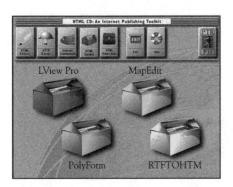

HTML Toolbox

- Mapedit
- LView Pro
- PolyForm
- RTFTOHTM. You will see an informational message about RTFTOHTM if you choose the RTFTOHTM icon. However, you cannot run it from the Menu since it is a DOS application.

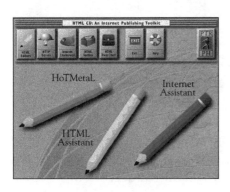

HTML Editors

- HoTMetaL
- HTML Assistant
- Internet Assistant/Microsoft Word

HTTP Server

Windows HTTP Server

Internet Chameleon: Automatic Internet

After you have used Automatic Internet to sign up for an Internet connection, you will be able to access the full suite of Internet Chameleon tools directly from the Internet Chameleon program group. Additional information about Internet Chameleon is provided later in this chapter.

HTML Document Treasure Chest

You will need to use a Web browser or HTML editor to view the files in the Treasure Chest. When you click on the Treasure Chest icon an informational message will be displayed.

Using the HTML Document Treasure Chest

In the HTML Document Treasure Chest you will find copies of the HTML examples in this book. In addition to the examples, we have also included a number of home page templates (both business and personal templates) as well as an icon catalog and numerous other useful documents.

The easiest way to find a specific document is to start with the treasure chest table of contents document. You will find the document in:

```
path\EXAMPLES\INDEX.HTM
```

path should be replaced with one of the following choices:

- The name of your CD drive if you are accessing the documents directly from the CD (e.g. "D:")
- "C:\HTMLCD" if you installed the treasure chest in the default location on your hard drive
- The path that you specified during the installation if you are using a non-standard location

To view the table of contents, start your favorite browser (if you don't have one, see the section "Getting Browsers" in Chapter 1 for help on obtaining browsers) and issue the command to open a local file. Alternatively, you may view documents by loading them into an HTML editor. If you plan on using any of the documents as templates for your own documents, you may prefer to do this. However, since most editors do not support navigation between documents, it will probably be easier to use a browser if you plan on looking at more than one document.

After the index file is loaded, you should see a screen that looks like this:

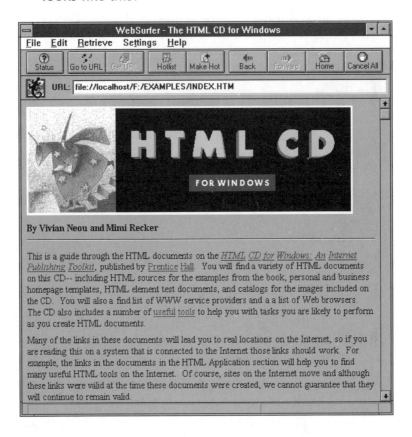

The table of contents appears immediately after the introductory section:

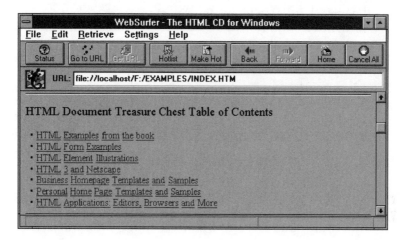

Click on the section in which you are interested to see a description of each document in that section. To view the document that interests you, simply click on the document's link.

Internet Chameleon

A special trial version of NetManage's Internet Chameleon is included on the CD. If your PC is not currently connected to the Internet, or if you do not currently have a Web browser on your PC, you can use this package to get started.

Internet Chameleon provides a complete set of tools to connect you to the Internet and to allow you to utilize all of the common Internet resources. It includes an e-mail program, Web browser, gopher client, FTP client, news reader, telnet client and archie client. It even comes with preconfigured connection scripts for a number of Internet Service Providers, so that you can automatically signup for Internet service.

You can use the software to make a free trial run of the Chameleon software. If you choose to use one of the providers available through Automatic Internet, the process of activating and configuring the software is completely automated—it only takes 5 to 10 minutes to have your system up and running on the Internet. If you choose to activate the software permanently, a software charge will apply. The demonstration period and other charges will be described when you contact each registration server.

System Requirements

In order to use this software, you will need to have a computer system that meets with at least these specifications:

- IBM or compatible PC (386 or higher)
- 4 megabytes of memory
- Mouse that works in Windows
- 8.5 megabytes of free disk space on a hard disk drive
- A modem that you can connect to a COM port, or an ISDN connection with an ISDN adapter card that supports COM port emulation or the new WinISDN driver standard
- DOS version 5 or higher
- Microsoft Windows 3.1 or higher running in enhanced mode
- CD drive

If you already have network software installed and want to try Internet Chameleon, you should be aware that there may be conflicts between Chameleon and your current software. If your system automatically starts some other network software, make sure that you disable it before you set up and start Chameleon. If you were already using the Chameleon Sampler from NetManage, it will be superseded by Internet Chameleon. The Sampler program group will be removed during the Internet Chameleon installation.

Installing Internet Chameleon

The Internet Chameleon installation will modify your AUTOEXEC.BAT and WIN.INI files. You may want to make copies of these files before proceeding with the installation. To install the package, insert your CD and choose "Run" from Program Manager. Replace the "f" in this example with the name of the drive that contains your CD. Your window should look like this:

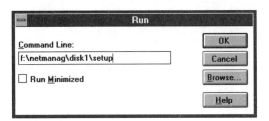

Click on the OK button to start the installation. You will first be prompted to enter the name of the directory where Instant Internet will be installed. It requires 7 megabytes of disk space, so make sure that you have enough space on your hard disk before proceeding.

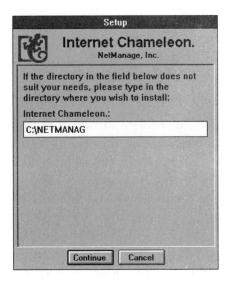

After entering the path for the directory where you want to install Internet Chameleon, click on Continue. You should now see the following screen indicating that you are done with the installation.

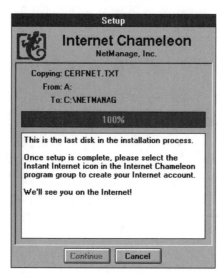

When the installation is complete, it will create a new program group containing the Automatic Internet utility and a Readme file. It should look like this:

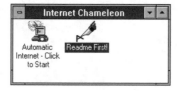

The first thing you should do is read the Readme First! file by double-clicking on that icon. This file contains the most recent information about the Internet Chameleon, including information that may not have been available when this book was written. The next step is to activate the Internet Chameleon by running the Automatic Internet application. Automatic Internet allows you to signup for service and configure your system in one step. Click on the Automatic Internet icon to get started. You will then see a window that looks something like this one:

The opening window in Automatic Internet:

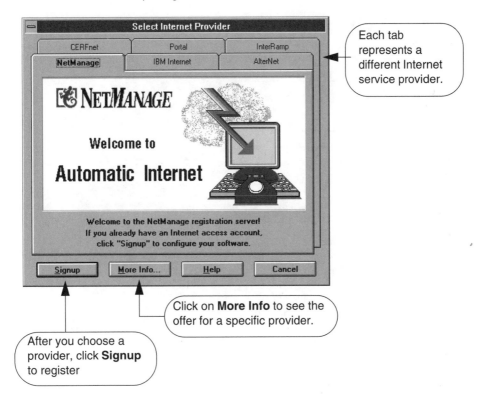

Each tab represents a different Internet service provider.

Click on **More Info** to see the offer for a specific provider.

After you choose a provider, click **Signup** to register

If you already have a provider, click on the NetManage tab to put in your configuration information and sign up for a demonstration serial number. Each of the other tabs is the name of an Internet Service provider. If you don't have a provider, you can click on any of these tabs to review the information for that provider. If you decide to use one of these providers, click the *Signup* button. You will be given a registration form to fill out:

Service Provider Registration Form

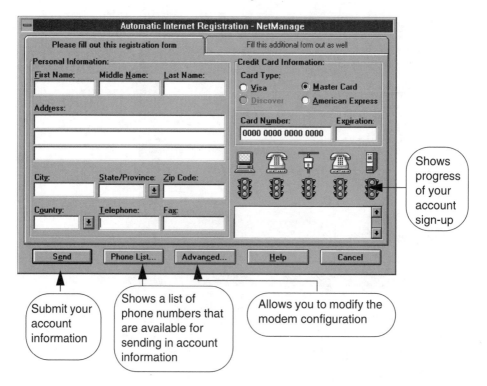

You will need to fill in all of the fields. Depending on the provider, there may be additional tabs requesting additional information. If there are such a tabs, you must choose each one and provide the information requested. When you have finished filling in all of the forms, click on the Phone List button. It will display a list of phone numbers that can be used to send your registration information to the registration server. Choose the number the closest to you. If needed, you can edit the number to add additional dialing information (such as a prefix of 9). Please note that all communication with the registration server is over a secure phone line, not the Internet. Your credit card will not be charged unless you explicitly sign up for a regular (nondemonstration) account and license.

Now go back and click the Send button. You will be given an opportunity to cancel the transaction after dialing into a registration server and before continuing with the sign-up process. Your credit card information will not be passed to the provider's server unless you agree to continue after receiving the initial hello message(s) and pricing information from the server.

As the registration proceeds, the area on the lower right of the window will display the status. The traffic lights signal the flow of information, and status messages will be displayed in the text box below the traffic lights. Note that you cannot type anything in this part of the window since it is only used for displaying status information. In a few minutes, the provider's server will return personalized account information to your system and automatically configure your software. A welcome message from your provider will be displayed. For example, if you choose to get a demonstration license from NetManage, you will see the following window:

You must reboot your system before using Internet Chameleon to connect to the Internet. After rebooting, run Custom to connect your system to the Internet.

Using Custom

Custom is the application that takes care of the connection process between your system and your provider. If you used Instant Internet to register with a service provider, Custom will start with an interface already defined for you. In this case, all you need to do to connect your system to the Internet is to click on the Connect menu item in Custom. However, if you are using a service provider that is not available through Instant

Internet, you will need to configure Custom before your system can be connected to the Internet. Custom can handle the following types of dial-up accounts:

- Serial Line Interface Protocol (SLIP)
- Compressed SLIP (CSLIP)
- Point-to-Point Protocol (PPP)
- Integrated Services Digital Network (ISDN)

You can get instructions on configuring Custom through the help menu in Custom.

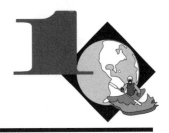

IN THIS CHAPTER YOU WILL LEARN

- HOW HTML ALLOWS YOU TO PUBLISH MULTIMEDIA DOCUMENTS ON THE WORD WIDE WEB
- HOW HTML AND DOCUMENT DISPLAY VARIES AMONG WEB BROWSERS
- HOW TO DOWNLOAD A VARIETY OF WEB BROWSERS

THE WORLD WIDE WEB AND BROWSERS

What's In This Chapter

In this chapter we will explain more about the World Wide Web and its relation to HTML. We'll explain how HTML is dependent on Web browsers. We will also explain how to download a variety of Web browsers on the Internet using the browser document included on the CD. If you are already familiar with the Web and Web browsers, skip to the section on the HTML templates on the CD at the end of this chapter.

HTML and the Internet

As we mentioned in the introduction, HTML is a hypermedia document description language used to publish documents on the World Wide Web. Since the Web spans the Internet, and the Internet is a global network, HTML documents can be, and frequently are, connected internationally. You might think of HTML documents as looking something like the picture in Figure 1–1.

From a practical standpoint this means that if you live in California and a colleague lives in New Zealand, the two of you could publish your work together—even though your portion of the work remains on a computer in California and your colleague's on a computer in New Zealand. How? It's simple—by using *links* to join your pieces of the work together. Thanks to the seamless integration of documents on the Web, your readers would be not be affected by the geographic separation of the physical pieces of actual work (although they may notice differences in transmission times between different pieces of the document).

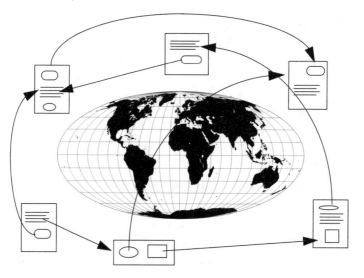

FIGURE 1–1   HTML Documents on the Internet

Let's look at a hypothetical set of documents in HTML to get a better understanding of how all of this fits together. It's time to introduce you to Kelly Kayaker. We will be developing a set of

HTML pages for Kelly in this book to illustrate how HTML works. Kelly's pages can be found on the CD, so you can use them as templates for your own HTML projects.

First, let us give you a little background on Kelly. She writes travel books for a small publishing company named Ozone Books. Kelly lives in Canada, and Ozone is based in New Zealand. Kelly will be breaking new ground for Ozone by developing a document on kayaking that will be published on the Web. Ozone is also planning to begin selling books on the Internet.

One part of Kelly's book will consist of pictures and descriptions of hot kayaking spots. She has friends all over the world who are helping her with these descriptions. Some of these friends would like to provide seasonal updates of their descriptions, so they want to keep their portions of the document on their own computers. Kelly is also planning to let people who read her document add comments to a "guest book." As a result, Kelly's document will be in pieces that are linked in this fashion:

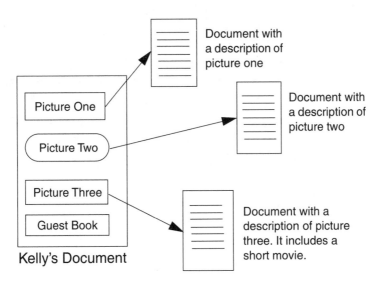

When readers look at Kelly's document with a browser (we'll tell you more about browsers in the next section), they will see a page of pictures. To read the descriptions that correspond to the pictures, the reader clicks on the picture, and the browser then gets the document with the description and displays it. The documents with the descriptions do not have to be on the same computer as Kelly's picture document—they don't even have to be the same type of computer! Even though the actual pieces of the work may be scattered on different computers all around the world, from the reader's standpoint the document is a single, cohesive piece of work.

The guest book will appear as a form, and people reading the document will have the opportunity to sign in and leave comments about it.

Browsers

We've mentioned browsers a number of times. Where do they fit into the picture? Browsers are the applications used to display HTML and other kinds of formatted documents. They understand HTML commands, and interpret the commands to format the document for display. Although there are many browsers now, the first widely used graphical browser was Mosaic from the National Center for Supercomputing Applications. As a result, many people refer to Web browsers as "Mosaic," although Mosaic is actually just the name of one type of Web browser. Figure 1–2 shows how the Web browser fits into the Web.

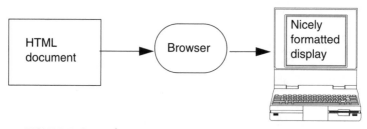

FIGURE 1–2   Web Browser

If you are already familiar with the Web, you are probably thinking "something is missing!" You are right. Figure 1–2 illustrates the flow of information for a local on-line help system, and local review of HTML files (for example, you will probably use a browser to review your document before publishing it on the Internet). There is another piece in this picture, the Web server. If your eyes are starting to glaze over because you thought you were going to learn about HTML in this book, not computer networking, please stick with us. You actually need to know this to effectively use HTML. We'll keep the networking stuff short and simple.

Browsers are applications called *clients*. They get most of their information from *servers*. We say most rather than all because browsers can get their information directly from local files, as illustrated in Figure 1–2. Servers are the applications that allow HTML files to be linked across the network. A Web server is a program that waits for requests to get documents; when it receives a request, it gets the appropriate document and sends it to the browser that made the request. Requests can come from the computer the server is on, or from computers on the other side of the world. The server doesn't care—as long as the request is valid, it will return the requested document. Figure 1–3 shows the flow of information when HTML documents are shared across a network.

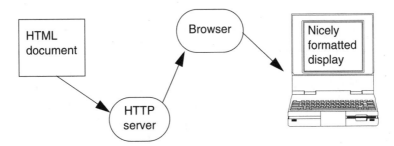

FIGURE 1–3 *Web Browser and Server*

Web servers talk to browsers by using a network protocol called the Hypertext Transport Protocol (HTTP). Protocols are the languages used by different applications on networks to talk to each other. Although HTTP is the primary protocol used to support the Web, Web browsers can actually get information from other types of servers that use different protocols; such as FTP, mail or gopher. As a result, you can put links in your HTML documents that will allow your readers to download documents and applications or to make a telnet connection to another computer. We'll explain how to do this in the section on Uniform Resource Locators (URLs) in "URLs and Links" on page 43.

Whew. That was a lot of jargon and acronyms. But now we're done with the network for a little while. Let's take a closer look at browsers now.

HTML and Browsers

HTML is used to define the *structure* of a document. However, the browser used to display the document dictates how each structural element should be rendered. *Although general element display guidelines are provided in the HTML specification, in practice there is wide variation in display between browsers.*

Browsers also vary widely in their recognition of HTML elements. Most browsers try to support version 2 of HTML; some browsers do not recognize anything above version 1, while others (most notably Netscape Navigator) use vendor-specific extensions to HTML. To muddy things even further, most browsers are also willing to accept documents that violate all of the specifications for HTML. When a browser encounters a noncompliant document, it will typically ignore noncompliant portions of the document and do its best to interpret the rest.

In other words, there is nothing to force you to write HTML documents that fully adhere to any of the HTML specifications. In fact, if you are writing for an audience that will be using a specific browser (for example, you may be writing in-house documentation for which your company has chosen a specific browser) you may want to become familiar with the way that browser handles HTML so you can tailor your documents in an appropriate fashion. However, if you are writing documents that will be published on the Internet, you will need to make sure that your documents look okay on a broad range of browsers.

To help you understand how much variation there is between browsers, each chapter in this book will use a different browser to display the examples. We have also provided a document on the CD that will help you locate and download a wide variety of Windows browsers across the Internet. We urge you to install at least two or three browsers to review your documents. As an incentive, let's take a quick look at the way different browsers display a simple HTML document. The HTML source we will display is this:

```
<P>The logical tags in HTML are:
<DL>
<DT><STRONG>Citation:&lt;CITE&gt;</STRONG>
<DD><CITE>This paragraph is in a citation tag</CITE>
<DT><STRONG>Code: &lt;CODE&gt;</STRONG>
<DD><CODE>CODE is intended for code examples, and is
typically displayed in a fixed-width font.</CODE>
<DT><STRONG>Emphasis: &lt;EM&gt;</STRONG>
<DD><EM>This paragraph is in an emphasis tag. It is usually
displayed in italics.</EM>
<DT><STRONG>Keyboard: &lt;KBD&gt; </STRONG>
<DD><KBD>This paragraph is in a keyboard tag. It is typically
displayed in a fixed-width font.</KBD>
<DT><STRONG>Sample: &lt;SAMPLE&gt;</STRONG>
<DD><SAMPLE>This paragraph is in a sample tag. The sample tag
is intended for sequences of literal characters.</SAMPLE>
<DT><STRONG>Emphasis: &lt;STRONG&gt;</STRONG>
<DD><STRONG>Strong Emphasis. It is usually displayed in a
boldface font.</STRONG>
<DT><STRONG>Variable Name: &lt;VAR&gt;</STRONG>
<DD><VAR>Variable Name. This is intended for variable
names</VAR>
</DL>
```

Now let's see how it looks in different browsers.

NCSA Mosaic

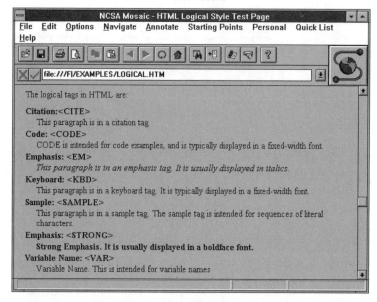

Netscape

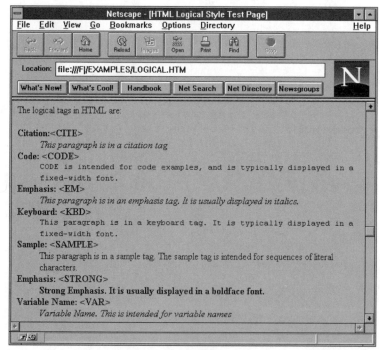

InternetWorks

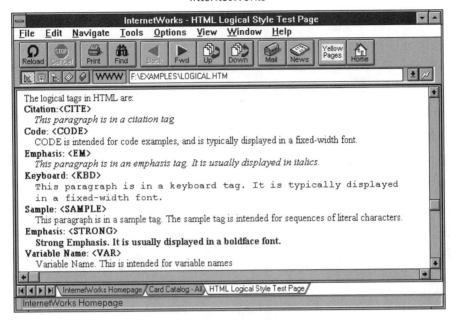

WinTapestry

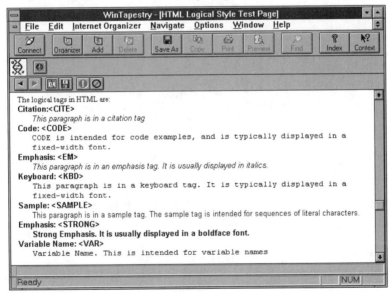

Air Mosaic

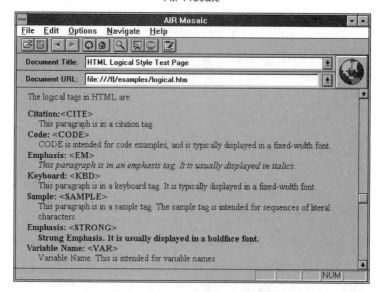

WebSurfer

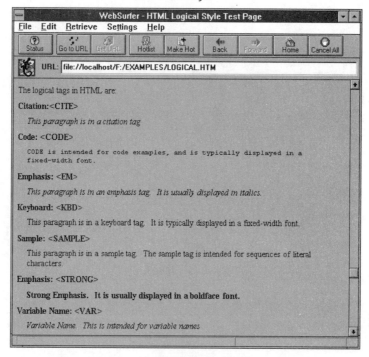

As you can see, these browsers display the same simple document in a variety of ways. From the background to line spacing to the fonts, nothing is consistent between browsers.

In more complex documents, the differences between browsers become even more obvious. Unfortunately, there is no simple solution to this problem. As we introduce new HTML elements, we make design recommendations that will help you to author documents that will look good regardless of the browser used to display them.

You can preview your document in most browsers by specifying the Open Local *or* Open File *command, which can usually be found in the* File *menu.* This allows you to see your document as it is being developed, and to correct potential errors. If you find a problem, correct it within the editing environment. Then use the *Reload* command to see if your changes have fixed the problem.

Getting Browsers

If you do not have any browsers, or only one, you are probably anxious to get some more now. On the CD we've included everything you need to get a wide variety of browsers. You can start with WebSurfer, a browser that is part of the NetManage Automatic Internet suite of applications on the CD. Once you activate this package (see "Using the CD" starting on page xxi for details), you can use WebSurfer along with the browser document on the CD to download:

- NCSA Mosaic
- Netscape Navigator
- Air Mosaic from Spry (demo version)
- Cello from Cornell Law School
- InternetWorks from NaviSoft
- Winweb from EINet
- WinTapestry from Frontier Technology
- Quarterdeck Mosaic

- Global-Wide Help and Information System (GWHIS) from Quadralay
- SlipKnot
- Lynx

To download these packages, all you need to do is load \EXAMPLES\BROWSER.HTM into WebSurfer. To do this, choose "Open Local File" from the Retrieve pulldown menu and enter the filename. You should see a page that looks like this:

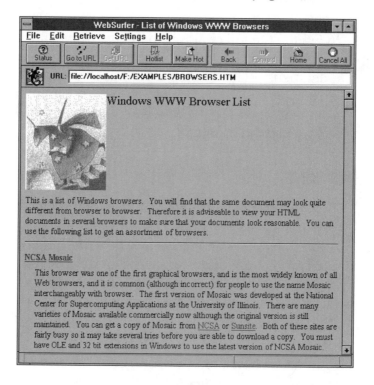

You will see the list of browsers along with some information about each one. When you choose the link in a browser's description, either the browser will be downloaded to your system, or you will be placed at a homepage for the browser that will provide you with information about the browser and an opportunity to download it.

Now let's see how to start an HTML document.

THE BASICS

What's In This Chapter

This chapter shows you how to create a basic HTML document. It discusses setting up your document and introduces the basic formatting commands. As mentioned in the last chapter, you will see how HTML documents look in different browsers. In this chapter we will be using NCSA Mosaic to display our examples.

Creating an HTML Document

HTML documents are written in plain text (ASCII). There are a number of ways to create an HTML document:

1. You can use your favorite editor and add in the HTML commands yourself.

2. You can use an HTML editor that inserts the commands in the appropriate locations for you.

3. You can also use a conversion utility that takes a document from some other format and converts it to HTML.

We discuss all of these methods in this book. We start with the text editor method, since it is important to understand how HTML works, even if you do use a system that inserts HTML commands for you.

The first step is to create a file to hold your HTML document. On a Windows/DOS system you need to create a file with the *.htm* file extension. If you will be authoring HTML documents on other systems, it is important to note that HTML documents on most other types of systems use file names with the extension *.html. Browsers and servers make some decisions on the way they deal with documents based on the file extension, so it is important to choose the correct extension for your document.*

In this chapter we will author a document on the sport of kayaking as an example. Hence, we call this file, kayak.htm. We have included a copy of this document on the CD.

HTML Document Tags: <HTML>, <HEAD>, and <BODY>

Several tags do not affect the presentation of documents but convey important information to browsers and users. As you will find, most browsers do not complain if you forget to put these tags in your document, but it is safer to include them.

First, HTML documents should contain an <HTML> tag. Note that the document should have a corresponding </HTML> at the end. HTML is *not* case sensitive. <HTML> is the same as <html> or <HtMl>.

The document should be organized into <HEAD> and <BODY> sections. Like an electronic mail message, the <HEAD> tags surround the introductory section, while the <BODY> tags surround the main part of the document.

Although these tags do not affect the presentation of a document, they are important. The HTTP protocol includes a "HEAD" command, which returns the information included in the head of a document. Although most browsers do not currently use this feature, many Web-searching robots use it to build their databases. If you want your documents to be catalogued in an understandable fashion, make sure that you include a HEAD section.

The TITLE element in a document must occur within the <HEAD> tags of the document, and it is the only element that goes in the head section. Within the <BODY>, the document can be structured in paragraphs, lists and so on, using HTML tags. The basic framework for our kayak document is shown in Figure 2–1.

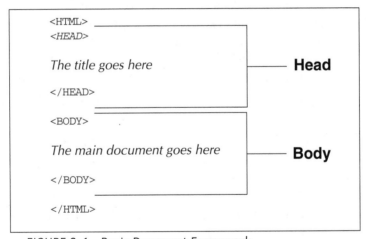

FIGURE 2–1   Basic Document Framework

Markup Tags

If you've used a WYSIWYG (What You See Is What You Get) word processing program such as Microsoft Word or WordPerfect, you have probably formatted your documents so that some words are displayed in italics or boldface. You have also probably designated portions of your text as titles, headings or lists.

HTML provides some of this functionality for documents that are published on the Internet. However, there is a significant difference between HTML and a WYSIWYG word processing system. Like many word processing systems, HTML allows you to define the *structure* of a document—you can specify such things as lists, titles, headings and so forth. However, the way these things will be displayed to the reader is determined by the browser used to display the document.

If you like to have complete control over the look of your document (for example, adjusting font sizes, or placing text on the page in a specific location), you will probably find working with HTML a bit frustrating. HTML was designed so that authors could mark up the text in documents to indicate *types* of text. However, since HTML was designed to allow the same document to be meaningfully displayed on a wide variety of platforms with vastly different capabilities, it is left up to the browser (which understands the limitations and abilities of the platform on which it is running) to decide how each type of text will be displayed.

Thus, you cannot specify that something should be displayed in a 9-point Courier font, or that an item designated as a heading will be centered and displayed in a bold 20-point font. These decisions are left up to the browser—and, as you will see, even on the same platform there is wide variation in how different browsers display the same document. In Chapter 3 we will provide some guidelines to make your documents look as good as possible in the wide variety of browsers that may be used to display them. But first, let's look at how different types of text are defined in HTML.

HTML commands use *markup tags* to specify structural elements in a document. These tags tell the browser about the type of text being displayed; such as headers, titles, lists or plain text.

HTML markup tags consist of a left-angle bracket (<), followed by the name of the tag, and then a right-angle bracket (>). Tags usually come in pairs in order to act as *containers* of the affected text. The second tag in a pair looks just like the first, except that a slash precedes the name. This second tag tells the browser that the command is done. Thus, an HTML statement looks something like this:

```
<TagName>Some Text</TagName>
```

Title: <TITLE>

The first essential item you should include in an HTML document is a title. We start our document with this title line:

```
<TITLE>The Sport of Kayaking</TITLE>
```

As you can see in this example, the markup tags for the title are <TITLE> and </TITLE>. Of course, since HTML is not case-sensitive, we could have written our tags in lower case:

```
<title>The Sport of Kayaking</title>
```

We will use upper case letters in the rest of our examples, but it is fine to use lower case tags if you prefer. In the above example, the title of the document is "The Sport of Kayaking."

A DOCUMENT MAY HAVE ONLY ONE TITLE.

Any HTML document should have a title that succinctly describes the contents of the document. This title, like the title of a book, can be used by readers to decide if they wish to view the entire document. If the title is too generic, the reader will be unable to determine whether the document is of any interest. For example, a bad title would be:

```
<TITLE>Introduction</TITLE>
```

This title does not tell the reader anything about the contents of the document. Since links (we'll explain more about links in the next chapter) may be made to any document from any other document, this title makes it difficult for readers to decide whether the document contains information they want. A better title would be:

```
<TITLE>Introduction to Kayaking</TITLE>
```

The following two titles are also poor choices. Although they tell something about the content of the document, they are too general to be useful:

```
<TITLE>Security</TITLE>
<TITLE>Games</TITLE>
```

Better alternatives would be:

```
<TITLE>Computer Security Hints</TITLE>
<TITLE>Games on the Internet: MUDs</TITLE>
```

Use descriptive yet succinct titles.

Browsers usually display the title of a document in a special area of the window. Although the HTML standard does not set a limit on the number of characters in a title, most browsers display only as much of the title as will fit into this section, which is typically no longer than one line. If you keep your title under 64 characters, you can be reasonably well assured that your title will fit into the allocated space.

Keep Titles Short! Titles with no more than five or six words have the greatest impact.

A title may not contain anchors, highlighting or paragraph tags (these types of tags are described later.) If you try to include these tags, the behavior from browser to browser is unpredictable (and, in most cases, undesirable). Some browsers may show the tags as part of the title, while some browsers may actually pull the text out of the title area and display it as part of the document.

Do not place any markup tags in a title!

We've provided a document on the CD that deliberately violates the guidelines for good title composition. You can find the file in \EXAMPLES\LONGTITL.HTM. Here's the beginning of the document:

```
<HTML>
<HEAD>
<TITLE>
Here's a Title That Won't Show Up
</TITLE>
<TITLE>This Is A Very Very <H1>Long Title</H1> That Tells You
Nothing
About The Document And May Not Fit In The Area That Browsers
Set Up For
Titles.</TITLE>
</HEAD>
<BODY>
<H1>Hints about Titles</H1>
<P>A HTML document can only have one title.</P>
```

And here's what happens when we load this document into Mosaic:

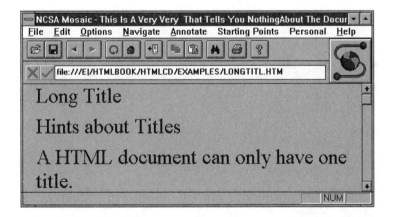

As you can see, a number of undesirable things happened. Our first title vanished without a trace. The document itself is displayed in a huge font. Why? Because we tried to include a header tag (explained later) in the title. "Long Title," which is displayed above "Hints about Titles," is actually part of the title. However, we placed a header tag around it, and as you can see the browser got confused and pulled it out of the title. In fact, it got so confused that it left the rest of the document in a header format. Of course, every browser will get confused in different ways when you violate the rules. Try loading this document into several different browsers and see for yourself.

Headings

Now we'll tell you about header tags. The next tag we use is H1:

```
<H1>White Water Kayaking</H1>
```

This is an example of a header tag, denoted by <H1>. The first header in our document is "White Water Kayaking." HTML allows you to specify up to six levels of headers, <H1> through <H6>. The first header, H1, is the largest, most prominent header. It is typically displayed in a large and bold font, while each subsequent header is displayed in an increasingly smaller size. Here are how the six levels of headers look in Mosaic:

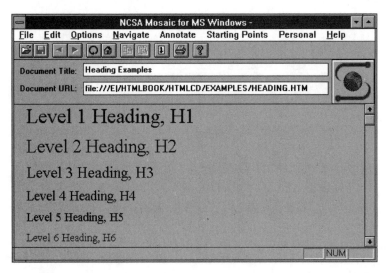

You can find this test document in \EXAMPLES\HEADING.HTM on the CD. Try loading it in several browsers to see the difference in the ways various browsers choose to display headings.

Paragraphs: <P>

Now we want to include some general text:

```
<P>Kayaking is an outdoor sport, practiced by adrenaline
junkies, in which enthusiasts paddle wild rivers and creeks
in small, enclosed boats. Most people are a bit nervous the
first time they kayak.</P>
```

The <P> specifies a paragraph break. Unlike most tags, it is an example of an *empty container* since it does not require an end tag. HTML performs automatic word wrap in documents, and ignores carriage returns. Therefore, you must explicitly signal paragraph breaks in text with the <P> tag. *If you do not include any paragraph breaks in your HTML text, it will appear as one, long paragraph.* Some exceptions do exist, as we will explain later. Let's digress from our kayaking document for a moment to illustrate this point.

Let's look at a short and simple HTML document. The document source looks as if there should be three paragraphs. However, notice that there are no P tags in this document.

```
<HTML>
<HEAD>
<TITLE>Paragraph Break Test Document</TITLE>
<HEAD>
<BODY>
<H1>Paragraph Break Test Document</H1>
This document illustrates the need to include paragraph tags in
your HTML sources. If you do not include &lt;P&gt; tags in your
documents, your document will appear as one long paragraph
(perhaps with some breaks if you use other elements such as
lists or headers). This document does not include any P tags.

Although there is a blank line before this sentence in the HTML
source, there is no P tag, so the browser will not recognize
the start of a new paragraph. It should appear as one long
paragraph in your browser.

In HTML 2, there is no requirement to close a P tag. However,
it is good practice to do so since HTML 3 introduces extra
attributes for the P tag (such as center) that will work more
cleanly if P tags are closed.
</BODY>
</HTML>
```

Now let's see how it looks in NCSA Mosaic:

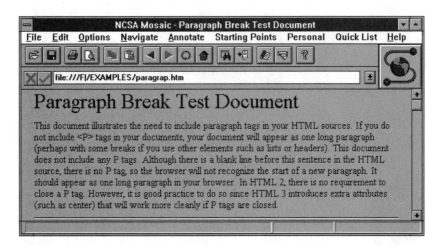

As you can see, the browser did not pay any attention to the blank lines in our HTML source, and placed the whole document in one long paragraph.

In future versions of HTML, the paragraph markup tag will be extended to include alignment attributes. As a result, it will become a container, like most other tags (although for compatibility with old documents, the requirement for a closing tag will not be enforced). Thus, a paragraph of text will be contained within <P> and </P> markers.

Since most browsers accept </P>, you can avoid having to go back and change your old HTML documents by treating the paragraph tag as a container, and using </P> now. One word of warning if you do this: many browsers treat <P> as an indicator that a paragraph has ended, so they add a blank line when they see <P>. If you put <P> at the beginning of a paragraph you may end up with more blank space in front of your paragraph than you want. You will need to decide if this additional space is acceptable.

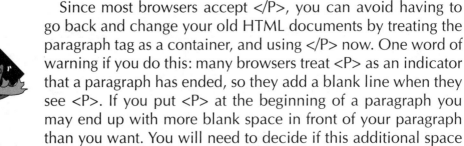

Horizontal Lines: <HR>

Sections between documents are often separated by a horizontal line that runs the length of the browser window. The <HR> tag produces a horizontal line in HTML. In our kayak document, we placed a line between the introductory paragraph and the rest of the document.

Lists

HTML provides several ways to display information in lists. These include:

- Unnumbered lists
- Numbered lists
- Menu lists
- Directory lists
- Definition lists

Specifying Items in Lists: <LI>

Lists share a common format. Like most HTML objects, you start and end lists with the appropriate markup tags. However, the tags used to mark items within a list are empty container tags (like paragraph tags, they only need a start tag.) For example:

```
<OL>
<LI>Paddles
<LI>Kayaks
</OL>
```

As you can see in this example, another markup tag is used to label each item in the list. With the exception of definition lists (which need two types of item tags since they have two types of items), items in lists are specified with the <LI> tag. You indicate that something is an item by starting it with the <LI> tag. Since this is an empty container tag there is no need to close the item (although you can add a closing </LI> if you prefer).

With the exception of items in a directory list (which should be kept under 20 characters), items in a list can be longer than a single sentence. If you wish to have multiple paragraphs within a list item, don't forget to separate them with the <P> paragraph separator.

Creating a List

The process of creating a list is simple. Here are the basic steps:

1. *Begin with the opening list tag for the type of list you wish to create.*
2. *Enter the <LI> tag, followed by a list item.*
3. *Continue entering list items, with an <LI> tag preceding each item. No closing tag is needed for items.*
4. *End the list by typing the appropriate closing container tag for your list.*

Unnumbered Lists: <UL>

Unnumbered lists, which are also known as unordered lists, are typically displayed by browsers with a bullet in front of each item. The markup tags for unnumbered lists are <UL> and </UL>. For example, in our kayak.htm document, we would specify an unordered list as follows:

```
Essential items to have while kayaking:
<UL>
<LI>Life jacket
<LI>Helmet
<LI>Spray skirt
<LI>Paddle
</UL>
```

When viewed with a browser, the above snippet would look like this:

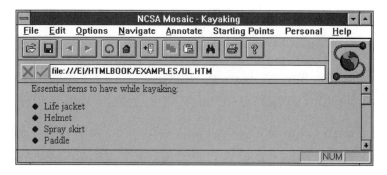

Numbered Lists: <OL>

Numbered, or ordered, lists have numbered items. The markup tags for ordered lists are <OL> and </OL>.

For example, in our kayak.html document, we would specify an ordered list as follows:

```
<P>Kayaking and other river sports are very popular
recreational activities in New Zealand. Popular rivers for
these sports are</P>
<OL>
<LI>The Shotover River, South Island
<LI>The Buller River, South Island
<LI>The Karamea River, South Island
<LI>The Rangitikei River, North Island
<LI>The Mohaka River, North Island
</OL>
```

When viewed in NCSA Mosaic, our ordered list looks like a this:

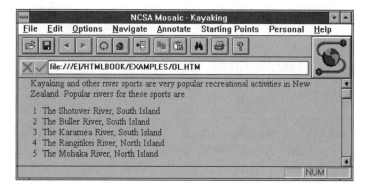

Directory List: <DIR>

Directory lists are intended for short lists. They should be enclosed in <DIR> and </DIR> tags. Each item should be no more than 20 characters. If space is available, the HTML specifications recommend that browsers try to display directory lists in multiple columns. However, in our tests with various browsers we have yet to find one that does this.

```
<P>Following is a list of kayaking resources you will find in
this document:</P>
<DIR>
<LI>Books
<LI>Magazines
<LI>Outfitters
<LI>River descriptions
<LI>Travel agencies
</DIR>
```

Now let's see how this looks in Mosaic:

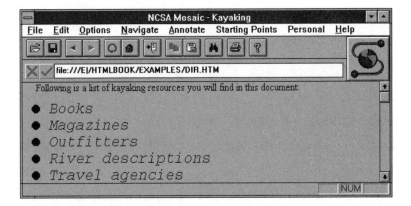

Menu List: <MENU>

A menu list functions much like an unordered list, except it is supposed to be displayed in a more compact style by browsers. We've found that menu lists look exactly like unordered lists in many browsers. However, as development on browsers continues this may change. For example, a new version of

NCSA Mosaic was released while we were writing this book—
in the old version, menus looked the same as unordered lists;
in the new version, menus have a completely different look.

A menu list is enclosed in <MENU> and </MENU> tags, and
each item in the list is preceded by the <LI> tag.

```
<P>Kayaking is especially rewarding on those rivers in the
United States that have been designated by Congress as part
of the Wild and Scenic River system. These rivers include:</P>
<MENU>
<LI>The Tuolumne River, California
<LI>The Chattooga River, Georgia
<LI>The Rogue River, Oregon
<LI>The Illinois River, Oregon
<LI>The Middle Fork of the Salmon, Idaho
<LI>The Selway River, Idaho
</MENU>
```

Now let's see how this section looks in NCSA Mosaic:

As you can see, the latest version of Mosaic at the time this
book is being written displays menu items in a bold italic font.

Definition Lists: <DL>

Definition lists should be used when specifying a set of terms
followed by their definitions. Most browsers format the definition text on a new line. Definition lists are specified as follows:

1. *Begin with an opening definition list <DL> tag.*
2. *Enter the <DT> tag, followed by the text for the defined term.*
3. *Enter the <DD> tag, followed by the text for the definition.*
4. *Continue entering definition terms with the <DT> tag, followed by their definitions, with the <DD> tag. No closing tags are needed.*
5. *Type the closing container tag, </DL>.*

For example, in our kayak.htm document, we would specify a definition list as follows:

```
Essential items to have while kayaking:
<DL>
<DT>Life jacket
<DD>A life jacket is essential while kayaking as it provides
flotation.
<DT>Helmet
<DD>A helmet protects the head against blows against rocks.
<DT>Spray skirt
<DD>The spray skirt fits between the torso of the kayaker and
the boat, and prevents water from swamping the kayak.
<DT>Paddle
<DD><P>A paddle allows the kayaker to navigate in the water.
</DL>
```

When viewed in Mosaic, the previous snippet would look something like this:

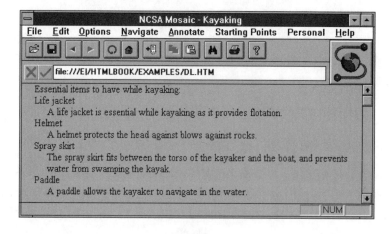

As with all list items, the <DT> and <DD> items can be multiple paragraphs. To make a multiple-paragraph item, use paragraph tags—do not try to do it by using multiple <DD> tags within a single definition.

Definition lists may also include the *compact* attribute, which tells browsers that compact rendering should be used. If you want to use the compact attribute, the start of your list should be:

```
<DL COMPACT>
```

This attribute should be used when the list is large or if you would like the items in the list to be small. When the attribute is on, browsers are supposed to reduce the amount of white space between successive dt/dd pairs, and may also reduce the width of the dt column. Although it doesn't hurt to include the compact attribute if you want your list to be displayed in this fashion, we have found that most browsers display description lists with the compact attribute no different than a description list without it. Table 2–1 describes the various tags used to create lists.

TABLE 2–1 List Tags

Command	Description
<OL></OL>	Numbered or ordered list.
<ULl></UL>	Unnumbered or unordered list.
<DIR></DIR>	Directory list. Looks like an unordered list in most browsers. List entries should be no longer than 20 characters.
<MENU></MENU>	Menu list. This list also looks similar to an unordered list in most browsers. The display is supposed to be more compact.
<LI>	Item in a list.
<DL></DL>	Definition list.
<DT>	Defined item in a definition list.
<DD>	Definition of an item in a definition list.

Nested Lists

The lists you use can be nested to an arbitrary level. When you nest lists, keep your poor readers in mind. Nest too deeply, and not only will you have an ugly document, you'll be guaranteed a confused audience!

We might use a nested list in our kayak document as follows:

```
Kayaking uses a dizzying array of specialized gear:
<OL>
<LI>Kayaks
<UL>
<LI>White water kayaks
<LI>Sea kayaks
<LI>Squirt kayaks
</UL>
<LI>Paddles
<UL>
<LI>Feathered
<LI>Dihedral
<LI>Break-down
</UL>
</OL>
```

Our HTML source looks like this in NCSA Mosaic:

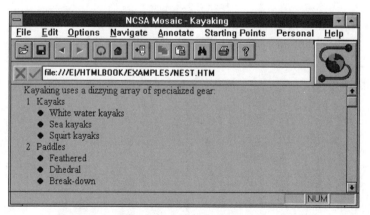

WHEN NESTING LISTS, DON'T FORGET TO CLOSE EACH LIST AND SUBLIST WITH THE APPROPRIATE TAG.

We found an interesting difference in the way that browsers display nested, unordered lists. Some browsers choose a different type of bullet for each level of nesting. We made a little test list to illustrate this:

```
<P>You can also nest unordered lists within each other.
Notice how some browsers change the bullets each level:</P>
<UL><LI>Level One
<UL><LI>Level Two
<UL><LI>Level Three
<UL><LI>Level Four
<UL><LI>Level Five
</UL></UL></UL></UL></UL>
```

Our favorite bullet changer is WinTapestry. Here's how Win-Tapestry displays our test list:

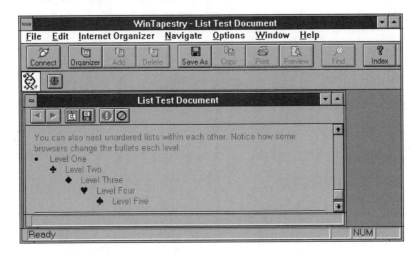

Although you can't count on it, this feature can add visual interest to your documents in some browsers.

Preformatted Text: <PRE>

Sometimes you don't want the Web browser to change the formatting of plain text. You may wish line breaks and spaces to be significant in a piece of text, not ignored by the browser. For example, you may need to display columns of data or show some computer program code. Another example would be a map drawn with ASCII characters. In all of these cases, you want the layout, spacing, and line breaks to be exactly reproduced by the browser.

The <PRE> tag tells the browser to display the text in a fixed-width font, and to faithfully reproduce spaces, line breaks, and tabs. The closing tag is, not surprisingly, </PRE>.

You should not nest other kinds of tags within preformatted text because browsers may interpret such tags strangely. The only exception is the anchor tag, <A>, which is explained in the next chapter.

ANCHOR TAGS ARE THE ONLY TAGS THAT ARE ALLOWED IN PREFORMATTED TEXT.

For example, in our kayaking document, we might want to have a silly ASCII drawing of a kayak paddle. In this example, spaces and line breaks are crucial:

```
<P>Here is a silly ASCII picture of a kayak paddle:</P>
<PRE>
```

```
</PRE>
```

This would be displayed in the browser as:

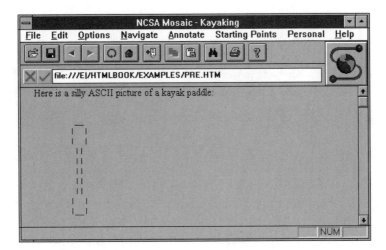

Long Quotations: <BLOCKQUOTE>

The <BLOCKQUOTE> tag is used to mark long quotations in documents. Browsers typically display quotations as indented text. For example, to include a quotation in our kayak document:

```
A first-time kayaker describes his experiences:
<BLOCKQUOTE>
<P>I found kayaking to be a thrilling sport.</P>
<P>At first, I was nervous about getting into such a small,
tipsy craft, but then I discovered its extreme
maneuverability.</P>
</BLOCKQUOTE>
```

The resulting text is displayed as:

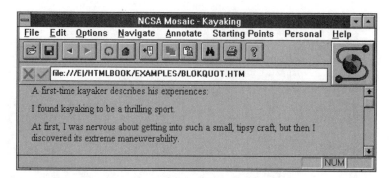

As you can see, NCSA Mosaic did not display our block-quote in an indented area. As we said before, you cannot count on all browsers to display documents the same way. So you can see that some browsers do treat this element as we expect it to be displayed, we will show you how this section looks in Netscape:

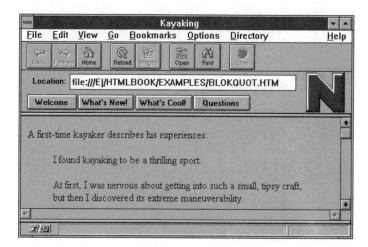

Line Breaks:

A line break is indicated by the <BR> tag. Unlike the <P> tag, an extra blank line is not inserted. The <BR> tag simply forces a line break in the text. We use a <BR> tag in our address example in the next section.

Addresses: <ADDRESS>

The <ADDRESS> tag is used to mark—surprise—addresses. Typically, it occurs at the end of documents, and is used to enclose the author's name and electronic mail address. Browsers usually display addresses in italic style. For example, the author of the kayak document might include the address as follows:

```
For more information, contact:
<ADDRESS>
Kelly Kayaker<BR>
kayaker@kayak.com
</ADDRESS>
```

This would be displayed in NCSA Mosaic as:

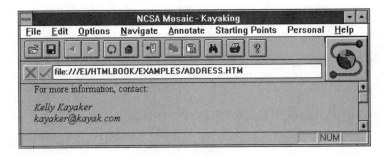

Comments: <! -->

Comments may be included in HTML documents by using the comment tags, <!-- and -->. Text appearing within comment tags will be ignored by browsers. *Comments cannot be nested within one another.* Comments are useful for embedding information for authors, such as document creation date. For example:

```
<!-- The file was created on Jan 1, 1995, by Kelly Kayaker-->
```

Many browsers do not treat embedded HTML tags in a comment correctly. Let's write some lines of HTML that have a nested comment line, and a comment line containing several HTML tags.

```
<P>The following line is &lt;!-- Comment --&gt; It should not
be displayed</P>
<!-- Comment -->
<P>Now we try a comment that contains a tag: &lt;!-- Testing
&lt;H1&gt;test&lt;/H2&gt; --&gt; If your browser handles tags in
comments, nothing should appear between the end of this
sentence and the word "Now" in the next paragraph.</P>
<!-- Testing <h1>test</h1> -->
<P>Now we try nesting some comments: &lt;!--&lt;!-- Testing
&lt;H1&gt;test&lt;/H2&gt; --&gt; Note that we only nest the
starting tag for the comment. Since "--&gt;" is defined to be
the end of a comment, the comment should end as soon as the
browser sees one -- there is no provision for nesting end tags
in the HTML standard. Nothing should appear between this
sentence and the horizontal rule if your browser can handle
nested comments.</P>
<!-- <!-- Testing <h1>test</h1> -->
```

NCSA Mosaic handles our test comments without any problems:

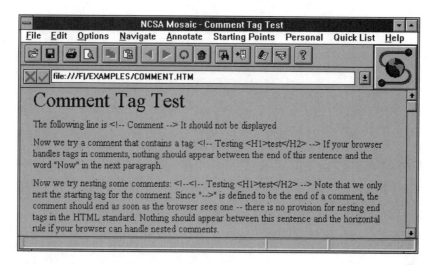

WebSurfer is confused by our nested comments:

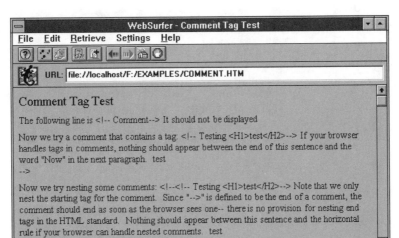

 Although the HTML specification does not restrict you from including HTML tags in a comment, it is better to be safe and avoid placing any tags in a comment. This means that you should not try to use a comment to prevent sections of a document from being displayed!

Logical and Physical Styles

The <ADDDRESS> tag is an example of a logical tag. It is intended to demark addresses, and it is left to the browser to determine how to display address fields. Most browsers choose to display addresses in italics, but this is not enforced; hence, it is called a logical style. Moreover, users may modify their browsers to display a logical style to their preferences. You can find a list of some other logical style tags in Table 2–2. In our tests of various browsers, we have found that browser support for the logical tags listed in this table is very uneven. The only tags consistently supported were STRONG and EM. Use the other tags with caution. You can check browser support for these tags by loading the \EXAMPLES\LOGICAL.HTM document.

TABLE 2–2 *Logical Style Tags*

Style Marker	Description
<CITE>	Used for bibliographic citations. Browsers usually display citations in italics.
<CODE>	Used to display snippets of computer code. Browsers usually display in a fixed-width font.
<EM>	Used to denote emphasis of the affected text. Browsers usually display emphasis in italics.
<KBD>	Used to denote user keyboard entry. Browsers often display in a bold fixed-width font.
<SAMP>	Used to denote a sequence of literal characters.
<STRONG>	Used to denote strong or important text. Browsers usually display in bold font.
<VAR>	Used to indicate a variable name.

Physical styles, on the other hand, specify the desired physical appearance of the affected text. Physical styles in HTML are listed in Table 2–3.

TABLE 2–3 *Physical Style Tags*

Command	Description
<B>	Bold style.
<I>	Italic style.
<TT>	Use typewriter text or fixed-width font.
<U>	Underline the text.

For both logical and physical styles, don't forget to include the closing tag to denote the end of the style.

Let's see how we can use these tags to dress up our documents. We'll go back to our description list, and add some physical and logical style commands:

```
<P>Essential items to have while kayaking:</P>
<DL>
<DT><STRONG>Life jacket</STRONG>
<DD>A life jacket is essential while kayaking as it provides
flotation.
<DT><B>Helmet</B>
<DD>A helmet protects the head against blows against rocks.
</DL>
<P>Other things you need include:</P>
<DL>
<DT><EM>Spray skirt</EM>
<DD>The spray skirt fits between the torso of the kayaker and
the boat, and prevents water from swamping the kayak.
<DT><I>Paddle</I>
<DD>A paddle allows the kayaker to navigate in the water.
</DL>
```

Now let's see how this looks:

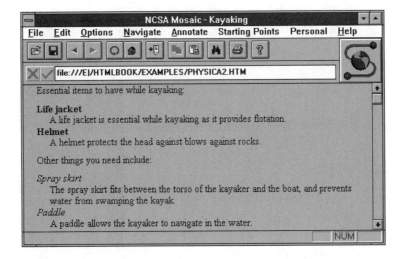

Did you notice that we did something a little unusual when we added our style commands? Although "Life jacket" and "Helmet" show up in a boldface font, we actually used different commands to make them appear that way. "Life jacket" is in a STRONG tag, and "Helmet" is in a B tag. As you can see, the browser treated these tags in a similar fashion. We did the same thing with "Spray skirt" and "Paddle." Spray skirt is in the logical tag, EM, and Paddle is in the physical tag, I. We don't recommend mixing the commands as we did in our sample document — we were only illustrating the similarity between these tags.

Since logical and physical styles can produce the same end result, there is some debate in the HTML community regarding the desirability of one form over the other. The consensus is that logical style markers should be used whenever possible since they give browsers greater flexibility in choosing the appropriate display for different elements. However, there are times when it might be necessary to use physical tags. For example, if you are providing instructions, you may want to put optional portions of commands in italics, and include a statement in your document explaining this convention. In this case you would need to be sure that certain portions of text really are in italics. Since browsers have more leeway on the rendering of <EM>, it would be safer to use <I> in a case like this.

We have included two documents—PHYSICAL.HTM and LOGICAL.HTM—on the CD that you can use to check how different elements look in different browsers.

Special Characters

HTML reserves four special ASCII characters for its own use. These are the left angle bracket (<), right angle bracket (>), ampersand (&) and quote ("). The alert reader will have noticed that the angle brackets are used to mark tags. The ampersand is used to signal the start of an escape sequence, while the quote is used around file names and URLs. These characters are frequently used in HTML documents, and browsers rely on these characters to interpret the documents.

If you wish to display these characters in your documents, you must use the escape sequences listed in Table 2–4.

TABLE 2–4 *Special Characters*

Escape sequence	Description
&lt;	The escape sequence for <
&gt;	The escape sequence for >
&amp;	The escape sequence for &
&quot;	The escape sequence for "

For example, you might want to display a section of HTML code in a document:

```
<P>Here are the escape sequences for some HTML characters:</P>
<PRE>
The escape sequence for &lt; is &amp;lt.
The escape sequence for &gt; is &amp;gt.
The escape sequence for &amp; is &amp;amp.
The escape sequence for &quot; is &amp;quot.
</PRE>
```

Here is how this looks in Mosaic:

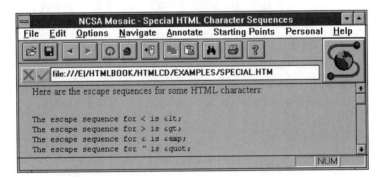

Unlike other HTML markers, escape sequences *are* case-sensitive. Escape sequences are also used in HTML for accented characters that occur in other languages. You can find a table of these in Appendix A.

The Kayaking Document

You can find a copy of the kayaking document on the CD in \EXAMPLES\KAYAK.HTM

The Good, the Bad and the Ugly

Let's sum up some of the lessons we've learned in this chapter:

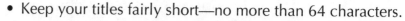

- Divide your documents into head and body parts.
- Don't forget closing tags.
- Never use more than one title in a document.
- Never use other tags in a title.
- Keep your titles fairly short—no more than 64 characters.
- Make your titles meaningful. For example, "Games" is a poor choice for a title; "Games on the Internet: MUDs" is better.
- When nesting lists, don't forget to close each list with the appropriate tag.
- Avoid HTML tags in comment fields—it is not a good idea to place portions of your document in a comment field to try to prevent it from being displayed. Browsers do not always handle tags within comment fields correctly.
- Look at your documents in more than one browser. Different browsers may display the same elements in dissimilar ways.

IN THIS CHAPTER YOU WILL LEARN

- WHAT A URL IS
- HOW TO LINK DOCUMENTS WITH URLs—THE "HYPER" PART OF HTML
- HOW TO LINK TO OTHER POPULAR NETWORK PROTOCOLS IN YOUR DOCUMENTS

In this chapter, we will be using the Netscape browser to display our documents. At the time this book was written, some network surveys indicate that Netscape was the most widely used Web browser—with around 70% of the market.

URLs AND LINKS

What's In This Chapter

This chapter introduces links—the "hyper" part of HTML. We also explain URLs and how to use them in links. We will be using the Netscape browser to display the examples in this chapter. At the time this book was written, some network surveys indicated that Netscape was the most widely used Web browser with somewhere around 70% of the market. Of course, this may change as more and more vendors bundle their own Web browsers with their network packages.

As a hypertext system, HTML allows you to link portions of a document to other locations that can be in either the same document or other documents. The links may be made from regions of text, icons, or graphics. They may point to a specific location within another document, or even to another section in the original document.

When a Web browser sees a link, it signals the available links to the user by underlining or coloring the link region. The link destination is communicated to the browser via a uniform resource locator (URL).

Uniform Resource Locators

In the previous chapters, we have mentioned URLs a number of times. You can think of URLs as addresses for documents on the Web. In order to make links you will need to understand what the different parts of a URL are. There are usually three parts in a URL: *protocol, hostname* and *filename*. These three parts are put together to make a URL as follows:

```
protocol://hostname/filename
```

A typical URL looks something like this:

```
http://www.ozone.com/kayak/top.html
```

In this example, "http:" indicates the name of the protocol that should be used for transfer, "www.ozone.com" is the name of the host, and "\kayak\top.html" is the name of the document. Now you may wonder why we are using the extension "html" rather than "htm" since htm is the actual extension. Even though htm is the extension used on Windows/DOS systems, html is used on most other systems.

Most browsers will automatically map references to a file with an "html" extension to a file with an "htm" extension on a Windows/DOS system. The majority of servers in use right now are not running on Window/DOS-based systems. It is likely that the pages you author on a Windows system will eventually end up on a server that supports files with an extension of "html" (even the Windows server included on the CD supports this). By taking advantage of this mapping feature by using "html" rather than "htm" in your filenames, you make your files more easily transportable across platforms.

Markup Tag: <A>

The link markup tag in HTML is <A> (denoting "anchor"). This is followed by the URL of the destination document. Then the content or name of the hypertext link (that is, the pointing link) is entered. The closing anchor tag is, of course, </A>.

Specifically, you specify a hypertext anchor in a document with the following somewhat cumbersome set of commands:

- Begin your anchor with "<A ". Don't forget the space after the A.
- Enter the URL of the destination document by typing HREF="*URL*".
- Enter ">".
- Enter the text that serves as the name or pointer to the destination document.
- Enter the closing container tag, </A>.

For example, we might wish to add to our kayak document a pointer to an FAQ on sea kayaking. The FAQ document is stored on another Web server, named www.intelenet.com, and the document is called /clubs/ckf/seakayaker. This link would be entered as follows:

```
Sea kayaking is also exciting. You can find out more about sea
kayaking in this
<A HREF="http://www.intelenet.com/clubs/ckf/seakayaker.html">
FAQ</A>.
```

Let's see how this looks in Netscape:

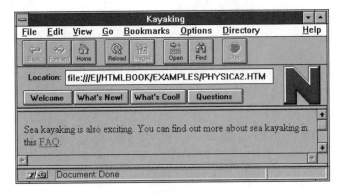

As you can see, the link shows up with an underline. It is also displayed in a different color.

Although the anchor tag is not case-sensitive, many systems (mostly UNIX) will not be able to find the file unless the path-name portion of the URL is treated as case-sensitive. This is not supposed to be the case according to the HTML specification, but in practice it is. Thus, http://ozone.com/myfile.htm is not necessarily the same as http://ozone.com/MyFile.htm. Make sure that you check your capitalization as well as spelling for URLs!

Partial Links

You can also make links that point to a file that is stored on the same machine and is in the same directory or subdirectory as the original document. In this case, you use a partial, or relative, URL as follows:

```
A number of <A HREF="magazine.htm">kayaking magazines</A> are
also available to help you learn more about the sport.
```

In this case, the browser assumes that the pointed-to document, magazine.htm, is located in the same directory as the original document, kayak.htm. It also assumes that the http protocol is used to retrieve the document.

In general, you should use partial links when pointing to related sets of documents. This way, it is easy to move entire sets of documents to a new location on the server if it becomes necessary. Be careful about trying to use relative URLs when your files are not on the same partition as your original file. These URLs may work correctly while checking your files with a browser locally, but will almost always fail when you try to access them through a server. For example, using an anchor that looks like this:

```
<A HREF="c:/html/magazine.htm">kayaking magazines</A>
```

may work correctly when you test your document with a browser locally; but when you move it to a server, you will probably find that the link no longer works. You should also avoid using ".." to try to transverse a directory tree in an upward direction. For example, you might be tempted to try something like the following:

```
<A HREF="../html/magazine.htm">kayaking magazines</A>
```

Like our previous example, this anchor works when the file is checked locally, but may not work correctly when moved to a server (depending on the server used). Rather than trying to use relative URLs when pointing to documents that are in neither the same directory or one of its subdirectories, you should use complete URLs. Note that some servers (primarily on UNIX systems) allow links to be made between unrelated directories. If you wish to make links between documents in unrelated directories, check with your site's webmaster to see whether this capability is supported by the local server.

You should use complete URLs when pointing to unrelated documents, or documents on other machines.

Specific Locations in Other Documents

In addition to pointing to other documents, links can be used to jump to specific locations within other documents, or even to another location within the same document.

For example, let's add a link within our kayak.htm document that specifically points to information about our favorite kayaking magazine in magazine.htm. To do this, we need to insert a named anchor to mark the location within magazine.htm. We name the destination location as follows:

```
<A NAME="wave">Wave~Length</A>
```

Then, when we create our link in the original document, kayak.htm, we include the URL pointing to the destination document, magazine.htm, as well as the name of the pointer to the desired destination anchor within the document. This is done using the hash mark (#), as follows:

```
<A HREF="magazine.htm#wave">Wave~Length</A>
```

Now when the reader clicks on the link "Wave~Length," not only will the reader be taken to the new file, magazine.htm, but directly to the specific location within that document. This is an especially useful feature when the destination document is long, and we don't want our reader to have to wade through a long document in order to find the section of interest.

Specific Locations within the Current Document

This notion of marking specific locations within documents using named anchors also applies within one document. Thus, we may choose to name several locations in one document, then have pointers to these locations within the same document. This is a quite useful feature if we wish to have a table of contents at the top of a long document. Readers may select items in the table of contents and be taken directly to that section of the document.

Naming anchors within one document works exactly the same way, except that the name of the destination document is omitted. Only the name of the anchor is included. For example, we may wish to put a pointer to the kayaking resource section at the top of the kayak document. First, we add a label to the beginning of the resource section, as follows:

```
<H2>Kayaking <A NAME="resources">Resources</A></H2>
```

Then, at the beginning of the document we add a link to this label:

```
<A HREF="#resources">kayaking resources</A></P>
```

Be careful when you reference links in the same document. Unlike links to other sites or files, which will usually cause browsers to leave your reader in the same location if something is wrong at the other end (for example, the other host is down or the browser is unable to find the file), browsers will not treat your readers kindly if something is wrong with the other end of a same-document link. Some browsers will dump your reader at the end of the document, while others may not do anything. Unlike links that go to other sites or files where you may have no control over the other end, you *do* have control over both ends of links within the same document. Make sure that you get it right!

Special Characters

URLs may include any alphanumeric character, and the symbols: hyphen (-), dollar sign ($), period (.), plus (+), exclamation point (!), star (*), left parenthesis "(", right parenthesis ")", single quote (') and underscore (_), typed in directly. If you're using a DOS or Windows system, the operating system limits you to these characters so you don't need to worry about putting something in a URL that will cause problems later.

However, you may occasionally want to make a link to a file on some other operating system that allows authors to be more creative with filenames. It is common for Macintosh filenames to include spaces, and it is not uncommon to find files with even more unusual characters in their names. When you run into this problem, you will need to encode the character. You encode characters by preceding the ASCII code for the character with a percent sign (%). For example, the ASCII code for the space character is 20. Thus, the URL for a file named "My Kayak" would be:

```
http://ozone.com/My%20Kayak
```

You can find an ASCII table in Appendix B, and on the CD in ASCII.HTM.

Other Ways to Use Links

Although at the beginning of this chapter we said that you can think of URLs as addresses for documents on the Web, they are actually much more than that. The key is the protocol portion of the URL. So far, all of our examples have used the Hypertext Transfer Protocol (http). However, you can specify protocols other than http, such as ftp, gopher, telnet, news or mail. By specifying the appropriate protocol in the URL, you can use links to send mail, transfer files or even make a telnet connection. One significant difference between the specification of the protocol and markup tags is that some browsers treat the protocol specification in a case-sensitive fashion. Therefore, it is not safe to assume that FTP is the same as ftp.

ALWAYS SPECIFY PROTOCOLS IN LOWER CASE.

A note of caution about the use of protocols other than http: as with markup tags, it is up to the browser to take the appropriate action for each protocol. Some browsers may not support all of the protocols. In these cases the browser will probably just ignore the reference.

We'll explain how to use some of the most popular protocols in URLs now.

FTP

When you specify FTP as the protocol in a URL, the browser will automatically make an anonymous FTP connection to the specified location, and transfer the requested file or provide a directory listing (depending on what you specify). Here is the format for an anonymous FTP URL:

```
ftp://hostname/directoryname/filename
```

Let's look at a few examples to see how this works. The following link will transfer a file called "kayak.gif" from the host ozone.com:

```
<A HREF="ftp://ozone.com/kayak.gif"> A Picture of a Kayak </A>
```

If a reader chooses this link, the browser will try to open an FTP connection to the host ozone.com and download the file kayak.gif. If you do not specify a filename, a directory listing will be provided:

```
Here are the files in our <A HREF="ftp://ozone.com/"> kayak
repository </A>.
```

Although ftp uses anonymous FTP as a default, you can also have the URL specify a particular user. We'll explain how to do this, but first a word of caution. After opening an FTP connection, browsers do not offer you the option of entering a password for the account if one is not provided. This means that you must include the password and account name as part of the URL if you want to use a specific account. This is a huge security hole since the password is not encrypted—anyone reading your document will be able to see it. Unless you have some special application that requires the use of a specific account, we strongly recommend that you avoid using this feature. The format for a URL that includes an account and password is:

```
ftp://username:password@hostname/path
```

For example, if we want to see a directory listing of Kelly Kayaker's account we could include the following in our kayaking document:

```
<p>Here is a <A HREF="ftp://kayaker:badidea@ozone.com/">
directory listing</A> of Kelly's account.
```

We have made extensive use of the ftp protocol in our browser.htm document (this is the document that you can use to get a variety of Windows browsers) on the CD. You should look at this document for more examples of this protocol.

File

The file protocol is for accessing files on a local disk. It is related to ftp because it will try to use FTP if you have specified a host other than the one on which the browser is being used. Here is the format for a file URL:

```
file://localhost/pathname
```

Mail

Using a link to send e-mail is an easy way to allow your readers to provide feedback about your document. The name for this protocol is *mailto*. Thus, the format for e-mail URLs is:

```
mailto:username@hostname
```

Two of the best places to put this option are in a short request for feedback at the beginning of the document, or as part of the address at the end of the document. Let's modify our kayak document to allow readers to send Kelly a message:

```
For more information contact:
<ADDRESS>Kelly Kayaker<BR>
<A HREF="mailto:kayaker@ozone.com"> kayaker@ozone.com </A>
</ADDRESS>
```

If the reader is using a browser that can send e-mail (note that WebSurfer in the Chameleon package does not offer this feature), kayaker@ozone.com will be highlighted in some fashion. If the reader clicks on it, it will provide a mail window that looks something like this:

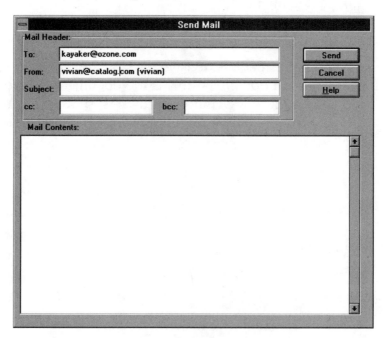

As you can see, the browser inserts the address specified in the URL in the "To" field.

Telnet

You can also use URLs to provide a telnet connection to the site of your choice. Telnet URLs appear in this format:

```
telnet://hostname:portnumber
```

You do not need to specify a port number if you want a connection made to the default telnet port. However, if you are making a link to a special service at a certain port, you will need to make the connection directly to that port. For example, the University of Michigan offers weather information on port 3000 on the host downwind.sprl.umich.edu. Let's incorporate this information in our kayak document:

```
It is important to know what the weather will be like before
going on a kayak trip. You can get National Weather Service
forecasts for any location from the  <A
HREF="telnet://downwind.sprl.umich.edu:3000"> University of
Michigan WEATHER UNDERGROUND</A>. <P>
```

When the reader chooses this link, the browser will call a helper application to make a telnet connection to port 3000 on the host downwind.sprl.umich.edu. You can try this yourself by loading the kayak document into a browser and choosing this link.

Gopher

Gopher is an information service developed at the University of Minnesota. It provides easy transfer of files because it encodes information about many types of files. However, since the Web includes similar file transfer facilities, it is usually easier to access files through http if a site offers both types of services. However, some sites still only offer gopher service. In this case, you will need to make a link through gopher. A gopher URL looks like this:

```
gopher://hostname:port/gophertype[item]
```

Gophertype is a single character indicating the type of thing to expect (see Table 3–1).

TABLE 3–1 Gophertypes

Type	Description
0	A text file.
1	A directory.
2	A CSO phone-book server.
3	Error.
4	A BinHexed Macintosh file.
5	A DOS binary archive of some sort.
6	A UNIX uuencoded file.
7	An Index-Search server.
8	The item points to a text-based telnet session.
9	The item is a binary file.
g	The item is a GIF format graphics file.
T	The item points to a text-based tn3270 session.
I	The item is some kind of image file.

The two most commonly used types are 0 (text) and 1 (directory). Let's add a link to a gopher site with kayaking information to our kayak document:

```
You can get more kayaking information from this <A
HREF="gopher://ftp.std.com/11/nonprofits/canoe.kayak">gopherse
rver</A>.
```

News

Newsgroups are an extensive set of electronic bulletin boards. There are newsgroups covering almost every conceivable topic. The news protocol allows you to make a link to a specific newsgroup. The format for URLs using this protocol is:

```
news:newsgroup
```

For example, we might want to make a link to the newsgroup rec.boats.paddle in our kayak document:

```
You can find more information about kayaks in the newsgroup
<A HREF="news:rec.boats.paddle"> rec.boats.paddle</A>.
```

You can also specify specific articles by replacing the name of the newsgroup with an article id in the URL. However, since news turns over so rapidly, this link would remain valid only a short time.

In order to use a newsgroup link, the reader's browser must support some news-reading mechanism, and must be configured to use a news (NNTP) server. This is a fairly new feature, and many browsers do not support it. While it is not your responsibility to make sure that your reader's browsers are set up correctly, if you make heavy use of news URLs, it might be helpful to your readers to include a warning about configuring their browsers to use an NNTP server before trying those links.

Link Trivia

There are a few things about links that we have not yet mentioned. We've left them for last, not because they are the best, but because right now they are not terribly important. Feel free to skip this section. We've told you about the attributes HREF and NAME in the anchor tag. We expect these tags to be the only ones you'll ever need to use. However, there are actually a number of other attributes that can be used with anchor tags, and so for completeness they are listed in Table 3–2. Browser support for these attributes is fairly spotty, and there is still debate about these attributes in the Web development community. For now, use them at your own risk.

TABLE 3–2 *Additional Anchor Tag Attributes*

Attribute	Description
REL	This is currently only proposed. It is supposed to give the relationship described by the link.
REV	Another proposed attribute. It is supposed to give the relationship described by the link in the opposite direction to REL.
URN	This stands for Uniform Resource Number, and is supposed to help the browser avoid reloading a document it has already acquired.
TITLE	This is only for information. It should provide the title of the document whose address is in the HREF attribute.
METHODS	This is supposed to provide information regarding the functions that the reader may perform on the object.

The Good, the Bad and the Ugly

Now that you know how to make links, it is time to go over some guidelines on when and where you should use them.

Don't fall into the *click here* trap. Many people have chosen to make links that look like this:

```
If you want to see my document on kayaking click <A
HREF="kayak.htm">here</A>.
```

While one "click here" in a document isn't necessarily a bad thing, it does not make good use of the browser's display features. Since most browsers highlight links, the links in a document are more conspicuous than the rest of the text. If most of your links are made to the same word, there is no way for the reader to quickly distinguish between the links. For example:

```
<UL>
<LI>Click <A HREF="bird.htm">here</A> for a document on birds.
<LI>Click <A HREF="cat.htm">here</A> for a document on cats.
```

```
<LI>Click <A HREF="dog.htm">here</A> for a document on dogs.
<LI>Click <A HREF="fish.htm">here</A> for a document on fish.
</UL>
```

When we see this in a browser, the word "here" leaps out. It is difficult to see what the links are actually for.

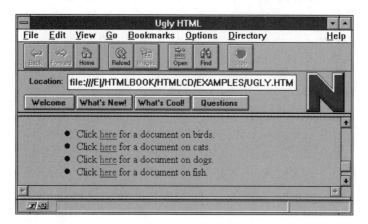

However, simply shifting the link over to the subject of each document and slightly rewriting each line clears up the problem.

```
<UL>
<LI>A document about <A HREF="bird.htm">birds</A>.
<LI>A document about <A HREF="cat.htm">cats</A>.
<LI>A document about <A HREF="dog.htm">dogs</A>.
<LI>A document about <A HREF="fish.htm">fish</A>.
</UL>
```

Now we have:

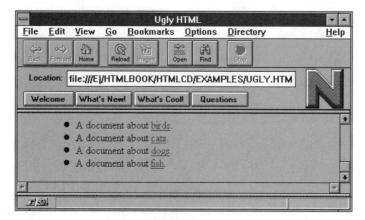

In our new and improved version, the topic of the document behind each link is easy to see.

It is easy to make links in inappropriate places. There are so many resources on the Internet, you may be tempted to make a link every time you mention something for which you have an Internet resource. Only place links where they really contribute something to the content of your document.

Finally, don't make your anchor text too long. While there is nothing to stop you from making a whole sentence into a link, doing this is unsightly and does not make it any easier for your reader to follow the link. Rather than using a long phrase as a link, choose the words in the phrase that most clearly describe the link and place your anchor tags around them.

IN THIS CHAPTER YOU WILL LEARN

- HOW TO INCLUDE IMAGES IN YOUR HTML DOCUMENTS
- HOW TO WORK WITH DIFFERENT TYPES OF GRAPHICS FORMATS
- WHY SOME FORMATS ARE BETTER THAN OTHERS
- HOW TO MAKE IMAGES WITH "CLICKABLE" HOT SPOTS
- HOW TO INTEGRATE VIDEO AND SOUND INTO YOUR HTML DOCUMENTS

MULTIMEDIA: IMAGES, VIDEO AND SOUND

What's In This Chapter

This chapter explains how to turn your HTML documents into multimedia presentations. We explain how to include images in your HTML documents. We will tell you about different types of graphics formats, explain why some are better than others for HTML, and show you how to make images with clickable "hot spots." We'll also discuss video and sound, and explain how to best incorporate them into your documents.

Images in HTML Documents: <IMG>

We spent much time discussing how to format text in your documents—but HTML also supports multimedia authoring on the Web. To make the best use of HTML's power, you also want to have pointers to or include multimedia elements such as images in your documents.

HTML supports the ability to display embedded images within textual documents. The syntax for an embedded image is similar to the one used for links. The image itself is pointed to with a URL, as follows:

```
<IMG SRC=URL_of_image>
```

Graphics Formats

Images may be stored in many formats. However, if a reader does not have a viewer for your image's format, he or she will not be able to see the image. You should always try to offer your images in a popular format to increase the likelihood that your readers will be able to view them.

On the CD you will find a copy of LViewPro, a shareware package that allows you to create, view, modify and transfer images between a number of different formats. You can use this package to make sure that your images are in a format your readers are able to view.

Table 4–1 displays many of the common file formats used on the Web, and their recognized file name extensions. Browsers use the file name extension to determine which viewer is needed for a particular image, so images *must* be given a file name extension that matches the image type.

Choosing an Image Format

As shown in Table 4–1, there are many formats that may be used to store images. However, most browsers only have built-in or "inline" support for one or two formats. While most browsers may be configured to support additional formats, it is up to the user to do so. Additionally, when a browser must use an external program to display an image, the image does not

TABLE 4–1 Common Multimedia File Extensions

Description	Extension
GIF image	.gif
JPEG image	.jpg or .jpeg
TIFF image	.tiff
XBM bitmap image	.xbm
Windows Bitmap image	.bmp
PostScript file	.ps
PICT image	.pict
AIFF sound	.aiff
AU sound	.au
QuickTime movie	.mov
MPEG movie	.mpeg or .mpg

appear in the browser window; instead, the browser runs the viewer program, and the image is displayed in the viewer program's window.

Since you cannot count on your readers to configure their browsers to support additional image formats, it is advisable to choose one of the widely supported formats for your images. Many tools exist to convert images from one format to another (including our favorite image tool, LViewPro), so even if you have images in a less common format it is a fairly straightfoward task to transfer them to one of the popular formats.

At this time the two most widely supported image formats are GIF and JPEG. JPEG stands for Joint Photographic Experts Group, which is the group that originally developed this standard. There is a related standard called MPEG that is used for video. We will discuss MPEG later, in the section on video.

JPEG stores information about the image by keeping track of the color changes in the image, rather than storing information about each pixel in the image. It is what is known as a *lossy* format because the final image is not exactly the same as the original. However, the human eye does not usually perceive the tiny differences introduced by JPEG. The big advantage offered by the JPEG storage format is that for certain types of images JPEG images typically take less storage space (and hence require less transmission time) than do equivalent GIF images. For example, the picture of Kelly Kayaker on the CD in JPEG format requires 26 kb of storage space, while the same picture in GIF format requires 122 kb of space. This dramatic difference in the storage requirement illustrates JPEG's strength in storing photographs and other images with a wide variety of shadings. This advantage does not hold for line drawings. For those types of images, GIF may require less storage space.

Although JPEG is popular, GIF formatted images are still the most common and have the widest support. We recommend offering your images in GIF format whenever possible.

Graphics Interchange Format (GIF)

As we mentioned in the previous section, the most common format for images on the Web is Graphics Interchange Format (GIF), which was developed by CompuServe. You can be fairly sure that if you provide images in GIF format, as long as the browser supports any image display, it will be able to display your image. If you already have a collection of images in some other format, consider converting them to GIF. You will find an application called LView Pro in the TOOLS directory on the CD that can be used to convert many formats to GIF.

Choosing the basic format for your image is only the first step in making the images in your documents look as good as possible. We will discuss other issues that should be considered later in this chapter.

We've included a number of GIF images in the GIF directory on the CD that you can use to experiment with images in documents. You are welcome to use these images as you wish.

Now let's add some pictures to our kayak document. It would be nice to have some pictures next to the choices in the table of contents at the beginning of the document. As you may recall, we had a table of contents that looked like this:

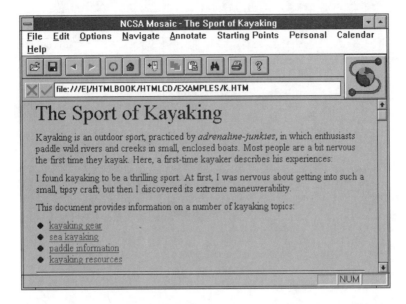

Those bullets are pretty boring, and we just happen to have some small GIF pictures that would work well in their place. We will put the image in the file KAYAK.GIF next to "kayaking gear," and the image in SEA.GIF in next to "sea kayaking." Here are the commands we use to add these images:

```
<P><A HREF="kayak.htm#gear"><IMG SRC="gif/kayak.gif">
kayaking gear</A>
<P><A HREF="kayak.htm#seakayak"><IMG SRC="gif/sea.gif">
sea kayaking</A>
```

If you look carefully at this example, you will see that we have placed the images inside an anchor tag. Although the images did not have to be inside the anchor, placing them there makes them a link. Now the reader can click on either the picture or the text to make the jump. As you will see, Mosaic also frames images that are links to let the reader know that the link is there. Most other browsers use a frame to indicate the presence of a link, although some browsers may use other methods to display the link.

Now let's see how our changes look in Mosaic:

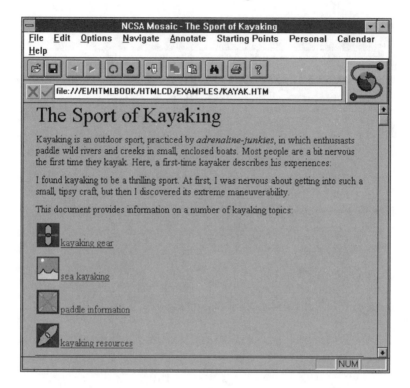

It's much fancier than our original list! Unfortunately there is a lot of wasted space since HTML currently doesn't provide a way to line things up in columns. This will change in the next version of HTML, but for now we have to approximate it. We do this by enclosing our table of contents in <PRE> tags, and adjusting our spacing to line up the images. Remember that line breaks are significant in areas that are tagged with <PRE>, so be careful not to accidently insert extra lines. The lines in our document are too long to show here in their entirety, but you can look at them on the CD in the document KAYAK2.HTM. Here we show you as much as will fit on the page:

```
<PRE>
<A HREF="kayak2.htm#gear"><IMG SRC="gif/kayak.gif"> kayaking gear</A>...
<A HREF="kayak2.htm#paddle"><IMG SRC="gif/paddle.gif"> paddle ...
</PRE>
```

We are going to make one more adjustment to the image and show you how it looks.

Aligning Images

Browsers generally display an embedded image with the bottom of the image aligned with the text in the document. For those of you who wish to align your images in some other manner, the IMG tag offers the ALIGN option. For aligning text with the top of an image, use ALIGN=TOP. For aligning text with the center of an image, use the ALIGN=MIDDLE tag. For example, if we want our kayak images to be aligned with the middle of the text baseline, we would change the image tags to include ALIGN=MIDDLE:

```
<IMG SRC="kayak.gif" ALIGN=MIDDLE>
```

Now let's take a look and see how PRE and ALIGN changed our document:

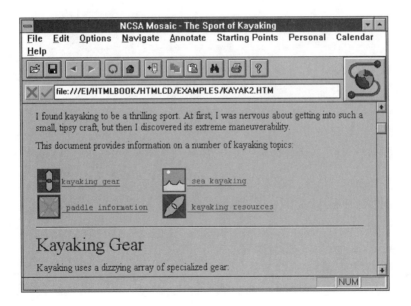

Images and Text-Only Browsers

Some browsers, such as Lynx, are not able to display images. Rather than simply ignoring those users, the ALT option allows you to display text to those users who use a browser that cannot display images.

With our kayak image, we may wish to substitute text indicating the content of the image for browsers that cannot display it, as follows:

```
<P><A HREF="kayak.htm#gear"><IMG SRC="gif/kayak.gif"
ALT="[Kayak Icon]"> kayaking gear</A>
<P><A HREF="kayak.htm#seakayak"><IMG SRC="gif/sea.gif"
ALT="[Sea Icon]"> sea kayaking</A>
<P><A HREF="kayak.htm#paddle"><IMG SRC="gif/paddle.gif"
ALT="[Paddle Icon]"> paddle information</A>
```

Users reading this document with a text-only browser will, instead of the embedded image, see the alternate text, such as "[Kayak Icon]." The following image shows how this section looks in Lynx.

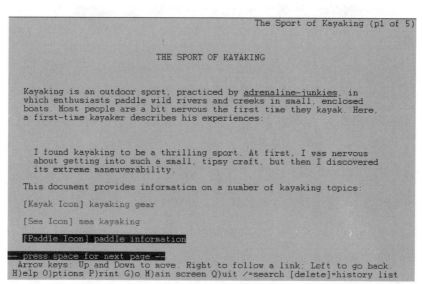

Transparent Backgrounds

Some images look better if their own backgrounds do not appear, giving them the appearance of floating on the browser's background. For example, if you have made a red button for your links, it would detract from the look of the button to have a white square background appear in back of it. If your image is in GIF89a format (or is in a format that can be converted to GIF89a), you can modify it so that the background is "transparent." What this means is that one color in the image is designated as the transparency color. When the image is displayed, this color is replaced with whatever background color is used by the display window. The key to transparency is in the version of GIF. There is actually more than one version of GIF. Most GIF images are in GIF87 format, which is an old version of GIF that does not support transparency.

It is a fairly simple process to convert your GIF files to the new format using LView Pro. We'll explain how to do this in the section about LView that's coming up.

Since there is no way to indicate that only the background is to be made transparent, your image's background must be a solid color, and the color must not be in use elsewhere in the image. As you can see, transparent backgrounds are not suited for many types of images. In particular, photographs do not work well with transparent backgrounds since their backgrounds are rarely solid colors, and it is difficult to make sure that the background color is not used elsewhere in the image. However, as mentioned, this technique is an excellent one to use with buttons and other icons.

A note of warning about design decisions for transparent backgrounds: not all browsers currently provide support for them. If a browser does not support transparency, it will display the image with the image's own background. One way to get around this problem is by choosing the background color to be the gray color many browsers use for their own backgrounds. This way, the image's background will still blend in with the browser's background even if the browser does not support transparent images. However, not all browsers use gray as a background color, so this is not an infallible technique.

Interlaced Images

Interlaced images are images in which the scan lines have been rearranged so that a low-resolution version of the image can be displayed quickly. The rest of the image is then filled in over four passes. Although storing images in this format does not speed up their transmission time, it does provide readers with a quick preview of the final image and helps to provide the impression that your document has loaded quickly. Although Netscape Navigator is the only browser we tested that has support for this format, we expect other browsers to begin supporting it as well. LViewPro can be used to convert non-interlaced images into interlaced images.

Thumbnails

It has been said that a picture is worth a thousand words. In the case of HTML and pictures, a picture can be worth much more than a thousand words—at least in the amount of time it takes to transfer the picture to your reader's system. Pictures can make a document look great, but if it takes your reader a couple of hours to transfer the document, odds are pretty high that he or she won't be willing to wait, no matter how great your pictures are. Image files are usually fairly large, and many people are still reading documents over slow phone lines. The answer? Thumbnail copies of your images. A thumbnail copy of an image is a small version (typically around one inch wide) that your readers can use to decide whether they want to get the full-size version.

As an example, we have a GIF picture of Kelly in her kayak. The full size picture is approximately 122 kb, but our thumbnail version is only 5 kb. By putting the thumbnail picture in our document with a link to the full size picture, we have saved our readers over 100 kb (unless they decide to get the full size picture). If your reader is using a 14.4b modem, this translates to approximately one minute. While one minute is not a lot of time, you can see how this adds up if you have any number of images at all.

LViewPro

How do you make thumbnail copies of pictures, use transparent backgrounds, and make sure that your images are in GIF format? A nifty shareware program called LViewPro can solve all of these problems for you. LViewPro is an image file editor for Microsoft Windows 3.1, Win32s and Windows NT. It can load and save image files in JPEG JFIF, GIF 87a or 89a, TIFF, Truevision Targa, Windows and OS/2 BMP, ZSoft's PCX, and PBMPLUS' PBM, PGM and PPM formats.

Installing LViewPro

If you did a full installation, LViewPro is already installed on your PC, and may be accessed from the HTML CD Menu. If you did not do a full installation and did not install the toolbox, you will need to run HTML CD Setup to install LViewPro. To do this, first make sure that the HTML CD is in your CD-ROM drive. Then click on the HTML CD Setup icon, and choose "Custom Installation". By default, Setup will place LViewPro in a subdirectory under C:\HTMLCD.

Now choose the Options button next to the HTML Toolbox, and choose LViewPro:

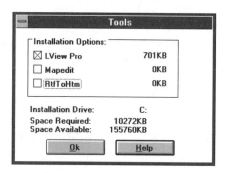

Next, click on Ok, and then on Install in the Custom Installation window. Unless you want to install or reinstall any of the other applications, make sure that they are not checked before you click on Install.

Starting LViewPro

After Setup is done, you can access LViewPro through the HTML CD Menu. You will find it in the Toolbox:

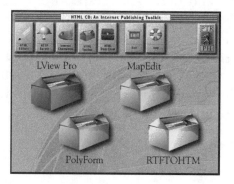

To start it, click on the toolbox icon under the LView Pro label. If you prefer, you may also create an icon for it in a program group by dragging it from the file manager into the group of your choice. You will find it in the subdirectory c:\htm-lcd\tools\lviewp1b\lviewp1b.exe. If you do this, you should then see the following icon in your program group:

Lviewp1b

Making Thumbnails

Now that L-View Pro is installed, let's see how to use it to translate Kelly's image from JPEG to GIF and make a thumbnail copy of it. First, we load the image by choosing "Open" from the File pulldown menu. We enter the name of the file, and then get the following screen:

To get a version of our image in GIF format, we choose "Save as" from the File menu, set the file type to GIF, and save the file:

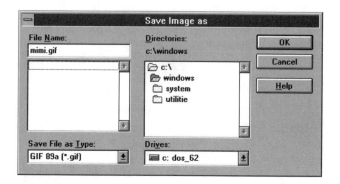

LView also knows about the GIF89 format (as you may recall, this is the version of GIF that allows "transparent" backgrounds), although in this example we choose GIF87. Now we have a GIF version of our image. Making a thumbnail version is just as easy. From the Edit pulldown menu, we choose "Resize" (you can also type <CTRL-R> as s shortcut). We enter "101" in the first box by "New size," and then hit a tab to let Lview fill in the second dimension. We then click on OK. Now we have a thumbnail-sized copy of our image. We go to "Save as" again and choose a new filename for our small image, and we're done.

Creating Transparent Backgrounds

As we mentioned in the section on transparent backgrounds, LView Pro can save an image with transparent color information. The procedure is fairly simple. First, use the Open command in the File menu to load your image into LViewPro. Next, choose Color Depth from the Retouch menu and make sure that the image is palette-based:

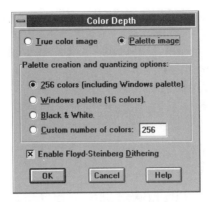

If the window comes up with the True color image button checked, simply click on the Palette Image button to convert the image to a palette-based format. Now choose Background Color from the Options menu. A window similar to the following should appear:

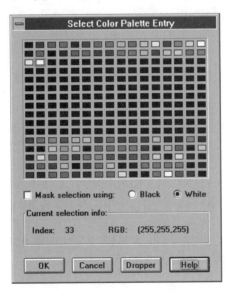

Select the palette entry for the color that you wish to make transparent. You do this by clicking either on the box with the color you want or the Dropper button, and then clicking on one of the pixels in the image. You may use the black and white masks to help you to verify whether you have chosen the correct color. Note that the currently chosen color will show up in the *Current selection info:* box. After you are satisfied with your choice, choose Save As from the File menu. Select GIF89a as the desired format, choose a filename, and you're done. You should load the image in a browser that supports transparent backgrounds (such as NCSA Mosaic or Netscape Navigator) to verify that the image is in the correct format.

Creating Interlaced Images

GIF files in either GIF87a or GIF89a format may also be saved with interlaced rows. To add this feature to your image, check Save GIFs Interlaced from the Options menu before saving your image in one of the GIF formats.

LView can be used to manipulate your images in many other ways as well, and there is an extensive help system that contains additional information about image formats. We think you will find it to be an invaluable tool.

Images with Clickable Spots: Image Maps

We've explained how to make images that are links. Now we'll show you how to do even fancier linking with images. Rather than making the entire image a single link, it is possible to make images with "hot spots" that have links. Readers can click on these spots to follow the link. For example, you could include the image of a map with hot spots that link points on the map to documents which describe those locations; or a picture of a car with each part of the car linked to a document describing how that part works.

Clickable images work by being associated with a coordinate map of the image that has links associated with specific coordinates. The association between the map and image is made by the server, so clickable images only work through a server. Here are the basic steps of making a clickable image:

1. *Get an image. The best images for this purpose should have well-defined sections and be in GIF format.*

2. *Decide what links you want to make to which sections of your image.*

3. *Make a coordinate map for your image. Different servers use different formats, so you will need to know the appropriate format for your server before you do this. You can make a map manually or with an application such as mapedit. We strongly recommend using an application to make the map.*

4. *Add information about your coordinate map to your Web server. If you are running your own server, you can do this yourself. If not, you'll need to ask the person in charge of your Web server to do it for you.*

5. *Make a document that includes your clickable image. You specify the image as being clickable by including the ISMAP attribute with the IMG tag.*

6. *Load your document in a browser and check it.*

Let's go through an example. We will make a weekly schedule of events for Kelly's kayak club. First, we need an image. We decide that we want an image with a square for each day of the week. There are many sources for images on the Internet, and you will find links to some of them in the icon catalog on the CD. However, our image is fairly simple, so we draw it with the drawing tool in our word processing application, and then use a screen grabber (you can use LView to make screen dumps) to convert it to GIF format. We place the image in a file called WEEK.GIF.

The next step is to make the image map. It is difficult to create an image map by hand since you would first need to have a tool that can display coordinates for points on a GIF image, and then you would need to locate the coordinates for each "hot spot" and manually enter them in the map file. Different servers use different formats for these maps, so you would also need to know the format for your server. Fortunately, we have included a program on the CD that automates this process for you.

Mapedit

Mapedit automates the process of image map creation by loading GIF images into a scrollable, resizable window. It allows you to outline polygons, circles and rectangles on top of your image, and link a URL to each item. Mapedit also allows you to go back and delete these "hot spots," set a default URL for clicks outside of the "hot" areas and associate comments of arbitrary length with each object. It even knows about the formats for the NCSA and CERN servers.

Installing Mapedit

If you did a full installation, Mapedit is already installed on your PC, and may be accessed from the HTML CD Menu. If you did not do a full installation and did not install the toolbox, you will need to run HTML CD Setup to install it. To do this, first make sure that the HTML CD is in your CD-ROM drive. Then click on the HTML CD Setup icon, and choose "Custom Installation". By default, Setup will place Mapedit in a subdirectory under C:\HTMLCD. If you wish to install it in another location, click on the "Set Location" button, and enter the alternate location.

Now choose the Options button next to the HTML Toolbox, and choose Mapedit in the Tools window:

Next, click on Ok, and then on Install in the Custom Installation window. Unless you want to install or reinstall any of the other applications, make sure that they are not checked before you click on Install.

Running Mapedit

After the installation is complete, you may run Mapedit from the HTML Menu by going to the toolbox section and choosing the toolbox icon under Mapedit:

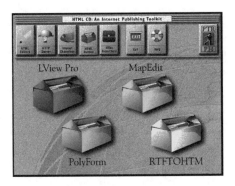

Alternatively you could create an icon for Mapedit in a program group by dragging Mapedit from the File Manager into the group. You will find Mapedit on your hard disk in :

```
TOOLS\MAPEDIT\MAPEDIT.EXE
```

under the top-level directory specified in Setup. After being copied to a program group, the following icon should appear:

Mapedit

Using Mapedit

Let's see how to use mapedit by making a map for Kelly's weekly planner. We click on the icon to start mapedit, and get the following screen:

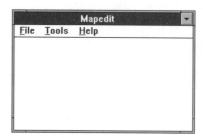

From the File pulldown menu, we choose Open/Create, and get this screen:

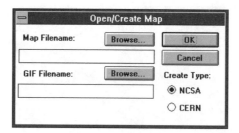

Now we enter the name of Kelly's Weekly Schedule image, week.gif, in the GIF Filename slot. Although there is no requirement to do so, the map file typically has the same name as the image file with the extension of "map." So we enter "week.map" in the Map Filename slot. We will be testing our map with the WHTTP server, which uses the NCSA format, so we choose NCSA under "Create Type."

Since this is a new map, the program notices that it doesn't exist, and asks us to confirm the setup. Make sure you check the box that matches your server under "Create Type."

It takes a little time to load the image into the program, so you need not be concerned if nothing happens immediately (there is no status bar to show you the progress of the load—you just have to be patient). After the image is loaded, it will appear in the mapedit window. Here is how Kelly's Weekly Schedule looks:

Now we want to make a link for each day of the week. In the Tools pulldown menu you have the option of choosing polygon, circle or rectangle for coordinate shapes. We choose rectangle since our planner has squares for each day of the week. Now we are ready to start making "hot spots." We start with Monday by clicking the left mouse button on one corner, and the right mouse button on another (note that with any of the shapes you can always hit the <Esc> button to cancel your outline). As soon as we hit the right mouse button we get this screen:

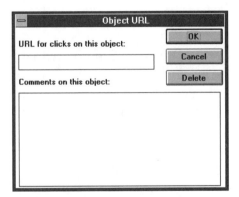

We've prepared a document named "monday.htm" that has a list of events on Monday, so we enter file://localhost/monday.htm" in the URL box. We repeat this procedure for each day.

We also have a general announcement file named "info.htm" that we want to display when people click on sections of the image that are not tied to a specific day. We do this by choosing "Edit default URL" from the File menu, and entering the URL for our file in the box. Now we do a preliminary check of our map using the "Test+Edit" option under the Tools menu. We click on each hot spot, and the URL box for that spot appears. After we are done, we choose "Save" under the File menu to save the map. Here is how our finished map looks:

```
default file://info.htm
rect moday.htm 8,6 62,62
#Tuesday's events
rect tuesday.htm 69,12 117,58
#Wednesday's Events
rect wednesda.htm 125,10 176,59
#Thursday's events
rect thursday.htm 182,12 233,55
#Friday's events
rect friday.htm 242,13 290,59
#Saturday's events
rect saturday.htm 301,12 349,62
#Sunday's events
rect sunday.htm 355,10 406,59
```

ISMAP

Now we create a document with the image. We use the ISMAP attribute to indicate that this is a "clickable image." ISMAP is an attribute that identifies an image as an image map. We place the image in an anchor tag that links it to the imagemap application in the server area. We are using WHT-TPD, so our line is specific to this server. You will need to get the appropriate command from the person in charge of your Web server. The line for the image would be:

```
<A HREF="/cgi-bin/imagemap.exe/week"><IMG SRC="week.gif"
ISMAP></A>
```

In \EXAMPLES\WEEKLY.HTM on the CD you can see the whole document. Since we are using the WHTTP server, and have control over it, we can add information about our image ourselves (you may need to coordinate this with the person in charge of your Web server.) We go to the file "conf\imagemap.cnf" in the WHTTPD directory, and add the line:

```
week: c:\gif\week.map
```

You will not be able to test a clickable image if you open a file locally with a browser. The server handles the mapping, so you can only access the hot spot functionality through a server.

Using Video in Your Web Pages

Video and animations are two of the most dramatic and eye-catching elements that you can include in your Web documents. The two most common formats used on the Web are:

Quicktime

A format, originally developed for the Macintosh, which allows users to view and edit video, animation, sound, text, music and other dynamic information. From a technical point of view, Quicktime supports two kinds of files: image files and time-based movie files.

MPEG (Moving Picture Expert Group)

A standard for digital video (sequences of images in time) and audio compression. MPEG is expected to become the industry standard for delivery of interactive television. There is a new version of MPEG (MPEG-2) which supports audio. Older MPEG files sometimes use .wav for audio. QuickTime also supports MPEG compressed video.

As usual with Web documents, the format used is specified via the file name extension. For Quicktime, use .qt or .mov as the extension. For MPEG, use .mpg or .mpe as the file name extension.

Desktop digital video is relatively new, so it's a moving target. There are many other variables that will affect the quality of your video presentations (only some of which you can control):

- The compression rate used when making the movie
- The program and setting used to translate between formats (for example, the program we used, SParkle, drops sound)

- The player program (MPEG players apparently vary widely in how well they support the standard)
- Player playback options (for example, having the player drop frames to keep up, or not)
- The CPU power of the machine used to play the video

A document named \EXAMPLES\VIDEO.HTM is provided on the CD that includes a number of videos. The Quicktime video that is part of this document was made with a black-and-white digital video camera called QuickCam, made by Connectix. Although it is a short clip—only about eight seconds long—it takes up 880K of disk space. If it was color, the clip would take up even more space. This should drive home the point that video storage requires large amounts of disk space.

We translated the clip into MPEG format, and now it only takes up about 180K. If you view the clip, you will see that we've lost both quality and sound!

In sum, if you plan to incorporate video into your Web documents, you must ensure that you have adequate disk space. In addition, you'll probably also want to have a fast server machine and a fairly high-bandwidth network connection. Otherwise, Web clients trying to retrieve video documents risk having to wait a long time while the video is transferred. Worse, if it takes too long, their network connection might abort partway through the process!

Links to Images, Sounds, Movies

Instead of embedding images, you may wish to include pointers in your document to external images, sound, movies and so on. This way, users can decide if they wish to load and view large nontext documents. To include a pointer to such files, the usual link syntax is used, and the external document is referred to via a URL. As with embedded images, the file name extension must be used to specify the file type. Browsers need to know the file type of a nontext document in order to use the appropriate viewer to display them.

The Good, the Bad and the Ugly

Turning a Web document into a multimedia presentation can be fun, but it is easy to get carried away. Here are some guidelines to keep your documents under control:

- Be nice to your readers. If you have a large image, offer either a thumbnail or a plain-text link to it. On a related note, for video and sound as well as images, it is a good idea to include the size of the multimedia element next to the link that will be used to retrieve it.

- Remember to use the ALT attribute so that readers without a graphical browser are not left out.

- If is often possible to reduce an image's storage requirements by reducing the number of colors in its palette. You can do this with LViewPro. Reducing the number of colors also reduces the likelihood that all of the available colors on your reader's system will get used up.

- In general, you should try to offer your images in GIF format.

- Interlaced images will allow readers with a browser that supports this format to see what the image looks like more quickly.

IN THIS CHAPTER YOU WILL LEARN

- How to create documents supporting user input

- How to use PolyForm, the CGI forms-handling application included on the CD

  Browser support for forms varies. Therefore, we will be using a number of different browsers to display our examples in this chapter.

FORMS AND THE COMMON GATEWAY INTERFACE (CGI)

What's In This Chapter

In this chapter, we describe how to create documents that contain tags supporting user input. We then describe how to write programs that process user input and send new output to users back through the Web server. These interactions are accomplished through the use of Common Gateway Interface (CGI) scripts. Browser support for forms varies quite a bit from browser to browser, so we will be using a number of different browsers to display our examples in this chapter.

Introduction

By definition, Web documents are interactive. If a document contains a hyperlink, users can individually select links and choose their own pathway through the information.

The Web also supports other ways for users to interact with documents. HTML version 2.0 and higher provides support for several kinds of user interactions. For example, Web documents can contain graphics with clickable regions, and support keyword searches of databases. Documents can also cause a program to be executed with the input to the program supplied by the user. The output from the program is then displayed to the user, typically in a new Web document. We call these kinds of documents "highly interactive documents".

In a typical scenario, user input and output is processed in the following manner. A Web document uses special HTML tags to collect user input. This document also specifies which program on the Web server should process the user input. After the user has entered the desired input, it is then packaged by the browser and sent to the server. The Web server recognizes that this particular browser request contains a user query and specifies a program. Accordingly, the server ships the user input to the responsible program, and continues being a Web server. In turn, the program is run using the input from the user. If the program has output—for example, a new Web document—the program sends the output to the server, which then ships it back to the requesting browser. In this way, the Web documents returned to users are specifically tailored to users' input. Figure 5-1 illustrates this process.

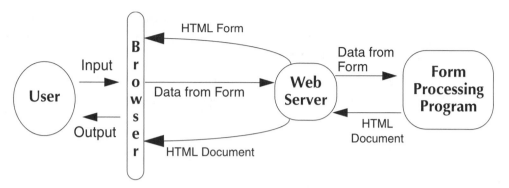

FIGURE 5–1   Flow of Information for Forms.

As with all HTML elements, forms depend on browsers. However, since forms are a relatively new element, browser support for forms varies wildly from browser to browser. This is one area where testing your documents in several browsers is especially important. We will display each of our examples in at least two browsers to give you some idea of the variety you can expect.

Although most browsers we tested support forms in some fashion, there are still many browsers that don't. When you use form elements in a document, you should warn your readers that they may not be able to access all the features by including a line stating that forms support is required.

Forms

HTML has several types of markup types that support higher levels of interaction with the user. We first describe the FORM tag.

Forms: <FORM>

The Form element is an HTML tag that is used to demark a data input form. A region using Forms is enclosed within the <FORM> </FORM> pair of markup tags. A Web document can contain several forms, but the Form element itself cannot be nested within other Form elements. However, forms can be embedded within other HTML tags. Similarly, within a Forms region, the usual HTML formatting tags can be inserted.

The Form element allows four possible attributes. They are ACTION, METHOD, SUBMIT and RESET. We explain these attributes in the following example.

Suppose we wish to author a user-survey questionnaire within a Web document. We would begin our Form as follows:

```
<HTML>
<HEAD>
<TITLE>Testing Forms</TITLE>
</HEAD>
<BODY>
<H1>User Survey</H1>
<FORM METHOD="POST" ACTION="http://ozone.com/cgi-bin
/survey.cgi">
</FORM>
```

The ACTION attribute specifies the destination URL to which the form should be submitted once it has been completed by the user. If no URL is specified, the URL of the current document containing the form is used. Here, our destination URL is:

```
http://ozone.com/cgi-bin/survey.cgi
```

In this example, the file "survey.cgi" is a CGI script that parses and collates users' responses. We have located the program in the directory called "cgi-bin." The actual location of CGI scripts or programs is dependent on how the server is set up, and must be discussed with your server administrator.

The method used to transmit the users' response is defined by both the access method contained in the URL and the value of the METHOD attribute. Thus, the value contained in the METHOD attribute must be compatible with the access method defined in the URL. The method attribute specifies the way in which the data from the user is encoded; the program that receives the user input naturally expects the user data to be encoded in this manner.

The default METHOD is GET. However, for most applications, we prefer the POST method. The reason for this preference will become clear in the section on CGI scripts. Note that the value of the METHOD attribute is case-sensitive on some systems!

As we will describe, a form is generally submitted by the user once the "Submit" button or "Return" key is pressed. When a form is submitted, the destination URL receives a string containing the selections and text entry made by the responding user. The method you choose determines how the data is sent to the server. The selection of a method is a server-side issue, and must be discussed with your Web server administrator. In the section on CGI scripts, we explain how to use CGI scripts to decode data sent via forms.

Each field within a form is defined by the following nested elements: INPUT, TEXTAREA, SELECT, and OPTION. These are described next. These fields must use the NAME attribute to identify the value selected by the user when the form is completed and submitted by the user. Thus, the submitted contents usually contain a stream of name/value pairs. The name is equal to the NAME attributes of the various elements within the Form. The value is equal to the entries made by the responding user.

Input: <INPUT>

The Input tag is a nested element within a Form, denoted by <INPUT>. It specifies the kind of input field presented to the user. The contents of the input field are then modifiable by the user.

For example, in our user survey, we may wish to ask the user's gender, by having the user click on a radio button. Our document would look like the following:

```
<HTML>
<TITLE>Testing Forms</TITLE>
<H1>User Survey</H1>
<FORM METHOD="POST" ACTION=" http://ozone.com/cgi-
bin/survey.cgi">
<B>What is your gender?</B>
<BR>
<INPUT NAME="gender" VALUE="male" TYPE=radio>Male
<INPUT NAME="gender" VALUE="female" TYPE=radio>Female
</FORM>
```

The Input tag uses the following, optional attributes: NAME, TYPE, CHECKED, ALIGN, MAXLENGTH, SIZE, SRC, and VALUE. These attributes are described in Table 5-1.

TABLE 5-1   Input Attributes

Attribute	Description
NAME	The name of the particular form item. This attribute is required for most input types. When parsing a user's input, the NAME value is used to provide a meaningful identifier for a field.
CHECKED	Indicates that a checkbox or radio button is selected.
ALIGN	When an image is used, this specifies the vertical alignment of the image. The syntax is the same as that of the <IMG> tag.
MAXLENGTH	Indicates the maximum number of characters that can be entered by users in a text field. If this attribute is not set, there is no limit on the number of characters.
SIZE	Specifies the size of the field and depends on its type.
SRC	Denotes URL for an image. This is used only with IMAGE type.
VALUE	Contains the initial value displayed to users. This attribute is required for radio buttons.
TYPE	Defines the type of data used in the field. The default is free-text input. The following types are definable: CHECKBOX, RADIO, HIDDEN, IMAGE, TEXT, PASSWORD, SUBMIT and RESET.

CHECKBOX Type

A checkbox is an item where several values can be selected at the same time. This type is submitted as separate name/value pairs, with a name/value pair submitted for each selected value. The default value for checkboxes is *on*.

There are two ways you could set up your checkboxes: set a unique name for each checkbox, or set a unique value for each checkbox.

The more common choice is to set a unique value for each checkbox. It is vital that you do at least one of these things; otherwise, you will not be able to distinguish between different boxes. For example:

```
<B>Why do you browse the Web?</B><BR>
<input NAME ="browse" TYPE=checkbox>Fun
<input NAME ="browse" TYPE=checkbox>Work
<input NAME ="browse" TYPE=checkbox>Research
<input NAME ="browse" TYPE=checkbox>Education
```

In this example no value is set, so all of the checkboxes would be returned with a name/value pair of "browse/on". There is no way to tell the difference between the boxes. One way to set up this set of checkboxes would be:

```
<B>Why do you browse the Web?</B><BR>
<input NAME="browse" VALUE="fun" TYPE=checkbox>Fun
<input NAME="browse" VALUE="work" TYPE=checkbox>Work
<input NAME="browse" VALUE="research" TYPE=checkbox>Research
<input NAME="browse" VALUE="education" TYPE=checkbox>Education
```

Now each checkbox will be submitted with a unique value. You can also define the initial setting for a checkbox by including the CHECKED attribute. When this attribute is set, the checkbox will appear to be selected when the form is first displayed or after the reset button is chosen. The reader can deselect the box by clicking on it.

RADIO Type

The RADIO type defines an item where only one value can be selected from a set of possibilities. A set is defined as the group of radio boxes with the same NAME attribute. Only the name and the selected value is returned. Note that you must set a value for each radio box. You can also set a default box by using the CHECKED attribute. However, you should be careful never to set more than one CHECKED radio box for in the same name set. Here is a sample set of radio boxes:

```
<B>What is your gender?</B> <BR>
<INPUT NAME="gender" VALUE="male" TYPE=radio>Male
<INPUT NAME="gender" VALUE="female" TYPE=radio>Female
```

Let's see how these elements look in browsers. Here our source is displayed in WinWeb from EINet:

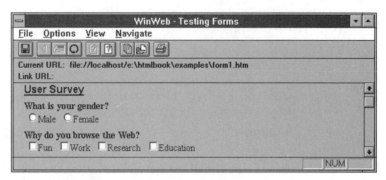

This is how the same source is displayed in WinTapestry from Frontier Technology.

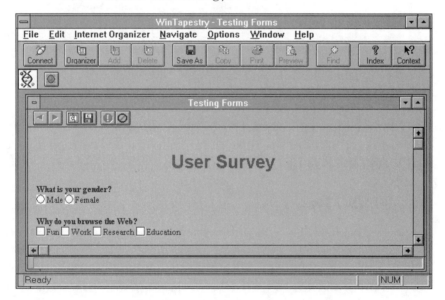

HIDDEN Type

No field is presented to the user (although a user looking at the source will be able to see that the field is there), but the contents of the field are returned in the submitted data. You might wonder what use there could be for an invisible field that does not allow user input. The primary use for this field is forms that provide some type of report or form back to the reader. For example, you might use this field to code user input in a way that is invisible to the user.

TEXT Type

This enables single-line text entry fields; it is used in conjunction with the MAXLENGTH and SIZE attributes. As you may recall, MAXLENGTH allows you to specify the number of characters that may be entered in the field, and SIZE allows you to specify the size of the field on the form.

Be careful to set MAXLENGTH to a value equal to or greater than SIZE. Otherwise, readers will be presented with an entry box that cannot be filled out completely.

Let's take a look at an example. Here is our document:

```
<P><B>First Name:</B> <INPUT NAME="fname" TYPE=text
MAXLENGTH=30 SIZE=30></P>
<P><B>Last Name:</B> <INPUT NAME="lname" TYPE=text
MAXLENGTH=30 SIZE=30></P>
<P><B>E-mail Address:</B> <INPUT NAME="eaddr" TYPE=text
MAXLENGTH=50 SIZE=50></P>
```

In WinTapestry, this source looks like this:

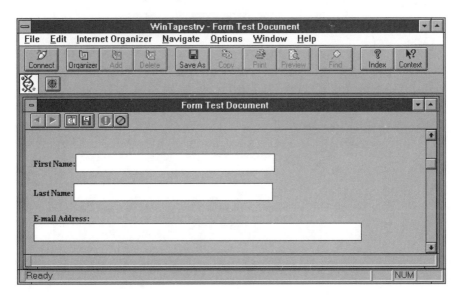

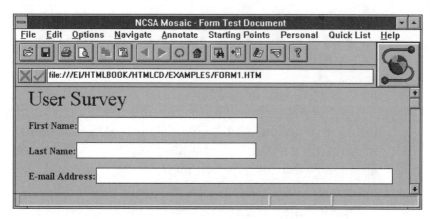

The above is how it looks in NCSA Mosaic.

As you may notice, the e-mail box is next to the label in the Mosaic example, but below the label in the WinTapestry example. We enclosed our box and label in the same paragraph tag, leaving it up to the browser to decide on placement. If you prefer to have your labels above the box, they should be placed in a separate paragraph or a <BR> tag could be used between the label and the form field.

If you want a multiline text entry, use TEXTAREA.

PASSWORD Type

This is the same as text, except the text is not displayed to the user. Like text, you can use the SIZE and MAXLENGTH attributes with this field.

```
<P><B>Enter a password to be used to retrieve survey
results:</B><BR>
<INPUT NAME="password" TYPE=text MAXLENGTH=50 SIZE=50></P>
```

This section in Netscape Navigator looks like this:

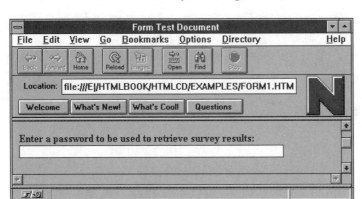

Do not allow the non-echoing characteristic of this field to lull you into a false sense of security. Although the reader (and anyone peeking over the reader's shoulder) will not be able to see whatever is typed in the field, the information is still exchanged with the server in a nonsecure fashion. You cannot rely on this field to provide real security.

SUBMIT and RESET Types

The SUBMIT button is used to submit the form's contents, as specified by the ACTION attribute. RESET resets the fields to their initial values. Both buttons may be used with the VALUE attribute to set the text that is displayed in the button. If you do not use the VALUE attribute, the buttons will be displayed with either SUBMIT or RESET. For example, we might end our survey with the following:

```
<P>Thank you for responding to this questionnaire.
<INPUT TYPE=SUBMIT>
<INPUT TYPE=RESET>
</FORM>
```

This source appears like this when in NCSA Mosaic:

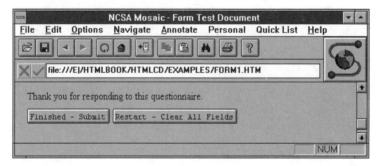

Now let's see how the addition of the VALUE attribute changes the buttons:

```
<P>Thank you for responding to this questionnaire.</P>
<P><INPUT TYPE=SUBMIT VALUE="Finished - Submit">
<INPUT TYPE=RESET VALUE="Restart - Clear All Fields"></P>
```

Here's how it looks now:

IMAGE Type

If you do not like the look of the plain button used with SUB-MIT, you may use the IMAGE type along with an image as an alternative to SUBMIT. The image type defines an image field that can be clicked on by the user with a pointing device, causing the form to be immediately submitted. The coordinates of the selected point are measured in pixel units from the upper left corner of the image. These are returned (once the form is submitted) in two name/value pairs. The x-coordinate is submitted under the name of the field with an x value appended, while the y-coordinate is submitted under the value of the field with a y value appended. This is discussed in greater detail in Chapter 4.

Let's look at an example now. We have the image of a submit button that we prefer over the standard submit button. Our image is in the file GIF\SUBMIT.GIF.

```
<P>Thank you for responding to this questionnaire.</P>
<P><input NAME="submit" TYPE=IMAGE SRC=GIF\SUBMIT.GIF
ALIGN=TOP></P>
```

Here is how this looks in Netscape Navigator:

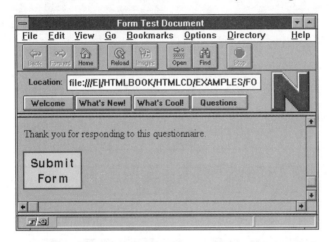

Note that the standard way for submitting forms is with the SUBMIT button, described earlier. In future versions of HTML, the IMAGE type is supposed to be folded into the SUBMIT type.

Textarea: <TEXTAREA>

The TEXTAREA tag is a nested element within a form, and is used when we wish to let users define more than one line of text. The tag creates a multiline text input region, which can contain prespecified text. The end tag, </TEXTAREA>, is required, even if the form is initially blank. The TEXTAREA tag uses two arguments, ROWS and COLS, to specify the height and width of the text box.

The following example displays a scrollable box into which the user can type text. The box begins with the following text:

```
<P>Please enter any additional comments here:
<TEXTAREA NAME="comments" ROWS=10 COLS=60>
</TEXTAREA></P>
```

This source looks like this in InternetWorks:

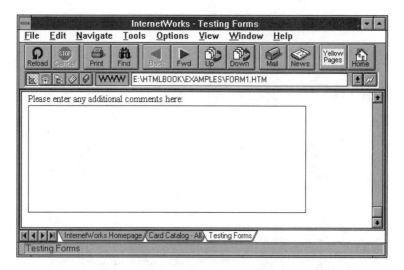

Here is how the same source looks in WebSurfer:

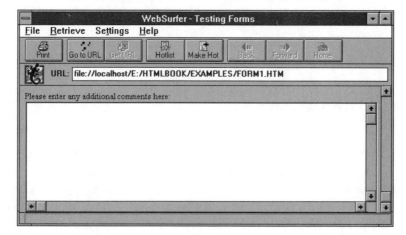

If you want to include default information, it should be placed within the <TEXTAREA> and </TEXTAREA> tags. Note that default information can be erased by the user. If default information is not erased, it will be returned as data by the form.

Select: <SELECT> and Option: <OPTION>

The SELECT and OPTION tags are nested elements within a form. Like the radio button, the Select element allows the user to choose one item from a finite set of alternatives. These alternatives are described by textual labels, using the OPTION element. The SELECT element is generally displayed in a compact manner as a pulldown list. Once the user has selected an option from the list, it becomes the visible element in the pulldown list.

The OPTION element can only occur within a SELECT element. It represents one choice in a list of alternatives. For example, in our survey we might have the following:

```
<P><B>Please select your occupation from the following
list</B>
<BR><SELECT NAME="occupation">
<OPTION>Student
<OPTION>Unemployed
<OPTION>Administrative
<OPTION>Professional
</SELECT><P>
```

In WebSurfer, the reader would see something like this:

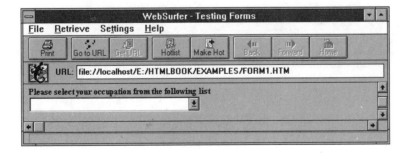

Here is what the reader would see in Netscape:

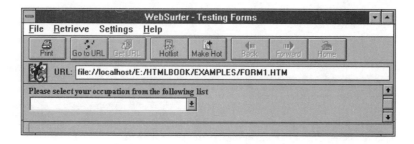

When the reader clicks on the pulldown arrow, the list of options will be displayed. Note that some browsers will display the first choice in the box, while others leave the box empty until the reader makes a choice.

You can use the MULTIPLE attribute with SELECT to allow readers to choose more than one option. We could modify our example to use the MULTIPLE attribute:

```
<BR><SELECT NAME="occupation" MULTIPLE>
```

Now let's see if and how this changes the display for this field in WebSurfer:

and in Netscape:

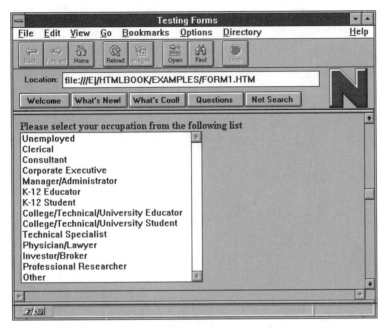

The WebSurfer display for SELECT with the MULTIPLE attribute looks suspiciously like the display for SELECT without MULTIPLE. And indeed, WebSurfer does not allow the reader to choose more than one option. On the other hand, Netscape has expanded the box, and allows the reader to choose more than one option. As you can see, using the MULTIPLE attribute can be dangerous because even browsers with some form support may not be able to use it.

The Complete Form

Our complete survey example, with three questions and a text-entry box, looks like the following:

```
<HTML>
<TITLE>Form Test Document</TITLE>
<H1>User Survey</H1>
<FORM METHOD=post ACTION=""http://ozone.com/cgi-bin/survey.cgi">
<P><B>First Name:</B> <INPUT NAME="fname" TYPE=text
MAXLENGTH=30 SIZE=30></P>
```

```
<P><B>Last Name:</B> <INPUT NAME="lname" TYPE=text MAXLENGTH=30
SIZE=30></P>
<P><B>E-mail Address:</B> <INPUT NAME="eaddr" TYPE=text
MAXLENGTH=50 SIZE=50></P>

<P><B>Enter a password to be used to retrieve survey
results:</B><BR>
<INPUT NAME="password" TYPE=text MAXLENGTH=50 SIZE=50></P>

<P><B>What is your gender?</B></P><BR>
<INPUT NAME="gender" VALUE="male" TYPE=radio>Male
<INPUT NAME="gender" VALUE="female" TYPE=radio>Female

<P> <B>Why do you browse the Web?</B><BR>
<input NAME="browse" VALUE="fun" TYPE=checkbox>Fun
<input NAME="browse" VALUE="work" TYPE=checkbox>Work
<input NAME="browse" VALUE="research" TYPE=checkbox>Research
<input NAME="browse" VALUE="education"
TYPE=checkbox>Education</P>

<P><B>Please select your occupation from the following list</B>
<BR><SELECT NAME="occupation">
<OPTION>Unemployed
<OPTION>Clerical
<OPTION>Consultant
<OPTION>Corporate Executive
<OPTION>Manager/Administrator
<OPTION>K-12 Educator
<OPTION>K-12 Student
<OPTION>College/Technical/University Educator
<OPTION>College/Technical/University Student
<OPTION>Technical Specialist
<OPTION>Physician/Lawyer
<OPTION>Investor/Broker
<OPTION>Professional Researcher
<OPTION>Other
</SELECT><P>

<P>Please enter any additional comments here:<BR>
<TEXTAREA NAME="comments" ROWS=2 COLS=60>
</TEXTAREA>
</P>
<P>Thank you for responding to this questionnaire.</P>
<P><INPUT TYPE=SUBMIT VALUE="Finished - Submit">
<INPUT TYPE=RESET Value="Restart - Clear All Fields"></P>
</FORM>
</HTML>
```

You can also find a copy of this form on the CD in:

\EXAMPLES\FORM1.HTM

HTML Tags: ISINDEX, ISMAP

Two additional HTML tags supporting user input are ISMAP and ISINDEX. The ISMAP tag was described in Chapter 4. The ISINDEX tag will not be described in detail here since it requires close interaction with the Web server and its administrator.

ISINDEX: <ISINDEX>

The **ISINDEX** element in a document signals to the browser that the requested document also serves as an index document. It should be placed in the HEAD portion of a document. The presence of this tag indicates that the user can perform keyword searches on the document. From a user's point of view, the browser displays a text-entry box in which the user may type search keywords.

We have added the ISINDEX tag to a short HTML document to illustrate the way some browsers provide a search box. Here is our document:

```
<HTML>
<HEAD>
<TITLE>ISINDEX Test Document</TITLE>
<ISINDEX>
</HEAD>
<BODY>
There is an ISINDEX tag in the head of this document. If your
browser has the capability to submit a search request, a
search box should appear when this document is displayed even
though there is no server with a search engine to do anything
with the text entered in the box.
</BODY>
</HTML>
```

Let's see how this looks in Air Mosaic:

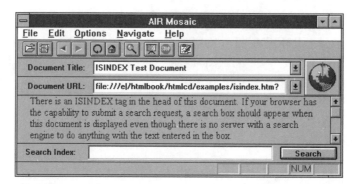

and in Netscape Navigator:

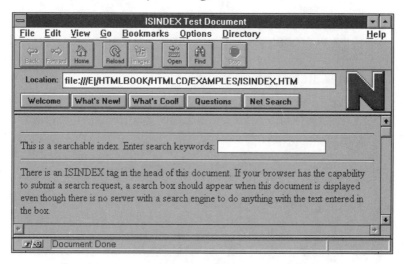

The browsers present the search box in different ways. Notice that the lack of a server and a search engine does not stop the browser from displaying the search box. Normally this tag is generated by the server, so there is no confusion about searchability. If you choose to add the tag manually, you should be careful to only add an ISINDEX tag to a document only if it is really set up for searches.

If everything has been set up correctly, the browser will capture the user input and send the query to the server. The browser does this by adding a question mark at the end of the document URL, followed by the list of desired keywords. These keywords are separated by the plus (+) sign.

For example, suppose we encounter a searchable Web document on the server OZONE.COM, named kayak-stores.html, which lists the addresses of kayak stores throughout the world. As a user, we can look for store locations within California by entering "California" in the keyword box. The query is sent by the browser to the server, as follows:

```
http://ozone.com/kayak-stores?California
```

Please note that in order for this query to work, the document must already be configured to perform keyword searches, and its Web server must already possess search engine software.

CGI Scripts

The Common Gateway Interface, or CGI, is a standard developed to allow external computer programs to interface with information servers, such as Web servers. Until recently, most CGI scripts on the Web were based on UNIX platforms. As the Web continues to grow, servers on a wider variety of platforms are becoming CGI-compliant. For example, the HTTP server for Windows included on the CD is a CGI-compliant server. The implementation of CGI scripts requires close interaction with the Web server and its administrator. Figure 5–2 illustrates the data flow between the Web server and external programs.

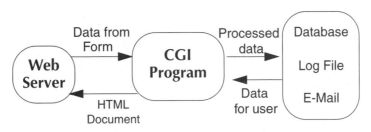

FIGURE 5–2   CGI Data Flow

Essentially, the standard allows a Web browser to cause a Web server to execute a program, which returns information to the server in a format readable by the browser. Some things you might use a CGI program to do include:

- Process the information from an order form and return a confirmation along with the total cost of the order
- Provide an interface to a searchable database, and return the result of a search to the client in HTML
- Process input from a guestbook, including logging information to a database or file, and returning a message to the client
- Provide the current hit count as part of a page each time someone accesses that page

CGI programs can be written in any programming or scripting language, such as C, Visual Basic, the DOS command interpreter or Perl. The standard assumes that the executable program resides in a prespecified location on the server. This location is usually the cgi-bin directory, although the HTTP server included on the CD allows you to keep your CGI programs in a number of directories.

CGI programs are executed on a server through the use of URLs. The URL in the ACTION attribute points to the desired Web server and the executable program. For example, the URL

```
http://ozone.com/cgi-bin/guestbook
```

requests that the CGI program named "guestbook" be run. The METHOD attribute specifies the method for sending the user's input to the program that will be run. Thus, a form tag using this URL along with the POST method would be:

```
<FORM METHOD=post ACTION="http://ozone.com/cgi-bin/guestbook">
```

Upon receiving the form's output, the server hands off control to the executable program. This program is run with the user's input. The server then returns the output from the program to the browser, usually as another Web document.

Post and Get

As previously mentioned, two methods can be used to access data in your form. These methods are POST and GET. The way in which you receive the encoded results of the form depends on which method is specified in the form. With GET, the parameters are appended to the URL, much like the ISINDEX tag. With POST, the program receives the input from standard input.

Note that the maximum length of a URL is limited by the browser and the server. With the POST method, there is no length limitation since user data comes from standard input. We therefore recommend using the POST method if the number of user input parameters is large, or if there is a <TEXTAREA> in your form. With the POST method, you do not run the risk of the URL length exceeding what the browser or server can handle. Of course, you can always write your script such that it handles both methods.

If you use the **POST** method (METHOD="POST"):

Your CGI script or program receives the encoded form input in its standard input stream. The server will *not* send an end-of-file (EOF) at the end of the data input. Therefore, you can use the CONTENT_LENGTH environment variable, which specifies how much data should be read from standard input.

If you use the **GET** method (METHOD="GET"):

Your CGI program receives the encoded form input in the QUERY_STRING environment variable.

Form Data

We have now told you where to find the output data from a form. Next, you need to decode this data. Recall that each form item should have a NAME tag. When the user enters information in that particular form item, this information is encoded in the form data. The name of the information is simply the NAME of the item tag, while the value is the information entered by the user.

Form data is then returned to the user as name/value pairs. Each pair is separated by the ampersand (&) character, while each pair of name and value is separated by the equal (=) character. These data are also URL encoded (see Chapter 3 for more information on URLs). For example, the space character becomes the plus character.

Let's look at a specific example now. We'll use an abbreviated version of the form that we developed in the previous section. Here is the completed form with answers checked off.

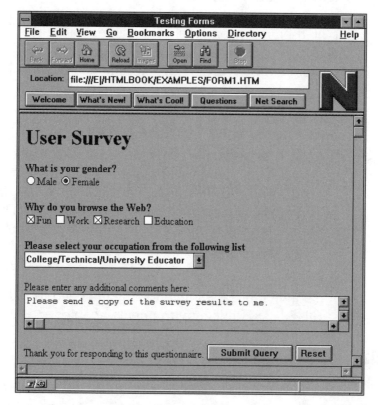

The output from these answers would look like this:

```
?gender=female&browse=fun&browse=research&occupation=College%2
FTechnical%2FUniversity+Educator&comments=Please+send+a+copy+o
f+the+survey+results+to+me.
```

Notice how each pair is separated by the & character. Each pair consists of the NAME, as specified in the form, and the VALUE selected by the user. The name/value pairs are separated by equal (=) signs, and spaces in the input fields are replaced with plus (+) signs.

The basic process in a CGI script is to split up the elements separated by ampersands. Each of these elements represents a name and value pair. Then each element is parsed to determine the value for each NAME item. Your program can then use these values to decide how to respond to the user.

On the CD, you will find several FORM examples. We have also included a general-purpose CGI forms-handling application that you can use with any form. This application is described in the next section.

PolyForm

PolyForm, by Mark Bracewell, is a shareware CGI forms-handling application that provides a central interface for writing and organizing your forms. You will find PolyForm in \POLYFORM on the CD.

PolyForm features include:

- Management of multiple independent scripts
- Saves data in text or HTML
- Can return client to any URL
- Beeper22—an application that allows PolyForm to e-mail submitted data to a fixed e-mail address, and/or send e-mail confirmation back to the client
- Runs Text and HTML Editors, and configures the scripts and related files, all from one interface.

Installation

Installing PolyForm is easy. Just run PolyForm's setup program, WGGSETUP, from the Program Manager or click on it in the File Manager.

WGGSETUP will install the files listed in Table 5-2.

TABLE 5-2   Files installed by WGGSETUP

File	Location
Polyform.exe and polyform.hlp	C:\HTTPD\CGI-WIN directory
beeper22.exe	C:\WINDOWS directory
polyform.ini	C:\WINDOWS directory
cmdialog.vbx and threed.vbx	C:\WINDOWS\SYSTEM or discard if you have a newer version
ipport.vbx and ipport.lic	C:\WINDOWS\SYSTEM

PolyForm also requires \WINDOWS\SYSTEM to contain VBRUN300.DLL. If you do not have it, it is available at ftp.portal.com in /pub/cbntmkr/vbrun300.dll. When the installation is complete, the following icon should appear in a program group:

PolyForm

To start PolyForm, click on the icon or choose PolyForm in the Toolbox in the HTML CD menu.

Setup

The first thing you need to do after installing PolyForm is to fill in the setup box. The setup box will appear automatically after the installation is completed. Here is how the setup window looks:

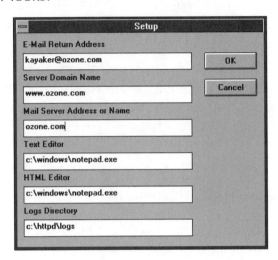

As an example, we've filled it in with Kelly Kayaker's information.

The E-mail Return Address should be the address that you want to show up in the "From" field for any e-mail that Poly-Form generates (such as an acknowledgment to the client).

The Server Domain Name is the name of the system on which your HTTP server is running. It will also accept an IP address.

The Mail Server Address or Name is the name or IP address of the system that PolyForm will use to send its e-mail messages. Unless you have an SMTP server running on your PC, don't put your PC's name in this box!

Text Editor is the path to the editor you wish to use to edit text files that PolyForm may create or modify (for example, if you choose plain text as your output file format).

HTML Editor is the path to the editor that you wish to use for editing the HTML files that PolyForm generates. Note that for both the Text Editor and HTML Editor fields, PolyForm does not check to see if the path is valid—if you put in an invalid path, it won't complain, but nothing will happen when you get to the portion of the program that sets up the text or HTML files.

Logs Directory should be the path for the directory where you want PolyForm to keep its logs.

You may change the setup at any time by clicking on the "Setup" button in the main PolyForm window. However, if you do make changes later you will have to exit from PolyForm and restart it to have the changes take effect.

Making a Script

PolyForm scripts handle the interaction between the server, PolyForm and your form. You create a script by filling out the main PolyForm Window and clicking on "Save." The PolyForm Window looks like this:

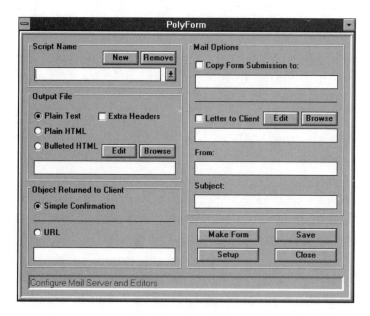

Script Name

This section allows you to pick a name for the script. The first eight characters of the script's name can only consist of characters that are allowed in DOS filenames since PolyForm uses those characters of the script's name as part of the recommended filename for the form and output files that go with the script. For example, if you have a script named "order", when you click on Make Form, PolyForm will open a browse box with "order.htm" as the recommended filename. If you named your script "order form", PolyForm cannot come up with a valid filename to recommend, so it punts and doesn't do anything. If you have chosen a valid script name, you are free to change the resulting recommended filename to anything you want.

Output File

The options in this box allow you to choose an output file for the data you receive from your form and to set a style for that data. There are three possible styles for your output file: text, plain HTML and bulleted HTML. You can also choose Extra Headers, which will cause PolyForm to try to include with each entry the name of the remote host, the host's IP address, the URL used to get to the form, and the browser name. However, whether PolyForm is able to do this will depend on the information that the browser returns to the server. Some browsers will not send the referral URL, while others send complete rubbish. Also the host name will be included only if the server is setup to do reverse name lookups.

After choosing the style that you prefer, pick a name for your output file. This is the file to which PolyForm will append data each time someone fills out your form. If you have selected an HTML style, your editor will fire up and give you the opportunity to format the file header and footer.

Note that there is nothing to stop you from changing data formats after the file is created (or from choosing a file with other information in it). If you do this, you will end up with a file that has different types of data—and will probably not be of much use if you plan to use a program to process the data.

Object Returned to Client

This box determines what PolyForm sends back to the client. If you choose Simple Confirmation, PolyForm will send back a bulleted list of the entries from the form.

If you select URL, you will need to enter a valid URL in the text box. It should be entered as you would a link in one of your pages; for example, "/" will send your home page. For a URL that is not local, enter the full URL; that is "http://wgg.com/" would send them to PolyForm's author's page.

Mail Options

If you wish to send e-mail when a form is submitted, you have a couple of options. These options are nonexclusive, so if you wish you can use both of them.

The first option allows you to send copies of the submitted data to a specific address. Choose this option by checking the Copy Form Submission to: box. You should also fill in the corresponding text box with the e-mail address to which the data is to be sent.

If you check Letter to Client, a form letter will be sent back to the user. There are a couple of things you must do to make this work correctly:

1. Provide the name of the file with your form letter in the text box under the Letter to Client checkbox. You can use a file that you have already created, or you can use the browse button to create a new file.

2. If you are using your own form, make sure that it includes a text field with the attribute "NAME=E-Mail." If you let PolyForm create the HTML template for you, it will automatically include this field if you have the Letter to Client box checked before you click on "Make Form."

If you choose one or both mail options, you should fill out the From and Subject fields. Note that the From field should contain a name (yours or a company name), not an e-mail address. The e-mail address that PolyForm uses in the From field comes from the e-mail address specified in the Setup window.

There is a security issue with regard to e-mail. E-mail generated by PolyForm is sent from your machine with your address. Since you cannot control the input from a form, a client can potentially have the form letter sent to an e-mail address other than its own. You will have to judge for yourself whether offering an e-mail confirmation with your form is worth the risk.

Creating the Script and Form

After you have completed the other boxes, push the Save button to create the PolyForm script.

If you do not already have a form made up, you can have PolyForm make a form template that corresponds to the options you have chosen by clicking on the Make Form button. When you click on this button, you will be prompted for a filename for the form. After a name is provided, the editor you specified for HTML will fire up and provide an outline for the form. Edit it as you wish and save it. You can use the Make

Form button again if you want to have more than one form reference the same script (just make sure that you use different filenames for each form). Note that PolyForm has a limit of 99 items in a form. PolyForm returns an entry for every item in the form, regardless of whether they have been filled in.

Linking an Existing Form to PolyForm

If you already have a form and want to link it to PolyForm, modify your FORM tag to use the POST method and to reference PolyForm along with the name of the script. The tag should be in the format:

```
<FORM METHOD="POST"
ACTION="http://server.name/cgi-win/polyform.exe/scriptname>
```

For example, if we have a script named "order," and if POLYFORM is in C:\HTTPD\CGI-WIN\POLYFORM.EXE, and our server is at ozone.com, our FORM tag would be as follows:

```
<FORM METHOD="POST"
ACTION="http://ozone.com/cgi-win/polyform.exe/order">
```

Once your scripts and forms are set up, you do not need to run PolyForm to process incoming data from your forms—the server will run it automatically when it is needed. Depending on how quickly it runs on your system, you may occasionally see an icon similar to this flash on your screen while it is running:

If you click on the icon, it will display the information from the SMTP server as it sends mail. At this point, if your server is running, you should be able to test your form by firing up a browser, loading the form, filling it out and submitting it.

Log Files

Beeper22, the application that handles e-mail for PolyForm, makes entries in a log file named:

```
C:\HTTPD\LOGS\BEEPER22
```

This log contains an entry for every e-mail message sent by Beeper22. It is useful for debugging since it records error messages from the mail server in addition to its own messages. Since this file does not get reset automatically, it is advisable to cycle this log file along with your HTTPD log files.

Getting More Help

PolyForm comes with an extensive on-line help system. To get to it, simply push the F1 key while you are in PolyForm.

PolyForm Example

Let's look at an example now. We will use PolyForm to process entries to Kelly Kayaker's guestbook. Since we already wrote the form for the guestbook, we do not want PolyForm to make the form for us. However, we need to make the script that will be linked into the form. We fill out the PolyForm window as follows:

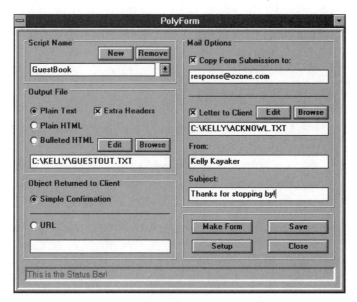

As you can see, we have named our script GuestBook. Since we do not plan to view the output with a browser, we chose Plain Text as the format for this file, which we named C:\KELLY\GUESTOUT. This file did not exist when we were setting up the script. We used the browse feature to get the output filename, and it noticed that the file was not there. When we entered the desired filename and clicked on OK, the browse box popped up a confirmation window:

Clicking on yes caused the file to be created with an informative header (which you can remove later if you prefer).

Next is the Object Returned to Client section. We wanted to allow Kelly's visitors to see that the information they've entered has been correctly received by the server, so we chose Simple Confirmation; this will cause a bulleted list of responses to be returned to the client after the form is submitted.

Finally we have the Mail Options section. Although we are collecting the information in a file, we wanted a backup copy via e-mail. To do this, we chose Copy Form Submission to:. We entered the special e-mail address that Kelly set up for these messages, response@ozone.com, in the text box. We also wanted to provide a note to the people who sign the guestbook, so we choose Letter to Client as well. We enter the path to our thank-you form letter, C:\KELLY\ACKNOWL.TXT, in the corresponding text box. Finally, we click on Save to create the script.

Now we need to link the script to our form. Since our script is named guestbook, our server is at ozone.com, and POLYFORM is in the standard location, our FORM tag would be as follows:

```
<FORM METHOD="POST"
ACTION="http://ozone.com/cgi-win/polyform.exe/guestbook">
```

Let's see what happens when we use the form now. Here is our form in NCSA Mosaic:

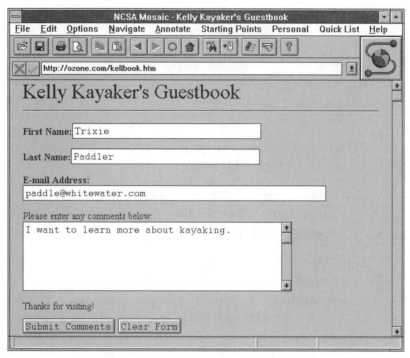

After clicking the Submit Comments button, PolyForm goes into action and returns the following:

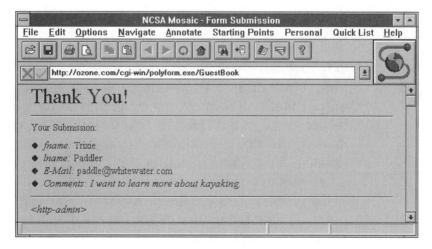

While we chose to set up our script to have PolyForm return a list of the responses, it would have been simple to have Poly-Form return some other URL, such as Kelly's home page instead. If you register PolyForm, you will also have the option of returning an HTML file of your own design that incorporates items from the form. You can find out more about the registered version of PolyForm below.

Errors

Here is a list of some of the error messages you may encounter while running PolyForm.

Error in /cgi-win/polyform.exe

An internal Visual Basic error has occurred in /cgi-win/polyform.exe.

Bad file name or number

Usually this means that one of the files needed by the script to complete its task is missing. One common cause of this is not specifying an output file, or specifying a file that does not exist. Note that there must be an output file, and it must exist prior to running the script. If it is an HTML file, it must contain the string:

```
<!--footer-->
```

on a line of its own. If Letter to Client is selected, the file to be sent must exist and be filled in.

Can't rename with different drive

Your TEMP directory must be on the same drive as your output file. PolyForm adds new entries to the output file by copying it to the TEMP directory, adding the new information, deleting the original file, and then renaming the updated file to the correct location. Since DOS does not allow files to be renamed across drives, the file will be lost in the process. To solve this problem you must put the output file on the same drive as your TEMP directory, or point your TEMP environment variable to the output file's drive. It will not work if your temp directory is on a RAM drive.

Registering PolyForm

If you plan to use forms with the HTTP server included on the CD, PolyForm's $12.00 registration fee is a bargain! When you register PolyForm, you will receive an ID that unlocks these additional features:

- You can write the text that is sent back as a confirmation to the client, and include in that text anything the client has submitted. For example, if your form asks the client's name, your reply could include "Hi Bob, thanks for visiting." You can try a demo of this function at:

  http://wgg.com/wgg/best/regdemo.html

- You can write to a comma-delimited file for import into a database. As an added bonus, the registered version comes with the Web's first realtime interactive forms tool, TalkBack—and registered users get all the updates as they are released.

You can register PolyForm through the Shareware Registration area (SWREG, ID 4174) on Compuserve, or by sending a check or money order for $12.00 to:

Willow Glen Graphics
440 Atlanta Ave.
San Jose, CA 95125

Security

CGI scripts are one of the most vulnerable aspects of the Web. These scripts are susceptible to tampering by malicious users, and we urge you to consult with Web administrators during implementation.

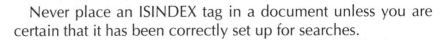

The Good, the Bad and the Ugly

Never place an ISINDEX tag in a document unless you are certain that it has been correctly set up for searches.

Never set the CHECKED attribute for more than one item in a set of radio boxes.

Make sure that you set a value for every radio box.

IN THIS CHAPTER YOU WILL LEARN

- THE NEW ELEMENTS AND ATTRIBUTES OF HTML 3
  (STILL UNDER DEVELOPMENT WHILE THIS BOOK WAS
  BEING WRITTEN)
- THE KEY FEATURES OF THE NETSCAPE EXTENSIONS
  TO HTML

THE FUTURE OF HTML: HTML 3 AND NETSCAPE EXTENSIONS

What's In This Chapter

This chapter discusses the future of HTML, and explains some of the features of HTML 3, such as the table element. Since HTML 3 was still under development at the time this book was written, it is impossible for us to describe all of its features here.

You will also find descriptions of all the nonstandard extensions to HTML available in the Netscape browser that we were able to find. We do not advocate the use of nonstandard HTML elements since they bypass the rigorous screening process that official HTML elements must pass and make it difficult for documents to look good when viewed by different types of browsers. However, we would be remiss in not mentioning these extensions due to the additional control they provide coupled with Netscape's huge market share.

The Future of HTML

HTML itself is evolving to meet the needs of the Internet. So far, the version of HTML described in this book is HTML Version 2, which is the version of HTML that most browsers are able to interpret. The main difference between HTML Version 1 and HTML Version 2 is the addition of support for forms in Version 2.

Even though Version 2 of HTML only recently completed the process for official recognition as the definition for HTML, a substantial amount of work has already been done on Version 3 of HTML. This new version adds support for tables and mathematical equations. It also provides better support for layout of images and text.

One of the most important features of HTML 3 is the addition of support for tables. Although the final details are still under discussion, some browsers such as NCSA Mosaic and Netscape have already included support for some of the changes. If you choose to use any of these elements in your documents, keep in mind that they are not supported by most browsers, and the definitions themselves may still change before being accepted officially. Most browsers ignore HTML 2 or HTML 3 commands.

A recommendation has also been made to use the filename convention of "ht3" rather than "htm" (and html3 vs html for non-Windows systems) so that it will be easier to distinguish between documents that have HTML 3 elements and ones that do not. However, since HTML 3 is still not widely used, it is okay to stick with the more familiar "htm" for now.

New Elements and Attributes in HTML 3

We will describe three new features here: text alignment, figures and tables. As with any HTML element, the usefulness of the element is dependent on support for that element by browsers. After extensive testing, we have found limited support in some Windows browsers for the elements described here. There is an experimental browser called Arena specifically for HTML 3 that provides better support, but it is currently only available on UNIX systems and is not in wide use.

We have included a document on the CD named "html3.htm" that includes samples of each of these features. You can easily determine whether a browser supports these features by loading this document into the browser you want to test. We expect that support for these features will be added to many browsers in the near future.

If you would like to learn about other HTML 3 elements, you can find a full description for it at the URL:

```
http://www.w3.org/hypertext/WWW/MarkUp/html3/CoverPage.html
```

Text Alignment

An ALIGN attribute has been defined for the paragraph tag that allows you to specify how the text is to be aligned. ALIGN may take one of four values: CENTER, LEFT, RIGHT, or JUS-TIFY. We found support for the CENTER argument in the Netscape browser:

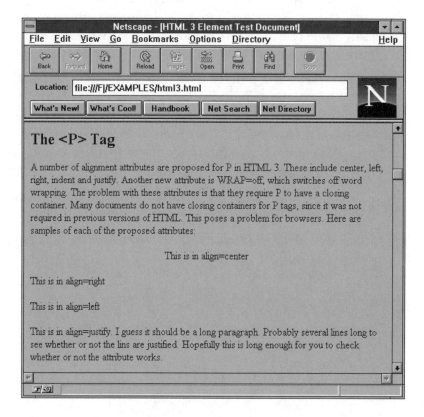

As you can see, RIGHT and JUSTIFY are not yet supported.

Figures: <FIG>

FIG is very similar to the IMG tag, but unlike IMG it also acts as a paragraph. FIG can take the ISMAP attribute, and allows the inclusion of images with "hot spots" without the need to go through a server. For example, we might use FIG as follows:

```
<P>The text in the following paragraphs will flow around the
figure if there is enough room. The browser is free to
position the caption at the top, bottom or sides of the
figure.
<FIG ISMAP SRC="gif/week.gif">
<CAPTION>Click on a day of the week for an event
listing</CAPTION>
A line drawing with a <A SHAPE="0.35,0.1&0.1,0.8&0.35,0.8"
HREF="week/monday.htm">triangle</A>
<A SHAPE="0.5,0.25&0.5,0.5&0.8,0.5&0.8,0.25"
HREF="week/tuesday.htm">rectangle</A>
</FIG>
```

We found limited support for FIG in the InternetWorks browser:

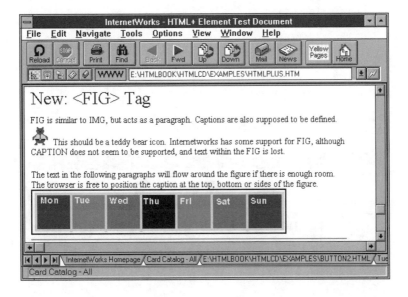

Tables: <TABLE>

The addition of tables is probably one of the most important extensions in HTML 3. The table tag allows you to format tables in your document. A table should be enclosed in the <TABLE></TABLE> tags. Within the table, the <TR> tag is used to designate rows. Individual cells are designated by <TH> for a header cell or <TD> for a data cell. A caption may also be included by using the <CAPTION></CAPTION> tags. We found support for tables in NCSA Mosaic, and will use Mosaic to display the examples in this section.

As you may recall from our chapter on images, we were having problems lining up our icons in the table of contents for our kayaking document. We ended up using the PRE tag to put things in neat columns, but the HTML source looked pretty messy. With the TABLE attribute, it is easy to make a table of contents in columns. We use the following snippet instead of our original:

```
<TABLE>
<TR><TD><A HREF="#gear"><IMG SRC="gif/kayak.gif" ALIGN=TOP>
kayaking gear</A>
<TD><A HREF="#seakayak"><IMG SRC="gif/sea.gif" ALIGN=TOP>
sea kayaking</A>
<TR><TD><A HREF="#paddle"><IMG SRC="gif/paddle.gif" ALIGN=TOP>
paddle information</A>
<TD><A HREF="#resources"><IMG SRC="gif/kayak2.gif" ALIGN=TOP>
kayaking resources</A>
</TABLE>
```

This then appears as follows:

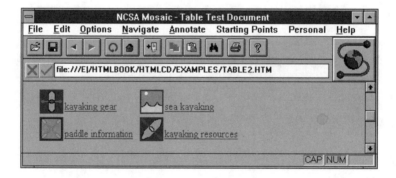

If you compare the source and the result with our HTML 2 version on page 65, you will see that both the source and output are better when using tables.

Some other attributes that are available with TABLE include:

ALIGN   This specifies horizontal alignment for the table itself. It can take one of six values: CENTER (center table between text margins — default value), RIGHT (flush with right margin), BLEEDLEFT (flush with left window border), BLEEDRIGHT (flush with right window margin), LEFT (flush with left text margin), and JUSTIFY (size the table to fill the space between left and right margins.)

BORDER   Render borders around the table.

COLSPEC   This attribute allows you to enter a list of column widths and alignment specifications. The columns are listed from left to right with an upper-case letter followed by a number, and entries delimited by spaces. The letter may be L (left), C (center), R (right align), J (justify if possible) or D (align on first decimal). The number specifies the width in ens or pixels, or as a fractional value of the table width, as specified in the associated units attribute; for example, COLSPEC="L20 C8 J30 R15".

UNITS   Specifies the choice of units for the COLSPEC attribute. It may be set to en (a typographical unit equal to half the point size—the default), relative (browser determines size based on the proportional width of each column) or pixels.

DP   Specifies the character to be used for the decimal point with the COLSPEC attribute; for example, dp="." (the default).

WIDTH   Specifies the width of the table according to the UNITS attribute. If UNITS=relative, the width is taken as a percentage of the width between the current left and right margins.

NCSA Mosaic did not seem to pay attention to most of these attributes, so our example only illustrates the use of borders and a caption (although we've included other attributes in our example for the time that support is added):

```
<TABLE BORDER UNITS=en COLSPEC="C20, D50" WIDTH 70>
<CAPTION><H3>Internet Growth<H3></CAPTION>
<TR><TH>Date <TH>Number of Hosts
<TR><TD>8/81 <TD> 213.0
<TR><TD>5/82 <TD> 235.0
<TR><TD>8/83 <TD> 562.0
<TR><TD>10/84<TD> 1,024.0
</TABLE>
```

In NCSA Mosaic, this table is displayed as follows:

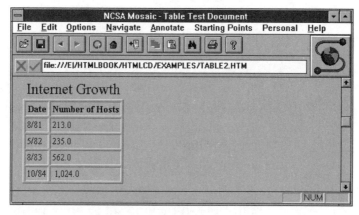

Within the table, elements are marked by the TD and TH tags, and rows are marked by TR. Here are two of the attributes that may be used with these tags:

ALIGN The ALIGN attribute allows you to specify the horizontal alignment of paragraphs within a table row. It make take one of five values:

left Flush left, the default for data cells (TD)

center Center the paragraphs, the default for header cells (TH)

justify Justify if practical, otherwise leave like left

right flush right

decimal Align on the first occurrence of a decimal point in the line.

Note: In the absence of the ALIGN attribute, the default may be overridden by the presence of an ALIGN attribute on the parent TR element, or by the COLSPEC attribute on the TABLE element. The COLSPEC attribute takes precedence over the TR element.

VALIGN   This attribute is used to explicitly specify the vertical alignment of material within a table row. Using it with an individual cell will override the setting for a row. It can take one of the following four values: top (align contents with the top of the cell—the default), middle (center contents vertically), bottom (place contents at the bottom of the cell), and baseline (ensure that all cells in a row share a baseline—only applies to the first text line for each cell.)

Now we will describe two more attributes that can be used with TH and TD to control cell size.

COLSPAN   The number of columns spanned by the cell. It allows you to merge cells across columns. It defaults to one.

ROWSPAN The number of rows spanned by the cell. This allows you to merge cells across rows. It defaults to one).

Let's look at a table example that uses some of these attributes. Here is a rather silly table:

```
<P>Here is a table with funny alignment and spanning columns
and rows:</P>
<TABLE BORDER>
<CAPTION><H3>A Very Silly Table</H3></CAPTION>
<TR><TH>Column One<TH>Column Two<TH>Column Three<TH>Column
Four
<TR ALIGN=CENTER><TD>La<TD>De<TD>Da<TD>Ta Dum!
<TR><TD COLSPAN=2>Next cell is right justified<TD
ALIGN=RIGHT>Da<TD>Ta Dum!
<TR><TD ROWSPAN=2>La De<TD>Da<TD>Ta Dum!<TD>Ta Dum!
<TR ALIGN=RIGHT><TD>Da<TD>Ta Dum!<TD>Ta Dum!
</TABLE>
```

And here is how our silly table looks:

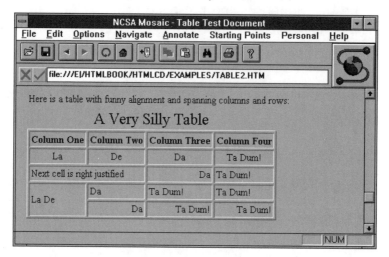

You can find all of these tables on the CD in the document \EXAMPLES\TABLE.HTM.

Document Background

An attribute has been added to the BODY tag to allow you to specify an image to be used as a background for your document. The format for this attribute is:

```
<BODY BACKGROUND="background.gif">
```

The only Windows browser we found that had support for this extension was Netscape Navigator. Netscape offers a number of GIF-format images suitable for backgrounds on their server. You can find these images at the URL:

```
http://home.netscape.com/assist/net_sites/bg/backgrounds.html
```

Netscape has also added support for a couple other attributes to the BODY tag. You will find more about those attributes in the next section.

Netscape and HTML

If you are an HTML purist, stop reading now! This section describes the nonstandard extensions to HTML that are available (at least at the time of this writing) in the Netscape browser. As we mentioned before, Netscape appears to be the most widely used browser, and these extensions allow you to have much greater control over the "look" of your document than standard HTML—but only if your readers are using Netscape Navigator.

However, at present these extensions are almost all guaranteed *not* to work with other browsers. Netscape has said that they will work with the standards bodies and other browser writers to try to make these extensions available in other browsers, so it is possible that at least some of these extensions may someday make it into the standard. Nevertheless, if your goal is to produce documents that look good in a wide variety of browsers, use these extensions to HTML at your own risk. You can check to see if any changes have been made to these extensions since this book was written by looking at:

```
http://home.netscape.com/home/services_docs/html-extensions.html
```

And now, for those of you who want to cater to Netscape users—the Netscape extensions.

Netscape Modifications to Existing Tags

As we mentioned in the previous section, Netscape Navigator supports a number of extra attributes for the BODY tag. We will now describe those extensions as well as Netscape-specific extensions to other HTML tags.

BODY

In addition to support for the HTML 3 BACKGROUND attribute, Netscape added a number of additional attributes that allow you to specify background, foreground, and link colors for your document. The background attribute is BGCOLOR, and is specified as follows:

```
<BODY BGCOLOR="#rrggbb">
```

#rrggbb is the hexadecimal red-blue-green triplet that represents the color to be used.

The foreground (text) color is specified with the TEXT attribute:

```
<BODY TEXT="#rrggbb">
```

Link colors are specified with the ALINK, LINK, and VLINK attributes:

```
<BODY ALINK="#rrggbb" LINK="#rrggbb" VLINK="#rrggbb">
```

ALINK stands for the active link, VLINK controls the color for visited links, and LINK specifies the color for all other links.

ISINDEX

This tag specifies that the document is searchable. Netscape has added a PROMPT attribute for this tag. If you do not like the default message (i.e., "This is a searchable index. Enter search keywords:"), you can use this attribute to enter an alternate message. In this example, we have set the prompt to "Enter the name of the celebrity you would like to find here:"

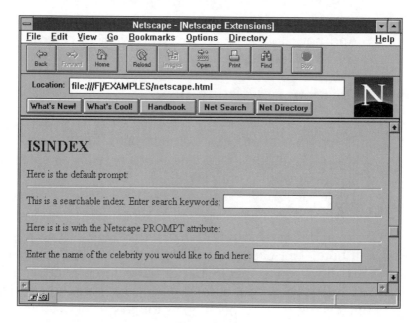

Horizontal Rule: <HR>

As you know, this tag draws a horizontal rule. Netscape has added four custom attributes:

SIZE   A number giving an indication of how thick the rule should be.

WIDTH   A number or percentage. The number is the number of pixels, the percentage is the width relative to the pagesize.

ALIGN   This may take one of three values: left, right or center (the default).

NOSHADE Use a plain line—no shading.

It is easier to see an illustration than to go into detail on what each of these attributes do. Here are some samples:

```
A plain &lt;HR&gt;<HR>
&lt;HR SIZE=5&gt;<HR SIZE=5>
&lt;HR SIZE=50&gt;<HR SIZE=50>
&lt;HR WIDTH=200&gt;<HR WIDTH=200>
&lt;HR WIDTH=70%&gt;<HR WIDTH=70%>
&lt;HR WIDTH=70% ALIGN=LEFT&gt;<HR WIDTH=70% ALIGN=LEFT>
&lt;HR WIDTH=70% ALIGN=RIGHT&gt;<HR WIDTH=70% ALIGN=RIGHT>
&lt;HR NOSHADE&gt;<HR NOSHADE>
```

Notice that we have used symbol names for "<" and ">" so that each line in our example will be labeled with the tag used to make it. Let's see how this looks:

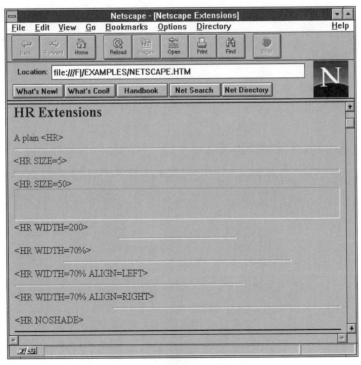

Unordered Lists: <UL>

Netscape has added a TYPE attribute to unordered lists. This attribute allows you to specify the type of bullet you would like to use with your list. Possible values are DISC, CIRCLE and SQUARE.

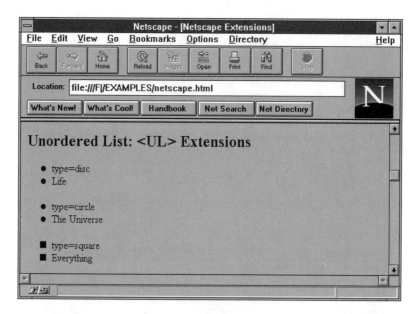

CIRCLE and DISC look the same to us, but since the documentation listed both of them we've included both here.

Ordered Lists: <OL>

Netscape has added a couple of attributes to ordered lists, too. A TYPE attribute has been added, with possible values being:

A	Upper-case letters
a	Lower-case letters
I	Large roman numerals
i	Small roman numerals
1	Numbers—the default

A START attribute has also been added so that you can designate a starting place other than one. The start should always be specified as a number—the browser will automatically translate it into whatever type is specified for the list.

Here is our sample list:

```
<OL TYPE=A>
<LI>one,<STRONG>TYPE=A</STRONG>
<LI>two</OL>
<OL TYPE=a START=3>
<LI>three, <STRONG>TYPE=a START=3</STRONG>
<LI>four</OL>
<OL TYPE=I START=5>
<LI>five, <STRONG>TYPE=I START=5</STRONG>
<LI>six</OL>
<OL TYPE=i START=7>
<LI>seven, <STRONG>TYPE=i START=7</STRONG>
<LI>eight</OL>
<OL TYPE=1 START=9>
<LI>nine, <STRONG>TYPE=1 START=9</STRONG>
<LI>ten</OL>
```

And here is how it looks:

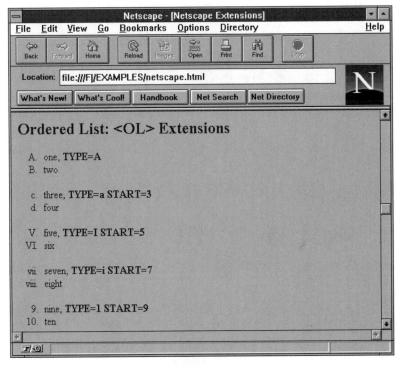

LI

A TYPE attribute has been added to the LI element. It takes the same values as TYPE for UL or OL (depending on the type of list you are in), and it changes the list type for that item and all subsequent items. A VALUE element has also been added for ordered lists so that you can change the count on the fly. Here's our test document:

```
<H2>LI Extensions</H2>
<H3>An Unordered List</H3>
<UL>
<LI TYPE=CIRCLE>CIRCLE
<LI TYPE=SQUARE>SQUARE
<LI TYPE=DISC>DISC
</UL>
<H3>An Ordered List</H3>
<OL>
<LI TYPE=A>TYPE=A
<LI TYPE=A>TYPE=a
<LI TYPE=I VALUE=100>TYPE=I VALUE=100
<LI TYPE=i>TYPE=i
<LI TYPE=1>TYPE=1
</OL>
```

And here is how it looks:

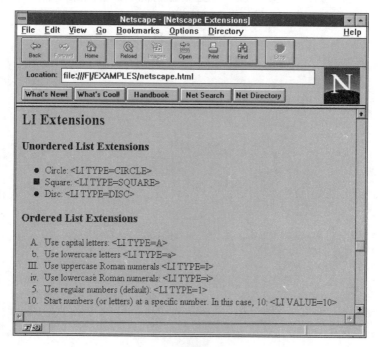

IMG

Many attributes were added to IMG. Netscape extended the alignment attribute for IMG. In addition to the original top, middle, and bottom options, Netscape has added left, right, texttop, absmiddle, baseline and absbottom. Four of these new options are:

TEXTTOP

Align the image with the top of the tallest text in the line (this is usually, but not always, the same as ALIGN=top).

ABSMIDDLE

Align the middle of the current line with the middle of the image. The difference between this option and the standard HTML middle option is that middle aligns the baseline of the current line with the middle of the image.

BASELINE

Align the bottom of the image with the baseline of the current line (identical to ALIGN=bottom). Since ALIGN=bottom is standard HTML, it is better to use it than this Netscape-only option.

ABSBOTTOM

Align the bottom of the image with the bottom of the current line.

Here is an example to illustrate the way these options place images:

```
<P>In the following examples notice how the alignment commands
affect the location of the baseline. If you plan on including
more than one image in a line, you should be careful of your
use of these alignment commands</P>
<PP>These images are aligned
<IMG SRC=gif/sailb2.gif ALIGN=texttop>
<IMG SRC=gif/sailb2.gif ALIGN=baseline>
<IMG SRC=gif/sailb2.gif ALIGN=absbottom>
<IMG SRC=gif/sailb2.gif ALIGN=absmiddle>
in this order: texttop, baseline, absbottom, absmiddle.</P>
<P>These images are aligned
<IMG SRC=gif/sailb2.gif ALIGN=baseline>
<IMG SRC=gif/sailb2.gif ALIGN=absmiddle>
```

```
<IMG SRC=gif/sailb2.gif ALIGN=absbottom>
<IMG SRC=gif/sailb2.gif ALIGN=texttop>
in this order: baseline, absmiddle, absbottom, texttop.</P>
<P>These images are aligned
<IMG SRC=gif/sailb2.gif ALIGN=texttop>
<IMG SRC=gif/sailb2.gif ALIGN=absmiddle>
<IMG SRC=gif/sailb2.gif ALIGN=absbottom>
<IMG SRC=gif/sailb2.gif ALIGN=baseline>
in this order: textop, absmiddle, absbottom, baseline.
```

Here is this section of the document:

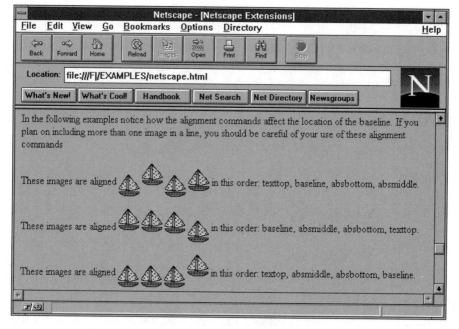

There are two more Netscape alignment options: left and right. These options "float" the image to the left or right margin rather than displaying it at the point in the text where the tag is placed.

LEFT   Floats the image down and over to the left margin (into the next available space there). Subsequent text will wrap around the right hand side of that image.

RIGHT   Aligns the image with the right margin, and wraps the text around the left.

Here is a paragraph using these options:

```
<P><IMG SRC=gif/sailb2.gif ALIGN=left> Now let's sail our
little boat on the left and right of this paragraph. This is an
example of floating images, where text will just go next to the
image rather than leaving space around it.
<IMG SRC=gif/sailb2.gif ALIGN=right> New attributes have been
added to the BR tag to allow you to cause the lines to be
displayed under the image. You can also use the Netscape VSPACE
and HSPACE attributes with IMG to leave extra vertical or
horizontal space around an image. </P>
```

Here is the way this paragraph looks in Netscape:

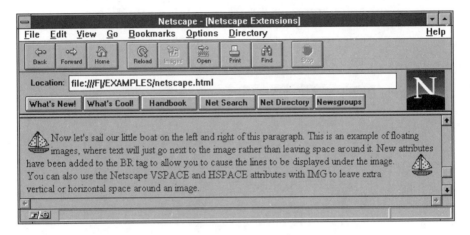

Other new attributes include:

WIDTH and HEIGHT

These attributes allow you to specify the size of the image. They are used to allow the browser to display documents with images more quickly by reserving space for the image without having to wait for the image to be downloaded to calculate the size.

BORDER

This attribute lets you control the thickness of the border around an image. You can confuse readers by setting BORDER=0 on images that are also part of anchors since this will eliminate the colored border normally placed around an image to indicate the presence of a link.

VSPACE and HSPACE

These attributes allow you to leave vertical or horizontal space around floating images.

Since the WIDTH and HEIGHT attributes only affect the way images are loaded by the browser, we can't show you an example here. However, we can show you an example of BORDER, VSPACE and HSPACE:

```
<P>Now we will place our <IMG SRC=gif/sailb2.gif ALIGN=left
BORDER=6 HSPACE=20 VSPACE=5> little sailboat on the left, give
it a border (BORDER=6) and give it some extra horizontal and
vertical space (HSPACE=20 VSPACE=5). Here is some extra
verbiage to make the paragraph longer so that you can see how
the wrapping and extra space looks.</P>
```

Here is this paragraph in Netscape:

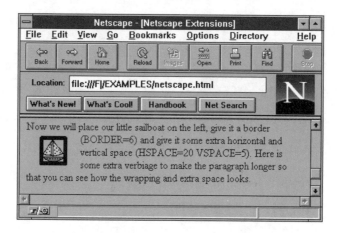

Line Break:

Added functionality was added to the BR tag to accommodate the addition of floating images. A CLEAR attribute was added, which breaks the line and moves down vertically until there is a clear margin. Values that CLEAR may take include ALL, LEFT or RIGHT. You should use the option that matches the side on which you placed your image. So if you have an image with ALIGN=RIGHT, use a BR tag with CLEAR=RIGHT to break the line and move down vertically until there is a clear right margin. If you have images on both sides of your paragraph, use CLEAR=ALL. Let's look at an example now.

```
<P> Here is an example using the CLEAR attribute with the BR
tag.

<IMG SRC=gif/tallsail.gif ALIGN=left BORDER=2>

We'll use a slightly taller boat so that you can see the break.
Since our image is on the left, let's use the LEFT option to
break this line.<BR CLEAR=LEFT>

<IMG SRC=gif/tallsail.gif ALIGN=right BORDER=2>

Now let's try a right linebreak. If it works correctly, there
should be clear space from the end of the paragraph and down to
the image's baseline. <BR CLEAR=RIGHT>
```

Here is how this snippet looks in Netscape Navigator:

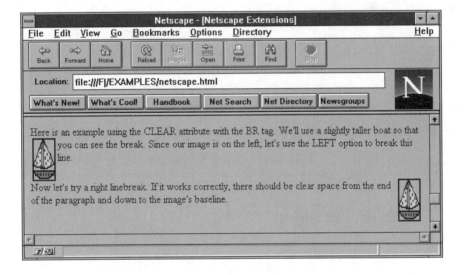

For comparison, let us look at a similar paragraph when we omit the CLEAR attribute:

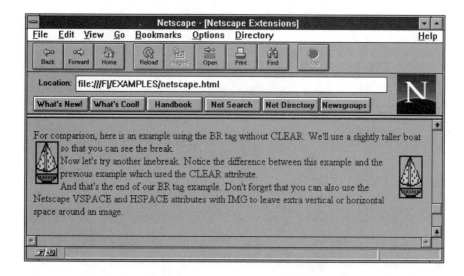

As you can see, the CLEAR attribute can be useful for putting comments about an image next to the image.

New Netscape Elements

Netscape has also added some elements that are not in the HTML specification.

Blink: <BLINK>

The BLINK tag does exactly that—makes your text blink on and off. Here's a sample from our netscape document:

```
<P><BLINK>Now you see me...</BLINK></P>
<P><BLINK>And now you don't</BLINK></P>
```

And here is how it looks:

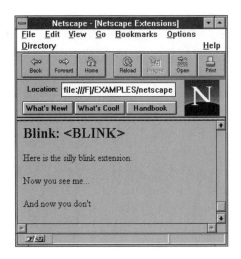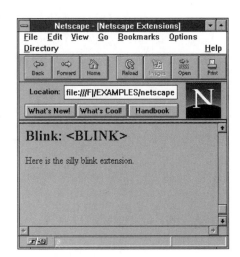

Sorry, we couldn't resist!

No Break: <NOBR>

The NOBR element stands for no break. This means all the text between the start and end of the NOBR elements cannot have line breaks inserted between them. Long text strings inside of NOBR elements can look rather odd.

Word Break: <WBR>

The WBR element stands for word break. This is for the very rare case when you have a NOBR section and you know exactly where you want it to break. It is also useful any time you want to give the Netscape Navigator help by telling it where a word is allowed to be broken. The WBR element does not force a line break (BR does that); it simply lets the Netscape Navigator know where a line break is allowed to be inserted if needed.

Font Size: <FONT SIZE=value>

The FONT SIZE tag allows you to change font size. Valid values range from one to seven, with the default being three. The value given to size can optionally have a '+' or '-' character in front of it to specify that it is relative to the current base font size. Here's our test document:

```
<H2>FONTSIZE</H2>
<FONT SIZE=1>1
<FONT SIZE=2>2
<FONT SIZE=3>3
<FONT SIZE=4>4
<FONT SIZE=5>5
<FONT SIZE=6>6
<FONT SIZE=7>7
<FONT SIZE=+3>6
<FONT SIZE=+2>5
<FONT SIZE=+1>4
<FONT SIZE=+0>3
<FONT SIZE=-1>2
<FONT SIZE=-2>1
```

In the first half of the document we use absolute values for the font size, and in the second half we use relative values to produce the same result. The relative values are based on the default base font size of 3. Now let's see how this looks:

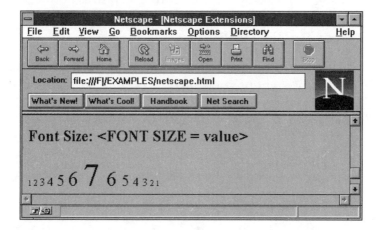

Base Font Size: <BASEFONT SIZE=value>

BASEFONT SIZE changes the base size of the font. Relative font size changes are based on this value, which defaults to 3, and has a valid range of 1-7. Here is an example:

```
<BASEFONT SIZE=1>1
<FONT SIZE=+2>3
<BASEFONT SIZE=3>3
<FONT SIZE=+2>5
<BASEFONT SIZE=5>5
<FONT SIZE=+2>7
<BASEFONT SIZE=7>7.
<FONT SIZE=-2>5
<BASEFONT SIZE=5>5
<FONT SIZE=-2>3
<BASEFONT SIZE=3>3
<FONT SIZE=-2>1
<BASEFONT SIZE=1>1
```

In our example we show how the same font size can be set using either the FONT SIZE tag, the BASEFONT SIZE tag, or a combination of the two. And here it is:

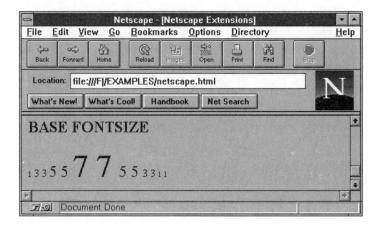

If the base font size is already set to the maximum size, trying to set a greater relative font size has no effect.

Center: <CENTER>

This tag allows you to center text. The text to be centered should be placed in <CENTER></CENTER> tags. It is similar to the HTML 3 "ALIGN=CENTER" attribute for the <P> tag. Sine Netscape also supports the ALIGN=CENTER attribute, we recommend using it over <CENTER> for compatibility with other browsers.

```
<CENTER>Here is some centered text!</CENTER>
<CENTER>We've finally reached the end!</CENTER>
<CENTER>Adi&oacute;s!!!</CENTER>
<CENTER>Auf Wiedersehen!</CENTER>
```

And here it is:

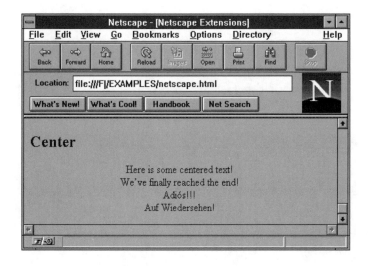

IN THIS CHAPTER, YOU WILL LEARN ESSENTIAL GUIDELINES FOR

- DESIGNING AND LAYING OUT WEB PAGES
- USING GRAPHICS
- SUPPORTING NAVIGATION IN WEB DOCUMENTS
- EFFICIENTLY USING SYSTEM RESOURCES

DESIGN GUIDELINES, STYLES AND TIPS

What's In This Chapter

This chapter pulls together the design guidelines mentioned as we described HTML tags in previous chapters, and introduces overall guidelines for laying out Web documents. In particular, we focus on the following aspects of Web document design:

- Designing and laying out Web pages
- Using graphics
- Supporting navigation in Web documents
- Efficiently using system resources

Introduction

Generally, books, magazine articles and papers are authored with particular audiences or readers in mind. Similarly, Web documents can be authored for a target audience. For example, Web documents containing company policy might be authored for members of that organization.

However, documents that are made part of the Internet World Wide Web are instantly available for browsing by its millions of global members. This means that the documents we author can be browsed by a hugely diverse population. In this case, it is almost impossible to know who our audience might be.

Moreover, users are not simply reading our Web documents—they are interacting with them. Our readers can select hyperlinks, navigate backwards and forwards between documents and Web sites, and generally choose their own pathway within information spaces in ways that we cannot fully anticipate.

These conditions present interesting and unique challenges for authors wishing to design interesting, appealing and effective Web documents. Although multimedia publishing is a recent desktop reality, little is known about the most effective ways to design digital documents that combine text, images, graphics, movies and sound in order to best present and convey the intended information.

Fortunately, fields such as human-computer interaction, graphic design, information design and instructional design combined with traditional typography contribute many useful techniques for improving the design and layout of effective Web documents.

Based on our experience in browsing and authoring documents for the Web, we have formulated a set of important authoring principles. Many of these principles have already been highlighted at appropriate spots in the book. In this chapter, we review and discuss these design principles, which authors should bear in mind when authoring Web documents.

In particular, we focus on the design and layout of Web pages, the use of graphics and support of navigation in Web documents, and the efficient use of system resources.

Of course, many of these issues are related. For example, a set of documents that are well designed usually enable users to effectively navigate within pages. Similarly, designers wishing for a strong graphical impact will take system and network resources into account. In short, the guidelines we present in the following section should be considered together.

Page Design and Layout

When authoring a set of related documents, it is important to keep a consistent design style and organization across documents. When authors use a repeated organization of text and graphics across documents, readers will come to know what to expect and where to locate pertinent information. Such patterns will help make your documents more understandable and legible.

Within one document, do not mix a large number of colors and fonts. While you may find this cute, it makes a bad visual impression.

Header Elements

In particular, you should have the following header elements at the top of each document. These elements should be positioned with the same screen location in each document.

- The title of the document. Do not confuse this with the title tag, which you should also include in the document. The title of the document should be included in a header tag at the beginning of the document.

- If applicable, a banner, logo, or seal identifying the organization or institution. This banner can also be a hyperlink that points back to the organization's top-level page.

Footer Elements

You should have the following elements at the bottom of documents (sometimes called footers). Again, these elements should be similarly positioned in all documents.

- The author of the document
- Author contact information, including e-mail address
- Last modification date of document
- A hyperlink to a top-level or home page
- Copyright status of document (if applicable)
- Links to related documents (if applicable)

The author and contact information are typically put within the <ADDRESS> tag. You may also want to put a mailto link in the e-mail address, and a hyperlink to the author's personal home page around the author's name. Here is an example:

```
<ADDRESS>
Kelly Kayaker, <A
HREF="mailto:kayaker@ozone.com">kayaker@ozone.com</A>
</ADDRESS>
<P>Last Updated: April 15, 1995<BR>&#169 1995 Ozone
Books</P>
<A HREF=index.htm><IMG SRC=gif/up.gif>Return to Home
Page</A>
```

Here is how our footer looks in Netscape Navigator:

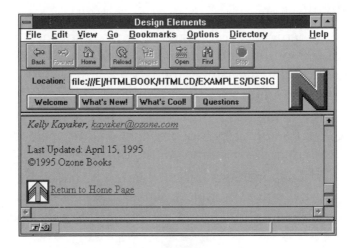

Using Graphics and Other Multimedia Items

The Web has made networked desktop publishing a reality for many people. Naturally, as authors, we are tempted to take maximum advantage of this new ability to integrate multimedia elements such as graphics, animations, audio and video into our documents.

However, there are many reasons to use such items with caution. Many users have limited network bandwidth and hence choose to browse the Web with images "turned off." Others access Web documents using text-only browsers, such as Lynx. These users are completely lost upon encountering a graphics-intensive page.

For example, don't use as your top-level document an image map on which users must click in order to select an area of interest within your Web document space. While this kind of top-level navigation approach may be visually appealing and supports graphical navigation, it also comes with the risk of losing users browsing without images. These graphics often take a long time to load for users connecting to the Web with a less than high-speed network connection. Many users will not have the patience for documents designed in this manner. Others will be incapable of viewing them.

Avoid using many small images in a single document. Although small images can be transferred quickly, a new network connection must be initiated for each image. This is very costly in terms of network usage. There are a couple of techniques that you should consider to minimize this problem. If you use multiple images for navigation, try to reuse the same images on all of your pages. Browsers usually cache images, and will be able to use them without needing to download them repeatedly. Alternatively, you could combine your images into a single image map. This way, only a single image will need to be transferred.

Image Style Issues

From the point of view of style, you should only use graphics to improve and enhance the presentation and content of your document. You shouldn't cram your page full of graphics, icons and buttons simply for their sex appeal. Make sure these offer real added value to your document and your document Web space. For example, an inlined graphic of your organization's logo used as a banner at the top of every page is an effective use of graphics since it provides a visual identity for documents. This banner can also be used as a hyperlink back to the organization's home page.

If you do choose to use images or image maps for navigation, be sure to offer an alternative. Either use the ALT tag or offer text-based URLs for users with text-only browsers.

When designing graphics for inclusion into Web documents, use a graphical format that most computer platforms can display. Presently, the two most common formats are GIF and JPEG. JPEG is generally a better encoding standard for larger images due to its high compression ratios. Note also that legal uncertainties currently surround GIF; as a result, JPEG may very likely emerge as the Web graphical standard.

Again, out of deference to network transfer time, try to keep the size of your inlined images as small as possible. If you have a large image, use a small icon representation to convey to users the content of a graphical image; then make the icon a hyperlink to the actual item. Using the icon representation, users can better decide if they wish to retrieve the entire image. You should also give users an estimate of the size of the full image. For example, next to the icon you might say "(Full image is 100K)." This will allow users to estimate network transfer time, and help them decide if they want the full image.

Finally, many authors make the mistake of designing wide images. The sides of these images then get chopped off when loaded in a browser set to the standard size. Avoid this problem by designing your graphics such that they fit within the standard browser size, which is usually on a 13-inch screen with 640 by 480 pixels.

Supporting Navigation

Navigation within and between sets of Web documents is an issue of paramount importance. Document design must support effective navigation among related documents, while avoiding the "lost in hyperspace" syndrome. In this syndrome, links are so convoluted and complex that users forget their location, cannot retrace their steps, and cannot locate items of interest. We now discuss supporting effective navigation for your users.

INCLUDE A TABLE OF CONTENTS.

Having to browse through a large document using a scroll bar is tiresome and disorienting, and makes navigation slow and cumbersome. It is better to keep your documents short and put a table of contents at the top of each high-level, introductory document. Items in the table of contents should be naturally hyperlinks to the actual items. The table of contents provides users with a overview of the document, and gives an estimate of the coverage. The hyperlinks allow users to quickly locate items of interest and form their individual information pathways.

There are a number of styles for tables of contents. For fairly short table of contents, it is popular to enclose the list in square brackets, with vertical bars separating the topics. For example:

```
<P>[<A HREF="kayak2.htm#gear">kayaking gear</A> |
<A HREF="kayak2.htm#seakayak">sea kayaking</A> |
<A HREF="kayak2.htm#paddle">paddle information</A> |
<A HREF="kayak2.htm#resources"> kayaking
resources</A>]</P>
```

Another simple style uses an unordered list:

```
<UL>
<LI><A HREF="kayak2.htm#gear">kayaking gear</A>
<LI> <A HREF="kayak2.htm#seakayak">sea kayaking</A>
<LI> <A HREF="kayak2.htm#paddle">paddle information</A>
<LI> <A HREF="kayak2.htm#resources"> kayaking
resources</A>
</UL>
```

Here is how these two table of contents types look in NCSA Mosaic:

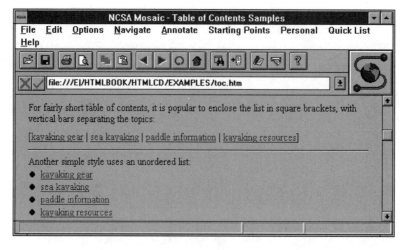

A fancier version of a table of contents uses clickable images. If you choose this style, make sure that you include a text description along with the picture. You should also include an ALT attribute with your image to further accommodate readers with line-mode browsers.

```
<P><A HREF="kayak.htm#gear"><IMG SRC="gif/kayak.gif"
ALT="[Kayak Icon]"> kayaking gear</A>
<P><A HREF="kayak.htm#seakayak"><IMG SRC="gif/sea.gif"
ALT="[Sea Icon]"> sea kayaking</A>
<P><A HREF="kayak.htm#paddle"><IMG SRC="gif/paddle.gif"
ALT="[Paddle Icon]"> paddle information</A>
<P><A HREF="kayak.htm#resources"><IMG
SRC="gif/kayak2.gif" ALT="[Kayak Icon]"> kayaking
resources</A></P>
```

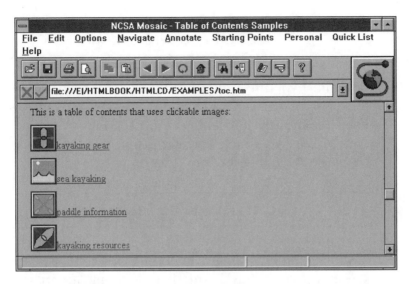

Here it is in the Lynx browser:

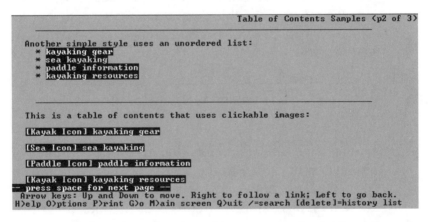

Notice that we placed our text in the ALT attribute in square brackets. Many linemode browsers do not do anything special to indicate that text comes from an ALT attribute. By putting our text in square brackets, we separate it visually from the rest of the document's text, and help to make it clear that it is an alternative to an image.

DON'T GO HYPERLINK-WILD.

While hyperlinks allow individual users to locate items of personal interest within large document spaces, they should be used judiciously. Presenting the user with too many options can be overwhelming and confusing. Find a happy medium, based on the content of your document.

DON'T FALL INTO THE "CLICK HERE" TRAP.

When implementing a hyperlink don't say, "If you want to see more, click here." This is redundant. It can also confuse readers since most browsers try to highlight links in some fashion. If you fall into this trap, your reader will be confronted with a page of "heres." Instead, embed the hyperlink within the referring text.

PROVIDE NAVIGATION BUTTONS.

In a large set of related documents, provide buttons that allow users to move to the "next" document in the series, the "previous" document in the series, and the top-level table of contents. For example, a computer manual stored as a set of Web documents can use the "Next" button to take the user to the subsequent section. Similarly, the "Previous" button will take the user to the preceding section. Finally, the "Top" button takes the user to the table of contents. These buttons can be represented as actual graphical buttons with hyperlinks to the appropriate page, or the buttons can simply be text hyperlinks. Supporting such navigation will allow users to effectively and quickly locate information of interest.

We have included a number of arrow icons on the CD that can be used as navigation buttons. You can find a catalog of these icons in \EXAMPLES\NAVIGATE.HTM. Here is an example of some navigational icons at the end of a document:

```
<A HREF=index.htm><IMG SRC=gif/larrow4.gif
ALIGN=middle>HTML CD Home Page</A>
<A HREF=next.htm><IMG SRC=gif/rarrow4.gif
ALIGN=middle>Next</A>
```

Here is how this looks in WinTapestry:

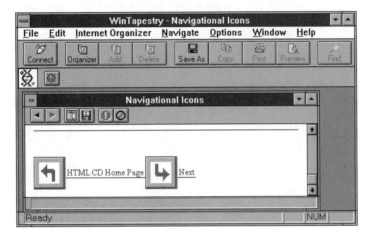

Use of System Resources

A number of concerns regarding appropriate use of system resources were discussed in the "Using Graphics" section.

Minimize Document Size

Recall that in a networked environment, delays can occur when transferring large documents. Moreover, users throughout the Internet have different amounts of bandwidth in their network connection. The larger the number of bytes in a document, the longer it takes for a browser to load it. Users without high-bandwidth connections will usually not have the patience to wait long periods of time for documents to be loaded.

Images, video, and audio, although compressed, contribute the largest number of bytes to documents. Therefore:

- Minimize the number of multimedia elements within documents in order to minimize byte size.
- Use icons (thumbnails) to convey to users the content of a graphical image.
- For large documents (e.g., graphics-intensive documents), provide users with an indication of the number of bytes in the image, video or audio segment. This number will help users estimate the required transfer time, given the nature of their network connection. Users can then decide if they are willing to load the entire document.

For example, rather than including large images directly in a document, provide a list of links to the images, with the size of each image included with its description:

```
Our trips feature:
<UL>
<LI>Exciting Rivers. <A HREF="terry.jpg">(Picture:
35K)</A>
<LI>Beautiful Scenery. <A HREF="lava.jpg">(Picture:
34K)</A>
<LI>Gourmet Food. <A HREF="cooking.gif">(Picture: 69K)</A>
</UL>
```

In Cello, this snippet looks like this:

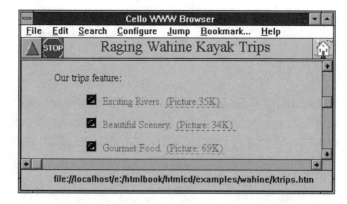

Readers can easily see how much space the pictures take up before deciding whether to download them.

Again, because of network delays and bandwidth limitations, many people choose to browse documents with images turned off. Others use browsers that can only display text. Therefore:

- Do not rely exclusively on images within your documents, or you run the risk of excluding many users who won't see your images.

- Don't use as your top-level document an image map users are supposed to click in order to select areas of interest within your Web document space. Users without image capabilities will be lost.

- Use the ALT tag or offer text-based URLs for users with text-only browsers.

Test Your Documents

It can be very frustrating to encounter a poorly or incorrectly formatted document on the Web. Users may form negative opinions about a Web site based on a single substandard document. Therefore:

- Always test the display of your documents before making them available to the Web community. If possible, test documents using multiple graphical and text-only browsers. Recall that different flavors of browsers may result in subtle variations in document display. You can use browsers.htm on the CD to download a wide variety of Windows browsers.

- Remember that browsers allow logical and physical styles to be modified by users. Therefore, don't rely on the appearance of a particular style. Instead, use styles with consistency.

- If your documents contain links, always check the accuracy of the URL. Make sure that you check your links both before and after your documents have been moved to a server. If you used relative paths in your URLs, some links may not work after your documents are moved to a server. There are a number of automated tools that you can use to check your URLs. We were unable to locate any Windows-based checkers, but many are available for UNIX systems.

Checking and Verifying Your Web Documents

Before making your Web pages public, you probably want to check them to ensure that they are using accurate and correct HTML. You probably also want to make sure that the links within pages are valid and don't point to nonexistent locations.

You could, of course, check everything by hand, but this is painstaking and time consuming. Fortunately, several tools are available for checking your HTML documents for errors and verifying link accuracy. These validation tools come in two general formats. First, they exist as software that can be downloaded and run on your own computer. Unfortunately, we were not able to find easily installable Windows-specific Web checking software utilities.

Fortunately, if you have Internet access, a second option is available. Validation services exist on Internet Web sites to which you can send the URL of the page you want checked. Typically, you use your Web browser to access the Web checking site. You are then usually presented with a form, which asks you to enter the URL of the document or documents you wish to have checked. You can also specify which version of HTML you are using. You then submit the form, and the checker then presents you with a new document listing the HTML errors found in your document. You must, of course, have Internet access for this service to work.

There are many such checking and verifying programs; we provide only the URLs of those that perform the services via the Internet.

For each of these services, you can use the listed URL and your Web browser in order to access the site.

The HaLSoft HTML Validation Service:

http://www.halsoft.com/html-val-svc/

Weblint:

http://www.khoros.unm.edu/staff/neilb

HTML Design

It is easy to write a document that can be displayed by a Web browser. Even a plain ASCII file can be linked into the Web. The difficult part of Web publishing is to make a *good* set of documents—ones that your readers will enjoy and be able to use easily. In this chapter we reviewed the guidelines that will help you to create a set of documents that do this. In the next chapter, we'll show you how to apply these principles to actual document design.

IN THIS CHAPTER, YOU WILL LEARN HOW TO CREATE
DIFFERENT TYPES OF HOME PAGES INCLUDING

- PERSONAL HOME PAGES
- BUSINESS HOME PAGES

*All of the home pages in this chapter can be found
on the CD.*

DESIGNING HOME PAGES

What's In This Chapter

This chapter explains how to author a number of types of home pages, including a personal, auto-biographical page, an on-line travel guide, and a set of pages for a business. You can find all of the pages in this chapter on the CD.

Personal Home Pages

One of the most popular uses for HTML is the creation of personal home pages. Many people choose to make their personal page act as their home page. We will present several sample pages to give you some ideas for your own page.

Kelly Kayaker's Home Page

In this example, we will create a personal home page for Kelly Kayaker. Kelly is a writer and editor of travel guides for a publishing company, called Ozone Books, Inc., which maintains a Web server on the host ozone.com. Kelly has two children, Ray and Neil. As hobbies, Kelly likes to bicycle, whitewater kayak, and play ultimate frisbee. Kelly is indeed a busy woman!

We begin by creating the file that will contain our initial document. Since it is an HTML document, we give it the .htm extension. We call our document kellhome.htm. Following good html practice, we include the following:

```
<HTML>
<HEAD>
<TITLE>Kelly Kayaker Home Page</TITLE>
</HEAD>
<BODY>
</BODY>
</HTML>
```

We include our closing tags so that we don't forget them, even though we are not yet done with the document.

We put Kelly's name in a large heading, and include a thumbnail picture of Kelly, which is linked to a full-size picture. We also include a section on Kelly's work. To minimize the size of the document, we use a black and white picture of Kelly. Where possible, we add the appropriate hyperlinks. For example, since Kelly works for a publishing company we include a link to the company's catalog. Now our document contains the following:

```
<H1>Kelly Kayaker
<A HREF="gif/kelly.gif"><IMG ALIGN=middle
SRC="gif/kellthum.gif" ALT="My photo"></A>
</H1>
I am a writer and editor of travel books at Ozone Books,
Inc., a small publishing company. I am currently writing a
book on kayaking. My book includes an
<A HREF=kelkayak.htm>HTML document about kayaking</A>.
<HR>
```

```
<H2>Ozone Books</H2> <A
HREF="http://ozone.com/ozone.html">Ozone Books, Inc</A>
is a small publishing company. We specialize in
<EM>travel books</EM>. <P> Our <A
HREF="http://ozone.com/catalogue.html">catalogue of
books</A> is available on the Web. Books can also be <A
HREF="http://ozone.com/order-form.html"> directly ordered
</A> on the Web
<HR>
```

Note that the links to Kelly's publishing company are to a different system, so we have used complete URLs for these files. Also note that these files are not on a Windows system since they have a file extension of "html." Here is the first part of Kelly's home page:

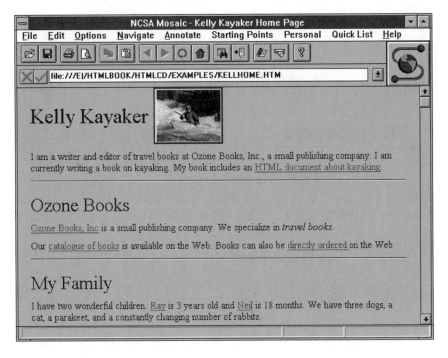

Now we add more personal information about Kelly—we describe her children, pets and hobbies. We have used partial URLs for the links in this section since they are Kelly's files, and are kept on the same system as her personal home page. Because we wish to keep the file small in order to minimize network transfer time, we have not directly included the GIF files of her children. Instead, users may load the images by clicking on the hyperlinks.

```
<H2>My Family</H2>
I have two wonderful children. <A HREF="ray.gif">Ray</A> is 3
years old and <A HREF="neil.gif">Neil</A> is 18 months. We
have three dogs, a cat, a parakeet, and a constantly changing
number of rabbits.
<HR>
<H2>My Hobbies</H2>
I have several hobbies that keep me very busy. I wish there
were more hours in the day!
<DL>
<DT><B>Bicycling</B>
<DD>I own a tandem bicycle, and my husband and I ride
frequently in the hills near our home.
<DT><B>White-water kayaking</B>
<DD>I have been <A HREF="kayak.htm">kayaking </A> for 5 years
in the rivers and creeks in the mountains near our home.
<DT><B>Ultimate Frisbee</B>
<DD>I play frisbee on a woman's ultimate frisbee team.
</DL>
<HR>
```

We end Kelly's page with an address. We make Kelly's e-mail address a "mailto" link, so that it will be easy for people to contact her over the Net.

```
<ADDRESS>Kelly Kayaker, <A
HREF="mailto:kelly@ozone.com">kelly@ozone.com</A><BR>
Ozone Books, Inc.</ADDRESS>
```

The rest of the file appears as follows:

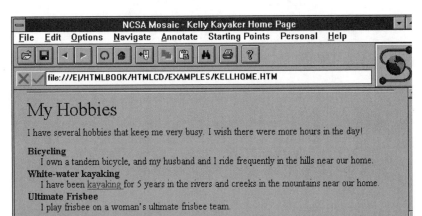

Kelly's Kayaking Document

On page 3 we described a kayaking document that Kelly was writing. The document consisted of a number of kayaking-related pictures, which were linked to documents about each picture. The descriptions of the pictures were written and maintained by Kelly's kayaking friends. The document ended with a guest book so that readers could leave comments about it. Let's take a look at that document now. Here is the first part:

```
<HTML>
<HEAD>
<TITLE>Kayaking with Kelly Kayaker and Friends</TITLE>
</HEAD>
<BODY>
<H1>Kayaking with Kelly Kayaker and Friends</H1>
<P><I>Page Under Construction</I></P>
<P>This is my kayaking hot spot list. I've gotten
together with some of my kayaking buddies to put together
descriptions of some of our favorite kayaking spots. I'm
looking for help with my descriptions of rivers in the US
and New Zealand. If you have an awesome run that you
would like to add to this list, please sign the guest
```

```
book at the end of the document or send me <A
HREF="mailto:kayaker@ozone.com">e-mail</A>. I'll be in
touch.<P>
<P>[ <A HREF=#newzealand>New Zealand</A> | <A
HREF=#usa>United
States</A> | <A HREF=#guest>Guest Book</A> ]
<HR>
```

Here it is in the InternetWorks browser:

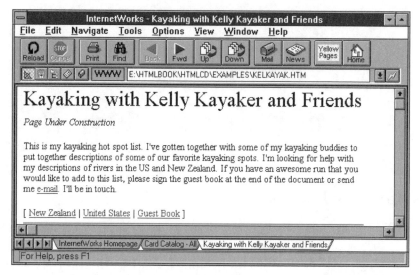

The first thing you should notice about this page is the *Page Under Construction* notice. Kelly is not really done with this page, but she wanted to make it available so that people could begin to use it. By putting a notice at the beginning of the document to let people know that it is a work in progress, people know that it is still rough, and this provides motivation to revisit the page later.

Right now the document is in one file. However, as more listings are added, the file will grow and may become too large to easily download and navigate. Kelly has planned for growth by including a table of contents at the beginning of the document. In the current document, the links point to locations within the same file. However, it will be easy for her to split sections into separate files as she adds more listings.

Here is the next part of the document:

```
<H2><A NAME=newzealand></A>New Zealand</H2>
<P>Kayaking and other river sports are very popular
recreational activities in New Zealand. Popular rivers
for these sports are:</P>
<H3><A HREF="http://river.net/funstuff/shot.html"><I>The
Shotover River, South Island</I></A></H3><P>A hair-
raising tale of a run down the
Shotover by Joe Paddle, Last Updated: Nov. 13, 1994
<P><A HREF="http://river.net/funstuff/picture.gif"><IMG
SRC=gif/mimithum.gif ALIGN=middle>Image of the Shotover
River, 65Kb</A></P>
<H3><A HREF="http://kayak.net/descrip/buller.htm"><I>The
Buller River, South Island</I></A></H3>
<P>A moving description of a solo journey down the Buller
by Sally Shooter, Last Updated: July 12, 1994</P>
<P><A HREF="http://river.net/funstuff/picture.gif"><IMG
SRC=gif/lavathum.gif ALIGN=middle>Image of the Buller
River, 78Kb</A></P>
```

Here it is in InternetWorks:

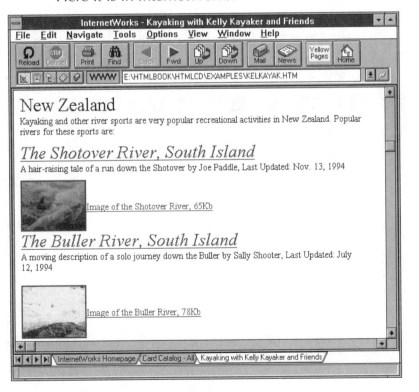

Notice that each link is accompanied by a brief description, and the date it was last updated. This makes it easy for people who may revisit the page to determine if anything has changed since their last visit. The thumbnail pictures, which are linked to full-size images, are labeled with the size of the full image to help readers decide if they want to download the picture.

The next section illustrates some useful design ideas for evolving pages.

```
<H3><A HREF="http://kayak.net/descrip/karamea.html"><I>The
Karamea River, South Island</I></A><IMG
SRC=gif/newred.gif></H3>
<P>The exciting saga of a blind kayaker's excursion down
the Karamea River by Darla Daring. Last Updated: April
10, 1995</P>
<P><A HREF="http://river.net/funstuff/picture.gif"><IMG
SRC=gif/terrthum.gif ALIGN=middle>Image of the Karamea River,
56Kb</A></P>
<H3><I>Still Under Construction...</I></H3>
<UL>
<LI>The Rangitikei River, North Island
<LI>The Mohaka River, North Island
</UL>
```

Here it is:

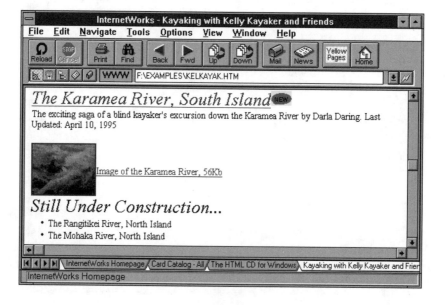

Kelly has only recently added the description for the Karamea River, so she includes an image of the word "new" in a red cloud. This makes it easy for people to notice the addition. Kelly has also left place holders for two other rivers that still need images and stories.

Kelly's Guest Book

Now let's look at the guest book. Kelly has requested that interested readers let her know if they have descriptions that they would like to add to her document. She also wants general comments about her page. She provides two methods for people to give her feedback. They can send her e-mail, or fill out the guest book form at the end of her document. The form is fairly simple since she only needs a few fields to get the information that she wants.

```
<H2><A NAME=guest></A>Kayaking Guest Book</H2>
<P>Like this page? Hate this page? Want to tell me about
your kayaking experiences? I'd like to hear from you --
please sign in!</P>
<FORM METHOD=post ACTION="http://ozone.com/cgi-bin/guest">
<P><B>First Name:</B> <INPUT NAME="fname" TYPE=text
MAXLENGTH=30 SIZE=30></P>
<P><B>Last Name:</B> <INPUT NAME="lname" TYPE=text
MAXLENGTH=30 SIZE=30></P>
<P><B>E-mail Address:</B> <INPUT NAME="eaddr" TYPE=text
MAXLENGTH=50></P>
<P><B>Tell me about your favorite kayaking run.</B><BR>
<TEXTAREA NAME="comments" ROWS=4 COLS=60>
</TEXTAREA>
</P>
<P>Thanks for visiting - come again soon.</P>
<P><INPUT TYPE=SUBMIT VALUE=" Finished - Submit ">
<INPUT TYPE=RESET Value=" Restart - Clear "></P>
```

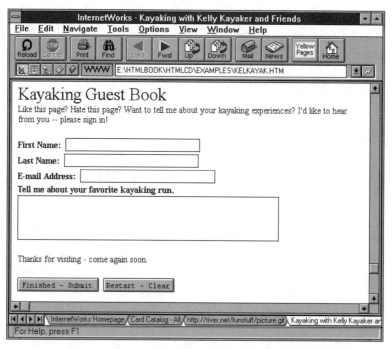

Kelly ends the page with her contact information, a last update date, and a copyright notice:

```
<HR>
<ADDRESS>Kelly Kayaker, <A
HREF="mailto:kelly@ozone.com">kelly@ozone.com</A><BR>
Ozone Books, Inc.<BR>
Last Update: April 15, 1995</ADDRESS>
<P>&#169 1995 Kelly Kayaker</P>
</BODY>
</HTML>
```

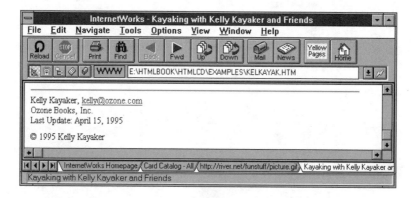

Mimi's Home Page

Now we'll look at a real home page—Mimi's. Mimi is a lecturer at a university in New Zealand. She has made it easy for readers to load her home page by leaving all images out of her top-level page. Instead, there are links to pages with images. In her description of her work history, she has included links to the pages for the places she has worked and studied.

```
<!DOCTYPE HTML PUBLIC "-//W3O//DTD W3 HTML 2.0//EN">
<HTML>
<HEAD>
<TITLE>Mimi Recker</TITLE>
</HEAD>
<BODY>
<H1><A HREF="mimipics.html">Mimi Recker</A></H1>
I am a lecturer affiliated with the University Teaching
Development Centre (UTDC) at  <A
HREF="http://www.vuw.ac.nz">Victoria University</A> in
Wellington, New Zealand.<P>
I received a Ph.D. from the <A
HREF="http://www.berkeley.edu">University of California,
Berkeley</A>, in 1992, and a B.A. from the <A
HREF="http://www.upenn.edu">University of
Pennsylvania</A>, both in the U.S.A.<BR>
More recently, I was employed as a research scientist in
the <A HREF="http://www.cc.gatech.edu">College of
Computing</A>, at  <A
HREF="http://www.gatech.edu">Georgia Tech</A>.
<P>
```

Let's see how this looks in the InternetWorks browser.

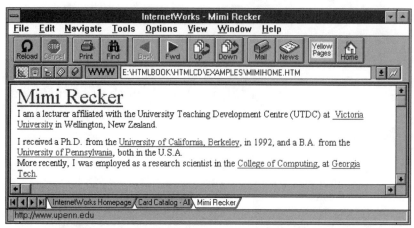

Rather than including her lengthy list of publications in her home page, Mimi keeps a separate document with a list of her publications and makes a link to this page. This keeps the top-level page clean, and makes it easy to maintain the list, which she may also want to incorporate in other documents. Mimi also provides a way for readers to contact her by including a "mailto" link to her e-mail address.

```
<H2>Some recent papers and publications</H2>
Click to see recent <A HREF="mimipubs.htm">papers and
publications</A>. Send <A
HREF="mailto:mimi.recker@vuw.ac.nz">email</A>
if you have trouble downloading a particular paper.
<HR>
<ADDRESS>UTDC<BR>
Victoria University of Wellington<BR>
P.O. Box 600<BR>
Wellington New Zealand<BR>
mimi.recker@vuw.ac.nz<BR>
+64 4-472.1000 x8868 </ADDRESS>
</BODY>
</HTML>
```

Here is the rest of Mimi's page:

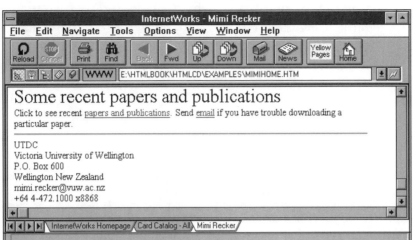

Business Home Pages

In this section we will present a couple examples of how a business might set up their home pages. When you set up home pages for a business, you should first decide what portions of your business are to be presented. Are you advertising the business as a whole? Do you want to give control of various pieces to different departments? Will you allow people to order your products through forms in some of your pages? Do you want customer feedback?

In our first example we will look at a small business. Our first example will be for Kelly Kayaker's publisher, Ozone Books, and its affiliate, Raging Wahine Adventures. Ozone Books is a publisher of travel books, and Raging Wahine Adventures is a travel company specializing in adventure expeditions.

We create a top-level page that includes a logo for each division of the company. We have placed both of the logos into the same image and created a map file for the image. Readers may click on the logo for a division to go to the home page for that division. We also include a short overview of both companies.

```
<HTML>
<HEAD>
<TITLE>OZONE BOOKS and RAGING WAHINE TRAVEL</TITLE>
</HEAD>
<BODY>
<A HREF="/cgi-win/imagemap.exe/obra>
<IMG SRC=wahine/obralogo.gif ISMAP></IMG></A>
<H1>Ozone Books & Raging Wahine Travel</H1>
<P>Welcome to Ozone Books and Raging Wahine Adventures.
Ozone Books and Raging Wahine have teamed together to
provide for all your adventure travel needs. Ozone books
is a publisher of travel books, specializing in adventure
travel. For those of you who prefer
firsthand experience, Raging Wahine Adventures provides
travel expeditions.</P>
```

So far, this is how our page looks:

Next, we add short summaries for each division. If you have several divisions in your company, you may wish to add a table of contents to make it easier for readers to find the section they want. However, since this company only has two divisions, we do not use a table of contents. The description for each division includes links to the division's home pages. Here is what we add:

```
<HR>
<H2><A HREF=ozone/index.htm>Ozone Books</A></H2>
<P>Ozone Books has been publishing and selling travel and
adventure books since 1987. We are based in Alberta, Canada.
We hope that you enjoy our <A
HREF=ozone/catalog.htm>catalog</A>. Our books are available
at many bookstores, or you may <A HREF=ozone/order.htm>order
them directly</A> from
us.</P>
<HR>
<H2><A HREF=wahine/raging.htm>Raging Wahine
Adventures</A></H2>
<P>Raging Wahine Adventures is an adventure travel company,
based in Wellington, New Zealand. We have been offering
adventure travel trips since 1988. We provide all levels of
trips -- from the backcountry novice to the most hardened
thrill-seeker.</P>
```

Notice that for the Ozone division, we have included links to Ozone's order form and catalog. This allows readers who may wish to place an order or look up a specific book to jump directly to the document of interest.

Finally, we end the page with contact information, as well as an e-mail address. The e-mail address is a mailto link, to make it as easy as possible for customers to contact the company:

```
<HR>
For more information, you may send us <A
HREF="mailto:queries@ozwa.com">
electronic mail</A>, or write to us at the address
below.<P>
We look forward to hearing from you.
<P>
<ADDRESS>
Raging Wahine Adventures and Ozone Books<BR>
P.O. Box 600<BR>
Wellington, New Zealand<BR>
<AHREF="mailto:queries@ozwa.com">queries@ozwa.com.nz</A><B
```

```
R>
</ADDRESS>
</BODY>
</HTML>
```

Here is how this section looks:

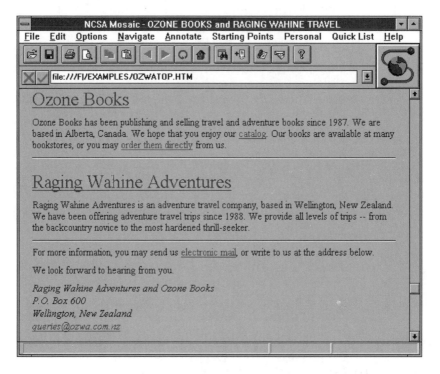

Now let's look at Ozone's pages. We divide Ozone's pages into two sections—one that describes books, and one that allows people to submit orders. Ozone's top-level page is a description of Ozone along with links to the other sections.

We start our top-level page with Ozone's logo. Notice that we have included the logo in a consistent location for all of the pages used in this company. Next, we include a short description of the company:

```
<HTML>
<HEAD>
<TITLE>OZONE BOOKS</TITLE>
</HEAD>
<IMG SRC=ozlogo.gif><H1>Ozone Books</H1>
Ozone Books publishes travel books.
```

Ozone's Order Form

Ozone Books sells books over the Internet. We will now develop an on-line form for book orders. In keeping with our desire to have a similar look for all of the business's home pages, we include a gif logo at the top of the form. However, since this is a form, we do not want to use up too much space with a logo, so we use a thumbnail version.

We start the form with some information about Ozone, and include contact numbers for telephone and fax support. It is always a good idea to provide alternate contact information since network problems may prevent people from reaching you via the Internet.

```
<HTML>
<HEAD>
<TITLE>Ozone Book Order Form</TITLE>
</HEAD>
<BODY>
<H1><IMG SRC=ozsmall.gif> Ozone Book Order Form</H1>
Thank you for choosing Ozone for your travel book needs.
In addition to Internet orders, we also accept orders
over the phone and via FAX. Our staff is available Monday
through Friday from 9 a.m. to 5 p.m. Eastern Standard
Time to take your orders and answer your questions. FAX
orders may be sent at any time. Phone Orders: (304) 555-
1368. FAX: (304) 555-3712.
<HR>
```

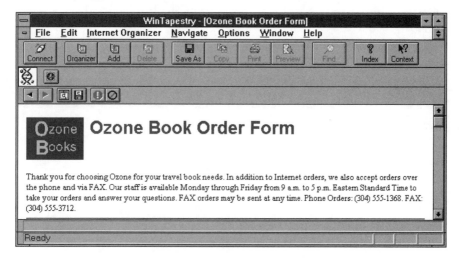

Next we provide areas for the customer's name and address:

```
<FORM METHOD=post ACTION="http://ozone.com/cgi-bin/orderform">
<PRE>
<B>First Name:</B>     <INPUT NAME="fname" TYPE=text MAXLENGTH=30 SIZE=30>
<B>Last Name:</B>      <INPUT NAME="lname" TYPE=text MAXLENGTH=30 SIZE=30>
<B>Address:</B>        <INPUT NAME="add1" TYPE=text MAXLENGTH=45 SIZE=45>
<B>Address:</B>        <INPUT NAME="add1" TYPE=text MAXLENGTH=45 SIZE=45>
<B>City:</B>           <INPUT NAME="city" TYPE=text MAXLENGTH=30 SIZE=20>
<B>State:</B>          <INPUT NAME="state" TYPE=text MAXLENGTH=2 SIZE=2>
<B>ZIP:</B>            <INPUT NAME="zip" TYPE=text MAXLENGTH=30 SIZE=10>
<B>E-mail:</B>         <INPUT NAME="eaddr" TYPE=text MAXLENGTH=50 SIZE=50>
<B>Daytime Phone:</B> <INPUT NAME="phonenum" TYPE=text MAXLENGTH=30 SIZE=20>
```

Notice that we put this section in a <PRE> tag in order to align our TEXT boxes.

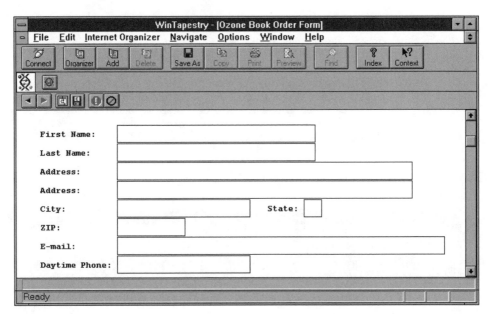

Next, we create the section for placing orders. Since we allow people to order gift certificates, we preload one of the lines with our gift certificate code. Note that customers can overwrite our predefined values in this line.

```
Product
Number  Title                             Qty    Price  Total
<INPUT NAME="PN1" TYPE=text MAXLENGTH=5 SIZE=5> ... SIZE=9>
<INPUT NAME="PN2" TYPE=text MAXLENGTH=5 SIZE=5> ... SIZE=9>
<INPUT NAME="PN3" TYPE=text MAXLENGTH=5 SIZE=5> ... SIZE=9>
<INPUT NAME="PN4" TYPE=text MAXLENGTH=5 SIZE=5> ... SIZE=9>
<INPUT NAME="PN5" TYPE=text MAXLENGTH=5 SIZE=5> ... SIZE=9>
<INPUT NAME="PN6" TYPE=text MAXLENGTH=5 SIZE=5> ... SIZE=9>
<INPUT NAME="GIFT" TYPE=text MAXLENGTH=5 SIZE=5 VALUE="GIFT"> <INPUT
NAME="TITLEG" VALUE="Gift Certificate" TYPE=text MAXLENGTH=40 SIZE=40>
<INPUT NAME="QTYG" VALUE=0 TYPE=text MAXLENGTH=5 SIZE=5><INPUT
NAME="PRICEG" VALUE=0 TYPE=text MAXLENGTH=6 SIZE=6><INPUT NAME="TOTALG"
VALUE=0 TYPE=text MAXLENGTH=9 SIZE=9>
Gift Certificate Recipient:
<B>First Name:</B> <INPUT NAME="fname" TYPE=text MAXLENGTH=30 SIZE=30>
<B>Last Name:</B>  <INPUT NAME="lname" TYPE=text MAXLENGTH=30 SIZE=30>
<B>Address:</B>    <INPUT NAME="add1" TYPE=text MAXLENGTH=50 SIZE=50>
<B>Address:</B>    <INPUT NAME="add2" TYPE=text MAXLENGTH=50 SIZE=50>
<B>City:</B>       <INPUT NAME="city" TYPE=text MAXLENGTH=30 SIZE=20>
<B>State:</B> <INPUT NAME="state" TYPE=text MAXLENGTH=2 SIZE=2>
<B>ZIP:</B> <INPUT NAME="zip" TYPE=text MAXLENGTH=30 SIZE=10> <B>Phone
Number:</B> <INPUT NAME="phonenum" TYPE=text MAXLENGTH=30 SIZE=20>
</PRE>
```

Note that in this example, most of the lines were too long to display here in their entirety. You can find the complete form on the CD in \EXAMPLES\OZONE\ORDER.HTM if you would like to see the complete lines.

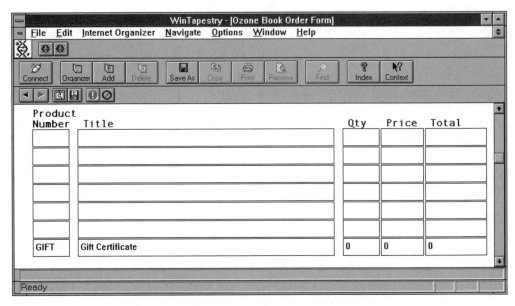

Our next section allows the customer to enter address information for a gift certificate. Since this section is essentially the same as the section for entering customer information, we will not display it here.

Now we include a payment section. We use radio boxes to allow the customer to pick one of four payment options.

```
<STRONG>Method of Payment:</STRONG>
<INPUT NAME="payment" VALUE="check" TYPE=radio>Check or
Money Order
<INPUT NAME="payment" VALUE="VISA" TYPE=radio>VISA
<INPUT NAME="payment" VALUE="Discover" TYPE=radio>Discover
<INPUT NAME="payment" VALUE="MC" TYPE=radio>MasterCard<BR>
```

Since Ozone Books does not have a secure server, they do not allow people to send their credit card information in the form. Instead, they request that customers call to confirm the order and provide a credit card number.

```
<STRONG>Important:</STRONG> We do not accept credit card
numbers over the Internet at this time. To complete your
order please call us within 48 hours to provide us with your
credit card number. At your request, we will retain your
credit card information in our files so that future orders
may be completed without additional calls. Credit card orders
which have not been completed with 48 hours will be
cancelled. Checks must be received within one week of the
order. Books will not be shipped until the check is
received.</P>
```

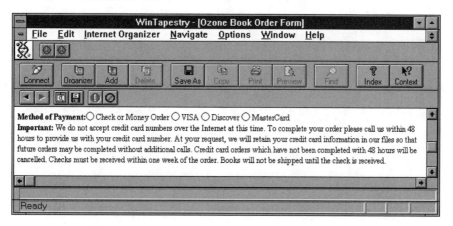

We end the input part of the form with a comment box so that our customers can give us feedback, and we provide submit and reset buttons.

```
<P>Please enter any additional comments here:<BR>
<TEXTAREA NAME="comments" ROWS=2 COLS=60>
</TEXTAREA>
</P>
</PRE>
<P>Thank you for your order!</P>
<P><INPUT TYPE=SUBMIT VALUE="Finished - Submit">
<INPUT TYPE=RESET Value="Restart - Clear All Fields"></P>
</FORM>
```

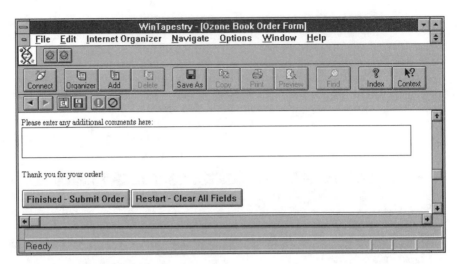

We finish off the form with some detailed information about Ozone's policies. At the very end we put our standard contact information along with some navigational buttons to allow customers to go back to the Ozone/Raging Wahine Home Page or to the Ozone Home Page.

```
For more information, you may send us
<A HREF="mailto:queries@ozwa.com">electronic mail</A>, or
write to us at the address below.<P>
We look forward to hearing from you.<P>
<ADDRESS>
Raging Wahine Adventures and Ozone Books<BR>
P.O. Box 600<BR>
Wellington, New Zealand<BR>
<A HREF="mailto:queries@ozwa.com">queries@ozwa.com.nz</A> <BR>
</ADDRESS>
<HR>
<A HREF="../ozwatop.htm"><IMG SRC="../gif/ozwahome.gif"
ALT="[Ozone/Wahine Home Page]"></A>
<A HREF="../wahine/raging.htm"><IMG SRC="../gif/wahihome.gif"
ALT="[Raging Wahine Home Page]"></A>
<A HREF="index.htm"><IMG SRC="../gif/ozhome.gif" ALT="[Ozone
Books Home Page]"></A>
</BODY>
</HTML>
```

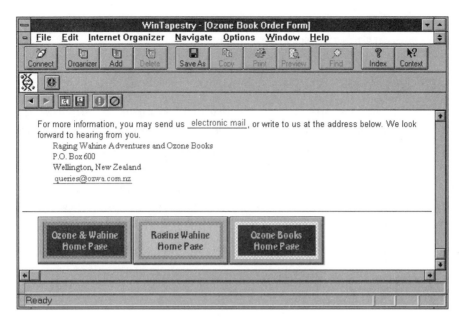

We included ALT values for each of our navigational buttons so that readers with linemode browsers or who have image loading turned off will still be able to use the links. For example, here it is in WinTapestry again, only this time with image loading turned off:

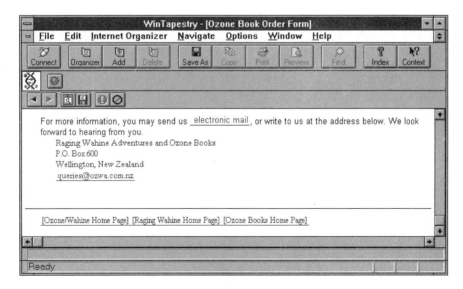

As you can see, the navigational links are usable even without the corresponding images.

Real Life Examples

We've presented a number of examples to illustrate the principles of good Web document design. However, you will find millions of other examples (both good and bad) on the Web itself. You can learn more about document design by looking at the HTML sources for any of these pages. Most Web browsers provide a way to view the source for the HTML document being displayed. Take advantage of this ability! Look at sources for both good and bad pages. This way, you will learn what to avoid as well as what to do.

WINDOWS HTTP
SERVER

What's In This Chapter

Robert Denny, the author of the HTTP server included on the CD, once said that his goal was to put a Web server on every home computer. We hope that this book and CD help him to reach this goal.

This chapter explains how to install and use the Windows HTTP server that is included on the CD.

Introduction

This server is based on the NCSA HTTP server. You can use this server to test your forms and image maps. You can even use it to publish yourself on the Internet. If you use this server for personal use, it's free! There is a nominal licensing fee for commercial use. Please see the software license agreement (one of the links that appears when you begin testing the server) that comes with the distribution for more details. We also go over some general tips and guidelines for running a Web server.

One important note before we get into the installation details—this is not a task for a novice. If you are not an experienced Windows user, you should find someone with more experience to help you. At a minimum, you should have experience updating your AUTOEXEC.BAT (if you are not sure what this file is, you definitely need to find some help!).

Before installing the server, you must have a Windows Socket (Winsock) 1.1-compliant network package installed on your system. The NetManage Internet Chameleon included on the CD is one such package. You can find instructions on the installation of the NetManage package in "Using the CD."

What This Server Can Do for You

We've touched briefly on the role that a server plays in the World Wide Web in earlier chapters. There are a number of ways that the server we've included on the CD can be of particular use for you as an HTML/Web author. We don't expect you to use this server to support a full-blown Web publishing business (the server can handle up to 16 simultaneous transactions), but it is perfect for small Web sites and for testing your HTML documents.

If you are writing HTML documents for a large site, you could run a personal server on your system, and let your colleagues check your documents before putting them on the primary server. Having control of your own server also makes it easy to test your image maps and forms.

Installing WHTTPD

If you did a full installation, WHTTPD is already installed on your PC, and may be accessed from the HTML CD Menu. If you did not do a full installation, you will need to run HTML CD Setup to install it. To do this, first make sure that the HTML CD is in your CD-ROM drive. Then click on the HTML CD Setup icon, and choose "Custom Installation".

Now make sure that WHTTPD is chosen and HTML Toolbox and HTML Document Treasure Chest are not:

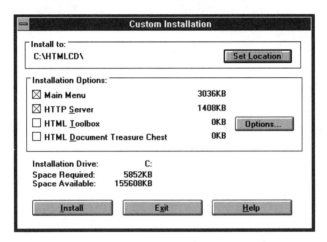

Note that Main Menu is always checked regardless of whether it has been installed already. Next, click on Install. Setup will place WHTTPD in C:\HTTPD. If you prefer, you may create an icon for it in a program group by dragging it from the file manager into the group of your choice. You will find it in C:\HTTPD\HTTPD.EXE. If you do this, you should then see the following icon in your program group:

Httpd

Setup will ask you if you want to update your AUTOEXEC.BAT to include time zone information needed by HTTPD. However it uses Eastern Standard Time as the default time zone. If you are in some other time zone, you will need to modify the time zone variable added by Setup, or just add the correct entry yourself. The time zone variable is TZ. It should be in the format *sssnddd*. *sss* should be replaced with the three-letter abbreviation for your time zone in standard time, *n* is the offset from Greenwich Mean Time, and *ddd* is your time zone in daylight savings time. For example, if you are on the East Coast of the United States, you would add the line:

```
SET TZ=EST5EDT
```

If you are not in an area that uses daylight savings time, omit the second set of letters. Now reboot your system so that this variable is in place.

Starting WHTTPD

The server is now ready to run. Before starting it, make sure that your system is connected to the network since the server will try to use the Domain Name System (DNS) to identify itself to clients. If DNS is not available, it may take up to 30 seconds for the server to start. If DNS is available, the server should start up fairly quickly. To start the server through the HTML CD Menu click on the large server icon.

Since WHTTPD normally runs in a minimized mode, you will see its welcome window displayed briefly:

after which it will be minimized. Don't worry—even though you won't be able to see its window, it is running. You will see it when you exit the HTML CD Menu.

Checking the Initial Setup

The server comes with a demonstration home page, which it will use until you set it up to use your own top-level page (we'll explain how to do this later). The demonstration home page contains an index that provides a number of tests which you can use to make sure that the server is working correctly. Before changing anything to customize the server, we strongly recommend that you take a test run with this default home page. To do this, start the browser of your choice (preferably one that handles forms) and give it the URL:

```
http://yourhostname
```

When you try this, make sure that you replace "yourhost-name" with your PC's name or IP number. If everything is working correctly, your browser should display a screen that looks something like the following screen.

A word of warning: The first few items in the Demonstration Checklist at the beginning of the Server Demonstration as well as some other references in the server's online documentation were written with a specific version of the NCSA Mosaic browser in mind. If you are not using that browser, whenever you see a reference to Mosaic, you will need to identify your browser's equivalent commands and use them instead.

Before you replace this page with your own top-level page, there are a couple of things you should do. Please read the software license agreement and make sure that your use of the server adheres to it. Next, choose the link for Server Demonstration & Test. You will be led through a set of tests that will allow you to check whether your server is running correctly, and will also show you some of the functionality provided by your server.

The demonstration provides examples of forms, imagemaps and audio as well as some of the more mundane features of HTML. If all the links in the demonstration work, your server is running correctly. You are now ready to customize the server to use your home pages.

Customizing the Server

Before proceeding, you must already have created a master home page for your server. If you haven't, you will need to do that first. You can find help on setting up your pages in Chapter 8, "Designing Home Pages." If you are running the server with the original files, stop it before you begin the next step.

Configuration Files

The server uses five configuration files, which are all kept in the C:\HTTPD\CONF directory. The files are described in Table 9-1.

TABLE 9–1 Server Configuration Files

File Name	Description
HTTPD.CNF	Primary server configuration file
SRM.CNF	Server resource map
ACCESS.CNF	Global access configuration file
IMAGEMAP.CNF	Imagemap configuration file
MIME.TYP	MIME types configuration file (do not modify this file)

Before making changes to any of the server configuration files, it is advisable to make a copy of the original. This way, if you make a mistake you can always start with a fresh copy. Of course, you can always get a copy by unpacking the package from the CD again, but it will probably be easier if you just make copies now.

There are a number of common attributes shared by all of the configuration files:

Use UNIX path syntax.

Use "/" in all configuration pathnames (this server started as the NCSA server, which was written for UNIX). For example, if you have a file named "c:\html\myfile.htm" and need to reference it in a configuration file, you would enter it as "c:/html/myfile.htm".

Configuration file entries are case-insensitive.

These files are not case sensitive.

Comment lines begin with #.

"#" must be the first character in the line, and comments must be in a line by themselves.

One directive per line.

Each line in these files consists of

```
directive data
```

where *directive* is a keyword httpd recognizes, followed by one space; *data* should be chosen specific to the directive.

Extra white space is ignored.

You can put extra spaces or tabs between directive and data. To embed a space in data without separating it from any subsequent arguments, use a "\" character before the space.

Loading Your Master Home Page

Once you have verified that your server is working correctly, you will probably want to replace the home page that comes with the server with one of your own home pages. There are a couple of ways you can do this:

1. Copy your pages into C:\HTTPD\HTDOCS, making sure that your primary page is named "index.txt".

2. Modify the DocumentRoot directive in SRM.CNF to point to the directory in which your top-level home page resides.

There are advantages and disadvantages to both of these methods. Let's look at the first option. On the plus side, if you copy your pages into the default directory, you will not need to make any changes to the configuration files (unless you are using forms or image maps). However, if your files are spread out across a number of directories, you may have to change links to accommodate the move to a new location. This can be cumbersome, and if you have a complex set of links that depend on files being in certain locations, it can be difficult to straighten them out after moving the files.

It is possible to define aliases for directories, but that would cancel the primary advantage of copying the files—avoiding changes to the configuration file.

With the second option, you will need to make more changes to the configuration files, making it slightly more likely that something in the server will break. However, the files are fairly flexible, and allow you to define aliases for directories so that you can maintain files anywhere on your system.

Copying Home Pages to Default Locations

To use the first option, you should have a master home page that uses relative links, and home pages in subdirectories that can easily be moved into a corresponding directory structure under HTDOCS. If your files are not set up in this fashion, you will probably find it easier to modify the configuration files to use the location where you already have your master home page.

If you've set up your master home page file so that its links are relative, all you need to do to make the server work with your pages is to move your directory tree into the HTDOCS directory, and name your master home page file:

```
\HTDOCS\INDEX.HTM
```

That's it! Now start the server and check it with your favorite browser.

Modifying Configuration Files

We chose to modify the configuration files to set up the master home page for our server. Let's look and see how we did it. We used the index file for the CD as our master home page. This file is in E:\EXAMPLES\MASTER.HTM on our system, since our CD drive is E:. We told the server about the location for our home pages with the *DocumentRoot* directive in C:\HTTPD\CONF\SRM.CNF. We go to the DocumentRoot section of the file and add our directive:

```
# DocumentRoot: The directory out of which you will
# serve your documents. By default, all requests are
# taken from this directory, but aliases may be used
# to point to other locations.
#
# DocumentRoot c:/httpd/htdocs
DocumentRoot e:/examples
```

As you can see, the default DocumentRoot location was already in the file—but only as a comment. We simply added our location beneath the sample line. Also, as you may recall, the server uses UNIX path syntax in its configuration files, so we use "/" rather than "\" in the pathname for our DocumentRoot directory name.

The next step is to tell the server which file in the directory to use as the master page. By default, the server looks for a file named *index.htm* in the directory designated in the Document-Root directory. Our file is named master.htm, so we need to tell the server about it. The directive for setting a new filename is *DirectoryIndex*. We go to this section of the SRM.CNF file, and add our directive.

```
# DirectoryIndex: Name of the file to use as a
# pre-written HTML directory index. This document, if
# present, will be opened when the server receives a
# request containing a URL for the directory, instead
# of generating a directory index.
#
# DirectoryIndex index.htm
DirectoryIndex master.htm
```

In our case, all of our files are in subdirectories beneath the DocumentRoot directory, so we don't need to do anything else—we're ready to test our server again and see if it is using the correct files. We double-click on our server icon to start it, and then use a browser to check it. If everything has gone on correctly, you should see your top-level page instead of the demo page. In our case we see:

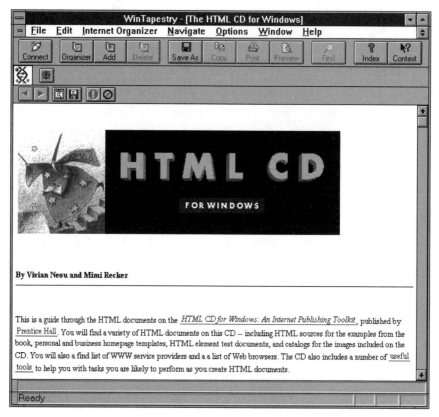

Aliasing Directories

If you want to make directories available that are not beneath your server's DocumentRoot directory, you will need to make maps to them in the Alias section of the SRM.CONF file. For example, if we have a directory named "c:\kellfile" that we wish to reference, we would make the following entry:

```
# Aliases: Add here as many aliases as you need, up to 20. One
# useful alias to have is one for the path to the icons used for
# the server-generated directory indexes. The paths given below in
# the AddIcon statements are relative.
#
# Format: Alias fakename realname
```

```
#
Alias /icons/ c:/httpd/icons/
Alias /kellfile/ c:/kellfile/
```

Once you have defined an alias, you can reference files in that directory through the alias. For example, if we have a file named "kaykbook.htm" in c\kellfile, we could construct a link to this file as follows:

```
<A HREF="/kellfile/kaykbook.html">Kayak book list</A>
```

Note that this link will probably not work when the file is viewed locally since the browser does not have access to the server's map file.

Notice that the configuration file comes with an alias for the icon directory that comes with the server. If you wish to use any of the icons in this directory, you should leave this alias in place. If you do not plan on using the icons, you can remove the entry or comment it out. If you do not remove the icon directory entry, and do not restrict access, anyone connecting to your server can access the icons through the URL:

```
http://your_host_name/icons/
```

You can add up to 20 aliases.

Redirection

If you move documents on your server, you may wish to have users automatically find the document at the new location. You can do this with the Redirect directive in /HTTPD/CONF/SRM.CONF. For example, if we move Ozone Book's directory, which was at /ozone/, to a new server at www.kayak.net, we would add the following line to our configuration file:

```
# Redirect allows you to tell clients about documents which used
to exist in
# your server's namespace, but do not anymore. This allows you
to tell the
# clients where to look for the relocated document.
#
# Format: Redirect fakename url
```

```
#
Redirect /ozone/ http://www.kayak.net/ozone/
```

When a user tries to view the document now, the server will tell the browser to get the document at the new location, and the user will automatically get the document at its new location.

Unless you plan to leave your redirection directive in your server forever (and run your server forever), you should be sure to make a note about the new location in the documents that have been moved so people who access your documents through bookmarks will know that they need to update their bookmark.

Errors

If your server does not start after you click on the httpd icon, you should check the HTTPD log file, which is kept in C:\HTTPD\HTTPD.log. Messages generated by the server as it starts are logged in this file. This includes errors that prevent the server from starting. For example, if you put an incorrect directory name in your DocumentRoot directive, you might see an entry like this:

```
Daemon startup: WinHttpd/1.4b (Shareware Non-Commercial License)
Syntax error on line 24 of c:/httpd/conf/srm.cnf:
f:/examples/html/ is not a valid directory.
```

For more information about HTTPD's log files, see the section on log files beginning on page 210.

Image Maps

One of the nice things about having your own server is that it gives you complete control over the interactive part of your documents, including the ability to test your image maps without having to go to anyone else. Before adding an image map to your server, you must have a map file for your image. If you don't already have a map file, you must create one before proceeding. You can find information about this process in the section on image maps starting on page 74.

There are four simple steps to setting up an image map:

1. *Copy your map file to \HTTPD\CONF\MAPS.*
2. *Add an entry for your image map to the image map configuration file, \HTTPD\CONF\IMAGEMAP.CNF.*
3. *Add the correct name (/cgi-win/imagemap.exe/mapname) of the link in your HTML source.*
4. *Test the link!*

Let's look at an example now. As you may recall, we had a weekly planner image map for Kelly. Our map file for Kelly's weekly planner is in a file called weekly.map. Note that these files are all on the CD, so you can try this yourself if you want to practice.

First, we copy the file to the server directory for image maps:

```
C:>copy e:\examples\weekly.map c:\httpd\conf\maps
```

Our next step is to add information about this image map to the configuration file, C:\HTTPD\CONF\IMAGEMAP.CNF.

The file looks like this:

```
# Default imagemap.cnf
#
imapdemo : c:\httpd\conf\maps\imapdemo.map
wizflow  : C:\httpd\conf\maps\wizflow.map
```

Since the server comes with a couple of test image maps, there are already entries in this file. We add the following line to this file:

```
week    :  C:\httpd\conf\maps\week.map
```

This tells the image map program that when the week image map is requested by the server, it can be found in c:\httpd\conf\maps\week.map. Notice that the map could be anywhere as long as you specify the correct path. However, it is easier to keep track of your maps if you keep them in a central location as we have done here.

Now we go back to the HTML document that references this image map, and add the link:

```
<A HREF="/cgi-win/imagemap.exe/week>
<IMG SRC="gif/week.gif" ISMAP></IMG></A>
```

This tells the server that the image map program should look for the mapname *week* when this link is chosen. The image map is now ready to use. You should always test your image maps after you have set them up to make sure that your links work correctly.

CGI and Forms

In order to use forms with this server, you will need something behind the server that can process data from a form and return information to the server. In turn, the server will pass this information back to the browser. You have a number of choices for the "something" that sits behind the server:

- PolyForm
- Native Windows CGI program
- DOS CGI program

In our opinion, PolyForm is by far the best and easiest option if you want to process forms. With PolyForm you don't need to do any programming or write any batch files. All you have to do is choose the options you want for responding to the client and storing your information, and PolyForm takes care of the rest. If you choose to use PolyForm, you should read the section on PolyForm beginning on page 109.

However, PolyForm does have some limitations; for example, if you are processing an order form and want to return the total cost for the order, there is no way to do it with PolyForm. In such a case you would have to use one of the other form-processing options: either a DOS script or a native Windows CGI program. Of these two options, we strongly recommend the Windows route.

Windows CGI Interface

The Windows CGI interface is a file-based interface. In other words, the server writes its information into a data file, which in turn is read by the back-end processing program. The processing program then returns any output to the server through another file.

A reference program written in Visual Basic has been provided with the server to simplify the task of writing native Windows CGI programs. Complete documentation on the interface for this mode is provided with the server in:

```
\HTTPD\HTDOCS\HTTPDDOC\INFO\WINCGI.HTM
```

You should refer to this document for complete instructions on the Windows CGI interface.

DOS CGI Interface

Since Windows does not have a native command interpreter, you will need some type of compiler if you want to use a Windows CGI program. DOS scripts have the slight benefit of not requiring the purchase of a compiler. Although we feel that this advantage is vastly outweighed by the inefficient way DOS scripts use your system's resources, we will describe a little about the use of DOS scripts for those of you who cannot, or do not want to, buy a compiler.

When you use a DOS script to process a form, it works by creating a virtual DOS window in which to run the script. If you do not believe this is a poor use of resources, just try running a server with one of these scripts while you try to do something else on your PC. A sample script comes with the HTTP server, so you can take the DOS CGI method for a test drive before deciding to use this form of CGI.

If you are still determined to use a DOS CGI script, you will find documentation on the DOS CGI in:

```
\HTTPD\HTDOCS\HTTPDDOC\SETUP\SCRIPTS\OVERVIEW.HTM
```

Access Control

WHTTPD allows you to control access to files by both user and directory. It also allows you to define which server functions may be performed in different document trees. You can use these systems independently or together.

The configuration file \HTTPD\CONF\ACCESS.CNF controls the overall access configuration. Table 9–2 lists the options for the directive in the file. The default file that comes with the distribution allows unlimited access to the server's document tree.

TABLE 9–2 ACCESS.CNF Directive Options

Option	Description
None	No features are enabled in the directory.
All	All features are enabled in the directory.
Indexes	The server allows users to request indexes in this directory. Disabling this option disables **only** the server-generated indexes. It does not stop the server from sending any precompiled index file it may find there (the name of which depends on DirectoryIndex).

User Authentication

User authentication allows you to require people to enter a username and password before accessing files in a specific directory. WHTTPD keeps its own password file, so its user authentication is completely independent of other systems such as NOS. The person trying to access the file *must* be using a browser that supports basic user authentication (most browsers do).

To set up user authentication, you will need to create a file named *#haccess.ctl* in the directory to which you want to restrict access. You may change this filename by setting the variable AccessFileName in \HTTPD\CONF\SRM.CNF to whatever filename you wish to use for your access control files. However, unless you specify otherwise, all of the access control files used by a single server **must** have the same name (they will just be in different directories). If you set this variable, make sure you check all of the directories where you have access control files to make sure they have the correct name. The file should contain the following lines:

```
AuthUserFile name and path of password file
AuthGroupFile name and path of user group file
AuthName ByPassword
AuthType Basic
<Limit GET>
require user username
</Limit>
```

For example, Kelly Kayaker has a directory named c:/kellwork, where she has a number of files that she only wants to allow her associate Bob Biker to view. She has set up a password file for this directory in c:/httpd/conf/kellpass.pwd. Since she wants to allow access to only one person, she does not need a real group file, so she uses the generic empty group file that comes with httpd, c:/httpd/conf/empty.pwd. Thus, the file c:/kellwork/#haccess.ctl would be as follows:

```
AuthUserFile c:/httpd/conf/kellpass.pwd
AuthGroupFile c:/httpd/conf/empty.pwd
AuthName ByPassword
AuthType Basic
<Limit GET>
require user bobbiker
</Limit>
```

Before authentication will work correctly, the user password file must be created. The user password file is created with the DOS program \HTTPD\SUPPORT\HTPASSWD.EXE.

HTPASSWD

HTPASSWD can be used to create or edit password files. The program is executed as follows:

```
htpasswd [-c] file user
```

The -c switch tells htpasswd to create a new password file of the specified name instead of editing an old one. *File* is the pathname of the user file you wish to edit or create. The *user* parameter is the name of the user you wish to add or edit.

IF YOU ISSUE THE HTPASSWD COMMAND WITH THE NAME OF AN EXISTING PASSWORD FILE, IT WILL OVERWRITE THE FILE.

For example, let's create a password file for Kelly Kayaker's files in c:\httpd\conf\kellpass.pwd. The user we want to create is bobbiker. We would issue this command:

```
                              MS-DOS Prompt
C:\>c:\httpd\support\htpasswd -c c:\httpd\conf\kellpass.pwd bobbiker
Adding password for bobbiker.
New password:
Re-type new password:

C:\>_
```

Notice that HTPASSWD does not echo the password as it is typed. When you want to change a password, issue the command without the "-c" switch. If htpasswd finds the user you specified, it will ask you to change the user's password. Type the new password (it will ask twice). httpd will then update the file. If htpasswd doesn't find the specified user, it will ask you to give the user an initial password. For example, if we were to change bobbiker's password we would issue the command as follows:

```
                              MS-DOS Prompt
C:\>c:\httpd\support\htpasswd c:\httpd\conf\kellpass.pwd bobbiker
Changing password for user bobbiker
New password:
Re-type new password:
        1 file(s) copied

C:\>_
```

Multiple Users

If you want to give access to a directory to more than one username/password pair, follow the same steps as for a single username/password, with the following additions:

Add users to the directory's access control file.

Use HTPASSWD without the -c flag to additional users to the password file for that area:

```
htpasswd c:\httpd\conf\kellpass.pwd katykayak
htpasswd c:\httpd\conf\kellpass.pwd billybike
```

Create a group file. Call it c:\httpd\conf\authgrp.pwd and have it look something like this:

```
endorphiners: billybike katykayak
```

where billybike and katykayak are the usernames that were added to the password file.

Next, modify the access control file (#haccess.ctl) in the directory to look like this:

```
AuthUserFile c:/httpd/conf/authusr.pwd
AuthGroupFile c:/httpd/conf/authgrp.pwd
AuthName ByPassword
AuthType Basic
<Limit GET>
require group endorphiners
</Limit>
```

Note that AuthGroupFile should point to your group file and that group *endorphiners* (rather than individual user bobbiker) is now required for access.

That's it. Now any user in group endorphiners can use his or her individual username and password to gain access to kell-work.

Verifying User Access Control Setup

After you are done setting up your user authentication files, be sure to check them. If they are working correctly, your browser should display an error when you try to access a restricted area with an invalid username and/or password. You should also find entries in \HTTPD\LOGS\ERROR.LOG for unsuccessful attempts to access restricted files:

```
[17/May/1995:21:07:27 -0600] user bobbiker: password mismatch
[17/May/1995:21:07:27 -0600] ozone.com authorization: Invalid
username or password
```

Successful requests should have entries showing the username along with the accessed file in \HTTPD\LOGS\ACCESS.LOG.

Host Filtering

Host filtering is used to limit access to specific machines. For example, you might want to limit access only to your company's machines.

Log Files

HTTPD logs information in three files:

- **\HTTPD\HTTPD.LOG**: Console log
- **\HTTPD\LOGS\ACCESS.LOG**: Log of all accesses
- **\HTTPD\LOGS\ERROR.LOG**: Log of all errors

The console log contains a recording of any system-related errors the server encounters (for example, if it is unable to use DNS, it will note that in the log). Each time you start HTTPD, it creates a new console log and wipes out the old one.

The access log contains a list of all queries made to the server. Each entry in the access log includes the name (or IP address) of the system from which the query originated, a date and time stamp, and the request that was made. For example:

```
128.23.20.12 - - [27/Mar/1995:19:50:34 -0600] "GET
/demo/index.htm HTTP/1.0" 200 8801
```

The error log contains a list of all the failed queries made to the server. You will probably find that most of the entries in this log are queries for files that do not exist. Each entry includes a date and time stamp and a description of the invalid query.

```
[10/May/1995:22:24:49 -0600] httpd: access to
f:/examples/cgitest.htm failed for 127.0.0.1, reason:
file does not exist
```

HTTPD does not automatically cycle the access and error logs—new entries are appended to the end of the logs. HTTPD comes with a couple of utilities you can use to help you maintain the log files. The application *logcycle* will rename the current logs to *logname.nnn*, where *nnn* is a number between 001 and 030, and *logname* is the name of the renamed log. The active log is always renamed *logname.001*, and any other log archives in the LOG directory will have their names moved up by one.

Logcycle works by sending a message to the HTTPD server, so HTTPD must be running for logcycle to work. If you try to use logcycle when HTTPD is not running, it will open a window and display an error message. Logcycle has three switches:

-a   Cycle the access log (the default)

-e   Cycle the error log

-h   Display a help message

If you run logcycle without a switch, only the access log will be cycled. The a and e switches may be combined to cycle both logs at the same time.

To run logcycle, choose Run from the File menu in the Program Manager. Enter the path for logcycle along with the switches you want to use, and click on OK. The following example illustrates the use of logcycle to cycle both logs:

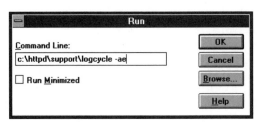

You may change the location(s) for the access and error logs by modifying the following lines in the HTTPD.CNF configuration file:

```
# ErrorLog: The location of the error log file. If
# this does not start with / or a drive spec
# (recommended!), ServerRoot is prepended to it.
# Format: ErrorLog <path/file>
#
# ErrorLog logs/error.log
# TransferLog: The location of the transfer log file.
# If this does not start with / or a drive spec
# (recommended!), ServerRoot is prepended to it.
#
# Format: TransferLog <path/file>
#
# TransferLog logs/access.log
```

WinCRON

The HTTPD kit includes a useful utility named WinCRON that allows you to execute tasks at specific times or intervals. If you plan to run your server continuously, you can use Win-CRON to automatically call logcycle at a preset time. You will find WinCRON in HTTP/SUPPORT. For WinCRON to do its job, it needs to run continuously. The easiest way to do this is to drag wincron.exe from the File Manager into your Startup folder. This way, WinCRON will automatically be started each time you start Windows. When WinCRON is running, you will see this icon:

WindowsCRON

To use WinCRON, click on the minimized icon. A popup menu will appear. Choose *Task*. You should see this window:

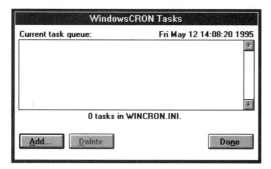

Click on the *Add* button to get the window for adding tasks. In the following example, we have made choices corresponding to a weekly cycle of both the error and access file logs on Sunday.

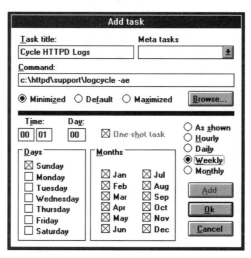

After filling out the form, click on *OK*. You will be returned to the task window, and the new entry should appear in the task queue. Although we chose to have WinCRON cycle both our logs at the same time, you can have the logs cycled at different intervals and times simply by making a separate WinCRON entry for each log. Also, remember that HTTPD *must* be running whenever you schedule the cycle for its logfile(s). For more information about WinCRON, refer to the online help option in WinCRON's popup menu.

General Server Guidelines

If you've read this far and followed the examples in this chapter, you're probably a server administrator now. If you're planning on making your server public, here are a couple tips to help make your server user-friendly and easy to manage.

- **Define a generic hostname for your server**. The convention for hostnames that act as web servers is www.domainname. For example, if we were to run a Web server for ozone.com, we would define a name, "www.ozone.com", which would point to the name of the machine running the server. This way, when you build your URLs or publicize them, you would use the alias hostname. If you need to move your server to another machine, you would only need to update the alias to point to the new machine rather than having to change all your URLs.

- **Provide a contact address in your documents**. The convention for the contact point for a server is the address

    webmaster@www.*domainname*

    If you do not already have an e-mail alias defined, you should add one for this address. You should point the alias to the e-mail address for the person in charge of the server. This is especially important for your master page, since people need a place to report problems.

You will find more hints on designing master home pages in Chapter 7, "Design Guidelines, Styles and Tips," beginning on page 149.

EDITORS, CONVERTERS AND VERIFIERS

What's In This Chapter

The number of HTML editors available for Windows has been increasing rapidly. When we started this book, we thought we would provide as many editors as we could find (and get permission to include), and let you decide which one you prefer. However, there are so many now, that we felt it would be too confusing to try to include them all. We've chosen a couple of our favorite standalone editors—HoTMetaL and HTML Assistant—and included them on the CD. We'll explain how to use them in this chapter.

For those of you who disagree with our choices, we have included an editor document on the CD that you can use to download some of the other Windows HTML editors available on the Internet.

The CD also includes a copy of Microsoft's Internet Assistant, an application that turns Microsoft Word into an HTML editor and browser.

You will also find instructions on the use of RTFTOHTM, a DOS application that can convert RTF to HTML.

HTML Editors

You can use just about any application that allows you to save text in an ASCII format to create an HTML document. Even a simple editor like Notepad can be used to create an HTML document. If you have most of the tags memorized, you may find it easier just to keep a browser open in one window, and your favorite ASCII editor open in another. This way you can reload your document in the browser to check on it as you go, and you don't have to learn how to use an additional application.

However, when you use an editor that doesn't know anything about HTML, it is up to you to remember all the HTML tags, and to verify that you've used them correctly. As HTML becomes more complicated, this becomes more and more difficult to do by hand. Fortunately, there are a wide range of HTML editors, and one is bound to meet your needs.

There are a number of features you should consider when choosing an HTML editor:

WYSIWYG

What You See Is What You Get. Editors used to create HTML documents range from plain ASCII editors, in which you type the tags (and hence see them), to editors that try to display the document as it would be seen in a browser. In between are editors that allow you to configure them with the browser of your choice and will automatically start the browser and display your document for you, and editors that show some tags and hide others (while showing the text in a formatted manner). Most editors that provide WYSIWYG HTML editing also allow you to set a switch to display the tags if you wish. Keep in mind that documents may look quite different in different browsers, and the editor can only show you its interpretation of the way in which the document will be displayed by a browser.

Add-on vs. standalone

Some HTML editors are add-ons for existing word processing applications, such as Microsoft Word. Others are standalone editors. If you already use a word processing application, you may find it easier to learn an add-on than to get a standalone application.

HTML verification

Some editors do no checking of the HTML tag usage. They will insert the tags for you, but if you use them incorrectly (such as putting text outside the tag or using invalid characters in your text), they will not notice or warn you. Other editors have extensive HTML rule-checking facilities and will always create HTML documents that adhere to the HTML standard (one of them anyway!). The drawback of an HTML-verifier editor is that it may be difficult to load documents that were created by some other source, which do not adhere to the standard.

HTML support level

As we mentioned earlier in the book, HTML is an evolving standard. Some editor maintainers have been aggressively updating their editors to support HTML 3 elements and even Netscape additions. Other editors do not offer these features, so you would have to type in extended tags yourself.

Price

HTML editors come in a wide range of prices. The editors on the CD and listed in our editor document are all available on the Internet. Some are freeware, others are demo versions of commercial products, while others are shareware. This is one area where price is not necessarily a good measure of quality. Some of the best editors are free or available for a nominal fee.

System requirements

In general, the more features an editor offers, the more resources your PC must have in order to run the editor. Some editors have fairly extensive memory requirements, which may make it difficult to run any other application while using the editor. This can be frustrating since many editors provide a link to a browser so that you can preview your document. If your system does not have enough memory, it may not be able to load both a browser and an editor at the same time.

The three HTML editors that you will find on the CD cover a wide range of these features. The demonstration version of HoTMetaL is the most fully featured editor on the CD—it is a standalone, WYSIWG HTML editor, and it also does HTML verification. Not surprisingly, it is also the most demanding of system resources. HTML Assistant is also a standalone editor, but it only inserts tags and does not do any verification. Internet Assistant from Microsoft is a free add-on for Microsoft Word. It turns Microsoft Word 6.0a into a browser and HTML editor.

HoTMetaL

We have included a demonstration version of HoTMetaL PRO on the CD. The demo is a fairly full-featured HTML editor in its own right, and you may use it at no charge. HoTMetaL can assist you in creating documents which will easily be made to conform to what may be more restrictive rules in future HTML software, and at the same time make it possible to continue to work with as many of the old or "legacy" documents as can be handled. HoTMetaL requires 8 megabytes of disk space and 6 megabytes of RAM.

You can find HoTMetaL in \EDITORS\HOTMETAL. To install it, either double-click on HMINST.EXE in the Windows file manager or choose *Run* from the *File* pulldown menu and enter the correct path.

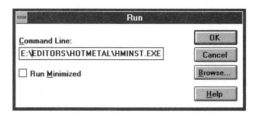

Setup will then start. If you wish to use HoTMetaL with the HTML CD Menu, it must be installed in C:\SQHM. If you have an earlier version of HoTMetaL installed in this directory, you should move it to another directory before continuing. Although Setup will give you an the opportunity to enter an alternate directory name, leave the default in place if you wish to use the HTML CD Menu.

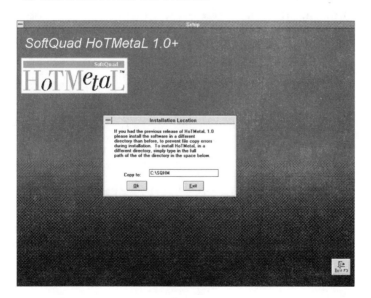

After setup is done loading HoTMetaL, it will create a program group with the HoTMetaL icon:

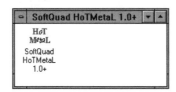

HoTMetaL Initialization File

HoTMetaL uses an initialization file named SQHM.INI, that normally resides in your C:\WINDOWS directory. The original file should look something like this:

```
[HoTMetaL]
Maximized=0
x=130
y=84
dx=475
dy=304
```

The entries in this file are in the format:

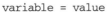

```
variable = value
```

You can run HoTMetaL without making any changes to the initialization file. However, although it is not required, we recommend that you set these three variables before starting HoTMetaL:

html_browser

Application to use for previewing documents

view_gif

Application used to view GIF format images

view_bmp

Application used to view bmp format images

HoTMetaL relies on external programs to display graphics (with the exception of GIF format images, which it can display inline). It also has a preview mode that allows you to see how

your document would look in your favorite browser. These three variables tell HoTMetaL where to find the applications that should be used to provide these display capabilities.

Changes made to the initialization file will only take effect when you start HoTMetaL after the file is updated. Although you can modify the file while HoTMetaL is running, we recommend that you do not run the program while you are making changes to the initialization file. This way, you can be sure that the changes you make will be in place when you run HoTMetaL.

Update SQHM.INI by opening it with your favorite text editor. The file must be saved in an ASCII format, so if you modify it with a word processing program such as Microsoft Word, make sure that you save it in a plain-text format. After you have loaded SQHM.INI in your editor, add a line for each variable you want to set. For example, let's see how to set up Netscape Navigator as the HTML browser and LViewPro as our image viewer. On our system, Netscape is in:

```
C:\NETSCAPE\NETSCAPE.EXE
```

So we add the following line to our SQHM.INI file:

```
html_browser=C:\NETSCAPE\NETSCAPE.EXE
```

Some browsers, such as Netmanage's WebSurfer, do not interact cleanly with HoTMetaL, and will not automatically load your document when you use the preview feature in HoT-MetaL. If you find that this is the case with the browser you have chosen, you will need to pick another browser if you want to use the preview feature. Both NCSA Mosaic and Netscape Navigator are known to work correctly.

We will use LViewPro as the image viewer for both image formats. We use the default location from HTML CD Setup to install LView Pro, so it is in:

```
C:\HTMLCD\TOOLS\LVIEWP1B\LVIEWP1B.EXE
```

We add the following lines to the initialization file:

```
view_gif=C:\HTMLCD\TOOLS\LVIEWP1B\LVIEWP1B.EXE
view_bmp=C:\HTMLCD\TOOLS\LVIEWP1B\LVIEWP1B.EXE
```

 There is one other variable that you may wish to set before starting HoTMetaL. HoTMetaL works by reading a rules file to determine which HTML elements are allowed in a document. The default rules file conforms to standard HTML. If you plan on authoring documents that are tailored for NetScape Navigator, you will need to tell HoTMetaL to use its NetScape rules file. You do this by adding the following line to the initialization file:

```
rules_file=html-net.mtl
```

Besides the variables mentioned here, there are others that you may wish to set after you become more familiar with HoT-MetaL. You can find documentation on them in the HoTMetaL manual, which is in the *DOC* directory in the file hotmetal.txt (ASCII version) or hotmetal.ps (PostScript version).

Creating HTML Documents in HoTMetaL

To start the program, click on the HoTMetaL icon. A splash screen with information about HoTMetaL will appear while the application is starting, and the following screen should appear:

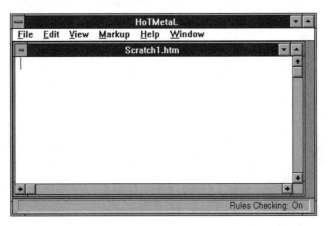

First, let's look at the procedure for creating a new document. You can use the default document window that appears with the first screen to begin your document. Place the cursor in the document window, and then type <CTRL-I> (hold down the control key and "i" at the same time) or choose Insert Element from the Markup pulldown menu. You should then see the following window:

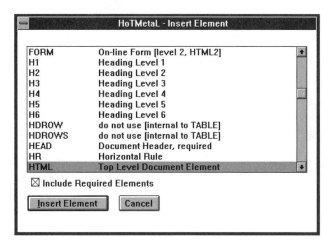

This window will show you a list of valid HTML elements that may be placed in the document at this point. Since you are starting a document, any element could be inserted. When appropriate, HoTMetaL will recommend an element by highlighting it in the list. In this case the choice makes sense, so we click on the HTML element to choose it. Before doing this, we make sure that the Include Required Elements box is checked. This option tells HoTMetaL to insert any other tags that might be required along with the one we have chosen. Now our screen looks like this:

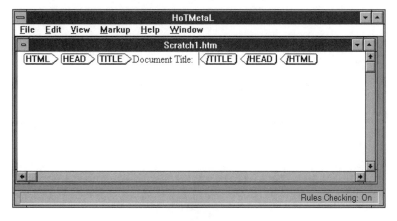

As you can see, HoTMetaL has inserted the TITLE and HEAD tags in our document along with the HTML tag. The *Document Title:* label in this screen is only there to indicate that the text following it is a title—the label will not be displayed as part of the document. At this point you should enter your document's title. After entering the title, move the cursor (with either your mouse or the arrow keys) to the point between /HEAD and /HTML and type <CTRL-I> again. You should see the following screen:

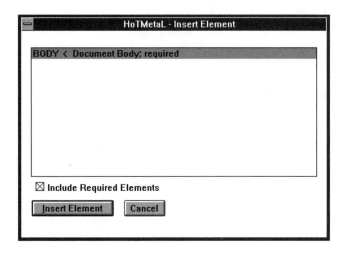

As you can see, only one element is legal at this point. To have HoTMetaL insert it, click on the Insert Element button. Now you are in the body of your document and may enter whatever element you wish—just type <CTRL-I> or choose Insert Element from the Markup menu.

View Options

HoTMetaL can act as a WYSIWYG editor (or as close to it as you can get when you are dealing with a markup language that will be displayed differently each time it is loaded into a different browser). The display format we have shown in our examples so far includes the tags. However, if you wish, you can ask HoTMetaL to hide the tags by choosing Hide Tags from the

View pulldown menu (or typing <CTRL-W>). Here is a simple document with tag view turned on:

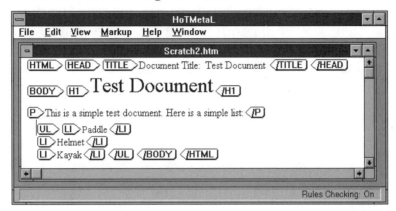

Now we type <CTRL-W> to turn tag view off, and here is the same document again:

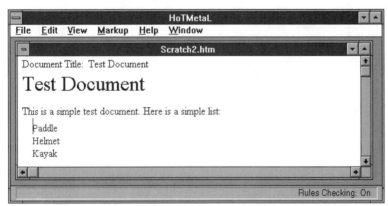

While it is sometimes useful to see your document without visible tags, it is more difficult to determine where your cursor is in relation to the tags. For example, if you wanted to insert something between the TITLE and HEAD tags, it would be difficult to find the right spot without seeing the tags.

Modifying Tags

Occasionally, you may wish to change the tag on a section of your document. The Change command in the Markup pulldown menu (which corresponds to the shortcut <CTRL-L>) allows you to do this. At any point in your document, you can type <CTRL-L> to see a list of valid element types to which you can convert the current element. For example, if we want to change our unordered list to an ordered list, we would place the cursor between the UL tag and the first LI tag. Then we type <CTRL-L>, and the following window appears:

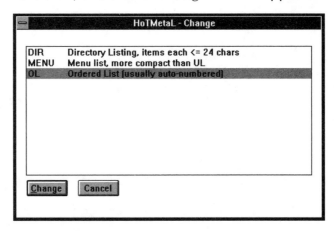

We choose the element type we wish to use and click on the Change button. You should then see the tags change to the new type in your document window.

Creating Links

Now let's look at how we add links to documents in HoT-MetaL. There are two ways to add anchor tags:

1. You can insert an anchor tag the same way any tag is added in HoTMetaL—by typing <CTRL-L> or choosing Insert from the Markup menu at the point where you want the tag to be added.

2. You can anchor existing text by highlighting the text and choosing Surround (or typing <CTRL-U>) from the Markup menu.

Once your anchor is in place, you will need to add attributes to it. Do this by choosing Edit SMGL Attributes from the

 Markup menu (or type F6). Note that you can only choose this option when the cursor is in the anchored area. If the option does not show up as an allowed choice when you go to the Markup menu, you will need to move your cursor to a point in the anchored area before proceeding. After this option has been chosen, the following window should appear:

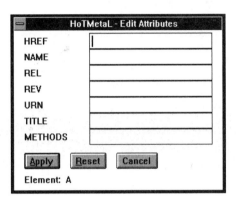

If you are creating a link to another location, enter the appropriate URL or relative location in the HREF box. If you are not sure what may be entered at this point, please refer to the chapter on "URLs and Links" . If you are creating a desti-nation anchor, enter the name of the label you wish to create in the Name box. Then click on Apply to finish creating the link.

Adding Images

The procedure for adding images to your documents is simi-lar to the procedure for adding an anchor. Place your cursor where you want the image to be inserted (make sure the loca-tion is valid for an image), and type <CTRL-I> to get the list of valid elements. Choose IMG from the list and click on the Insert Element button. Make sure that your cursor is in the IMG tags, and then choose Edit SMGL Attributes from the Markup menu (or type F6). The following window should appear:

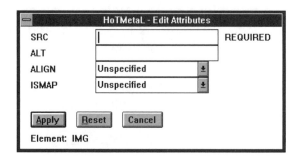

Enter the path to your image in the format

```
file:///c|/pathname/image.gif
```

where "c" should be replaced with the partition on which your file is located, and pathname and image.gif should be replaced with the path and filename for your image. For example, if we wanted to add a picture of a kayak to our document, and our picture is in f:\examples\gif\bigkayak.gif, we would enter the following in the SRC box:

```
file:///f|/examples/gif/bigkayak.gif
```

We also want to provide information for our readers who do not have graphic display browsers, so we enter "Picture of a Kayak" in the ALT box. We choose TOP in the Align box. If this image is going to be a clickable image, we could also choose ISMAP from the ISMAP menu. Then we click on Apply to enter our changes. Since our image is in GIF format, and HoTMetaL can display inline GIF images, the image appears in our document window:

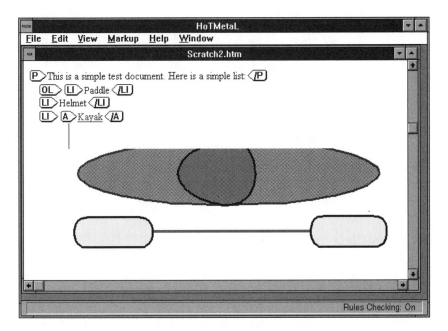

If you prefer to see the tag rather than the image, you can choose "Hide Inline Image" from the View menu. Also note that the image will not be displayed if it is not in GIF format. In this case, if you want to see the image with an external viewer (and you have configured a viewer for that image type in your initialization file), you can choose "Show Image" from the View menu to see the image.

Entering Special Characters

One of our favorite features in HoTMetaL is its ability to enter special and reserved characters automatically. For example, rather than having to remember < for "<", you can just type "<" and HoTMetaL will automatically insert the correct HTML tag for that character. If you want to enter a character that does not appear on the keyboard, you can choose Insert Character Entity (or type <CTRL-E>) from the Markup menu, and the following screen will appear:

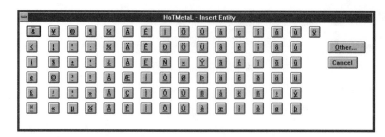

Click on the characters you wish to insert (or click on Other to see additional choices), and then close the window when you are done.

Creating Forms

It is easy to create forms in HoTMetaL. To illustrate, we will show you how to create Kelly's guest book (see page 173) using HoTMetaL. As with all HTML documents, we start by telling HoTMetaL to insert the HTML and HEAD tags. At the Document Title: prompt, we enter the title for our document: Kayaking with Kelly Kayaker and Friends.

Next, we move our cursor to the point between the closing HEAD and HTML tags and insert a BODY tag. We enter our heading and introductory paragraph:

Now we are ready to create our form. Kelly's guestbook consists of three text boxes for the guest's name and e-mail address, and one textarea for comments. We will also add another set of boxes not found in the original guestbook—a set of radio boxes to allow the guest to indicate their kayaking expertise level.

We start the form by inserting a form tag after our paragraph by choosing FORM from the list of elements:

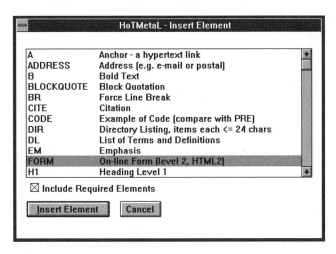

Next, we need to provide the attributes for the form. To do this we make sure that the cursor is between the FORM tags, and then choose Edit SGML Attributes from the Markup menu. We want to use the POST method and the CGI program at http://ozone.com/cgi-bin/guest with our form. We fill out the window as follows:

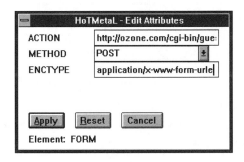

Now we are ready to enter the form itself. We start a paragraph and enter the text for the labels, followed by the type of input field we wish to use. For example, our first field is labeled "First Name:", and is associated with an input field of type "text". To create this field we enter "First Name" and then type <CTRL-I> to get the element insertion list. We choose input from the list:

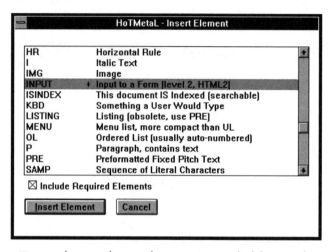

To set the attributes for our input field, we choose "Edit SGML Attributes" from the Markup menu, and fill it out as follows:

Notice that all of the legal attributes available with the Input field are listed, although some of them (such as CHECKED) are not applicable for the type of field we chose. We enter the information for our Last Name and E-Mail address fields in a similar fashion. The next field is a TEXTAREA for reader comments. As with our other fields, we place our input field along with its label in a paragraph field. When we insert the TEXTAREA field, the SGML attribute window for the field will automatically appear. We fill it out as follows:

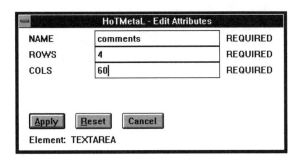

The next fields we wish to add are a set of radio checkboxes for readers to indicate their kayaking experience level. The procedure for radio checkboxes is the same as for TEXT types: insert an element of type INPUT, and then edit the SGML attributes. Remember that you must use the same NAME field for related radio checkboxes. You should also fill in the VALUE field. For example, this is how we fill in the first box:

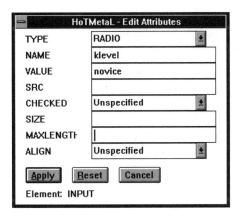

We end our form with the usual SUBMIT and RESET buttons by entering two more input fields of types SUBMIT and RESET. Our completed form looks like this in HoTMetaL:

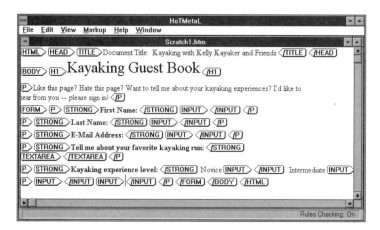

We have chosen Netscape Navigator as our preview browser. Although we have not yet saved the file, we wish to see how it looks in a browser. When we choose the Preview option from the File menu (which corresponds to the shortcut <CTRL-M>), HoTMetaL asks whether we want to preview the document even though it has not been saved. We answer yes, and HoTMetaL fires up Netscape.

If you want to make changes and then preview your document again, choose the Reload option in Netscape after choosing Preview in HoTMetaL (if you exited from NetScape, you only need to choose Preview in HoTMetaL).

Opening Existing HTML Documents

HoTMetaL also allows you to open and edit HTML documents that were created with other editors. You open these documents the same way you open any document—by choosing Open from the File menu, and entering the name of the document.

If you used an editor that didn't enforce strict rule-checking to create the document, you may have noncompliant elements in it. When HoTMetaL runs into noncompliant elements, it will pop up a window with a description of the error and its location in the document. For example:

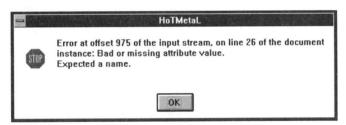

When you click the OK button, HoTMetaL will provide another window with a number of options:

If you choose Import Through Filter, HoTMetaL will use a special filter that will try to correct the noncompliant elements in your document. If you think your document is fairly close to being compliant to the standard, this is the easiest choice (and has the added benefit of automatically correcting HTML errors you may have made). Import Through Filter will pop up another window asking for a filename for the corrected version of your document:

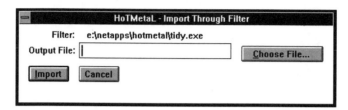

Enter the filename you want to use for your corrected document, and HoTMetaL will correct the document and then display it.

If you prefer to correct your document yourself, choose "Open as Text" rather than the filter. HoTMetaL will then open your document and place the cursor at the point in the document where it found a problem. You can then correct the problem and reopen the file. You may need to do this repeatedly until all of the errors are found and corrected.

HoTMetaL PRO

The following are additional features that you will find in the full version of HoTMetaL PRO:

- Spellchecker, dictionary and thesaurus
- URL editor
- Forms support
- Split paragraph
- Remove tags
- Color control
- Table and macro support
- Microsoft Windows Help
- Printed manual
- Homepage template
- Support

HTML Assistant

To install HTML Assistant, run \editors\htmlasst\htmlasst.exe from the Program Manager. It will give you the opportunity to specify the installation directory, and also to decide whether you want it to make backup copies of any files it modifies during the installation procedure. If you wish to use HTML Assistant with the HTML CD Menu, you must specify C:\HTMLASST as the installation directory. It will then give you the opportunity to specify a program group in which you wish to have the HTML icon placed. When it is done with the installation it will ask you if you wish to see the README file. The HTML Assistant icon should also appear in the program group that you specified:

HTML
Assistant

Internet Assistant

Internet Assistant for Microsoft Word version 1.02 (IA) is an upgrade to Microsoft Word that turns Word into an HTML browser and editor. If you are already familiar with Word, you will probably find it easy to learn IA. This product lets users browse the Web from within a single, easy-to-use program. However, because IA is designed to hide the details of HTML, it is sometimes difficult to use if you want to do something specific with HTML. This was especially noticeable when trying to create forms with IA. IA also does not support the Netscape extensions or any of the new HTML 3 tags (such as tables).

You must have an English, French or German copy of Microsoft Word 6.0a before you can install IA. If you have version 6.0 you can get a free upgrade on Microsoft's Web site at www.microsoft.com. Also, if you have an earlier version of Internet Assistant you should remove it before installing this version (remove IA by running SETUP for the version of IA that you have, and choosing Remove All).

Once you are sure that you have met these conditions, you may install IA by running \EDITORS\IA\SETUP.EXE from the program manager (or double click on it from the file manager). As part of the upgrade it will create a subdirectory named INTERNET in your Word directory.

Using IA as a Browser

After the upgrade is completed, you can access Internet Assistant's features from Word. To use IA as a browser, choose Browse Web from the File menu. The menu bar will then change to browser mode, and IA's default browser page will be loaded. You should see a window similar to this one:

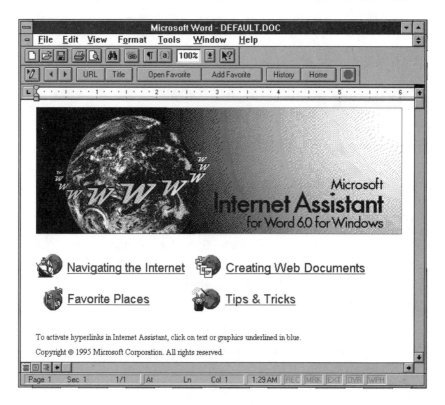

Since this is neither a book or chapter about Web browsers, we won't go into additional detail about IA's browser features. If you wish to use it, there is fairly extensive online help available to guide you in its use.

Creating HTML Documents with IA

In this section we will show you how to use some of the basic features in IA to create HTML documents.

To create an HTML document, choose New from the File menu. In the dialog box, you should see Html as an option:

Choose it, and click on OK to open the HTML document template. Your toolbar should now look like this:

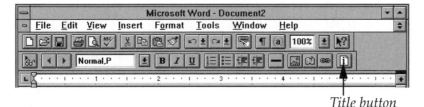

Title button

 As you can see, when you are in HTML mode most of the Word commands which would generate invalid HTML code are disabled. For example, the Font and point size boxes in the Formatting toolbar do not appear in HTML mode. However, some commands, such as tabs, are still available. HTML 2.0

239

does not support tabs, so if you use them, the formatting information associated with them will be lost when your document is saved in HTML.

Document Title

As with any HTML document, the first element you should create is the document's title. You can do this by choosing HTML Document Info... from the File pulldown menu or by clicking on the title button.

You will be given a dialog box in which to enter your document's title:

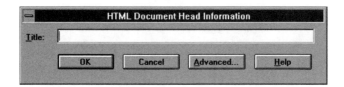

Since titles are not displayed as part of an HTML document, the title you enter will not be visible when you view the document in Word. Don't worry; it really is there, and will be displayed in the title area of the browser used to view the document.

Adding Text

Let's see how to add text to a document by creating a copy of the document that we used as an illustration in our section on HoTMetaL. First we add a heading to our document. We do this by choosing Heading 1, H1 from the list of HTML elements in the Style box. After adding our heading, we add a normal paragraph and an unordered list using the same procedure. Now our screen looks like this:

Style box

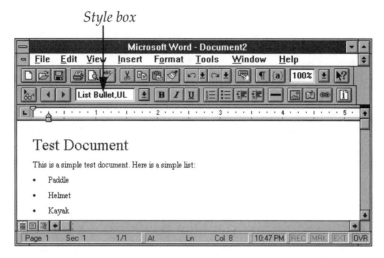

If you wish to add an HTML element that is not available from the Style box, you can type in raw HTML by choosing HTML Markup from the Insert pulldown menu. Elements which are entered in this fashion will be displayed with an HTML Markup note rather than as formatted text.

Forms

To add a form to your document, choose Form Field from the Insert pulldown menu. The following dialog box and toolbar will appear:

Although you can enter your first field from the dialog box, you will probably find it easier to enter the rest of the fields from the toolbar. Choose the types of input you would like, and they will be added to your form.

The version of IA on the CD does not support the TEXTAREA or RADIOBOX input formats. If you wish to use these types of fields, you can enter them via the HTML Markup command described in the previous section. Note that the IA browser mode also does not display these fields, so you will need to use another browser to see whether the fields are working as expected.

To choose the submission method for the form, create a SUBMIT field. You will be given the following dialog box:

Hyperlinks

To add a link, choose Hyperlink from the Insert pulldown menu or the insert hyperlink button on the toolbar. The following dialog box should appear:

You may either create a link over existing text by first highlighting the text, or you may add the text for the link when you create the link by entering the text you would like to use for the link in the Text to Display box.

To enter the link, choose the tab for the type of link you would like to make, enter the relevant information, and click the OK button. As you can see, IA provides three choices for link types: to Local Document, to URL and to Bookmark. To Local Document allows you to make a link to another file, and to URL allows you to make a link to a URL.

To Bookmark allows you to make a link to a specific location in the same document (e.g., a named anchor). Before using Bookmark, you must have already defined a bookmark. You can create a bookmark by choosing Bookmark from the Edit menu. Bookmark does seem to have a limitation — we could not find a way to create a link to a specific location in another document.

After creating the link, the text will be displayed as a link. You can check the link by double-clicking on it.

Learning More About IA

We have only covered some of the basic features available in IA. For detailed information about the HTML editor features in IA, please refer to the online help in Word or http://www.microsoft.com.

Converters

Converters take text in one format and translate it into another. For example, if you have a set of documents in FrameMaker that you wish to offer on the Web, you could use a converter to translate your documents into HTML. Unfortunately, most of the converters we found were written for UNIX systems or require Perl. Installing and using Perl goes beyond the scope of this book. For those of you who would like to try it, we have included a document on the CD that you can use to download Perl along with a number of the conversion tools that require it. You can find this document in \EXAMPLES\MORETOOL.HTM.

For those of you who don't want to deal with Perl, we have included a DOS-based converter on the CD that translates RTF to HTML. Rich Text Format (RTF) is a format created by Microsoft to allow documents to be transferred between Microsoft Word and other word processing packages. Many word processing packages (including WordPerfect and FrameMaker) have filters that allow you to save your files in RTF.

RTFTOHTM

On the CD you will find a DOS application by Chris Hector named RTFTOHTM that can convert RTF files into HTML. The converter and associated files are located in:

```
\FILTERS\TOOLS
```

To install this program, make a copy of this directory and its contents on your hard drive. Remember that this is a DOS program, so you will need to run it at the DOS prompt. It is not as easy to use as most of the Windows-based applications included on the CD. If you have never modified a configuration file, you should probably find someone to help you with this application. You will find a detailed manual for RTF-TOHTM at:

```
ftp://ftp.cray.com/src/WWWstuff/RTF/Users_Guide_ToC.html
```

RTFTOHTM converts formatted text into its equivalent HTML markup. Here is how it handles formatting commands:

- Bold, italic, underlined, and courier text will be tagged with <B>, <I>, <U>, or <TT>.
- Tables will be formatted using <PRE> (there is currently no support for the table element).
- Footnotes are placed in a separate document with hypertext links to them.
- Table of contents entries and paragraphs with the style "heading 1..6" will generate a hypertext Table of Contents in a separate file, and each table of contents entry is linked to the appropriate location in the main document.
- The original table of contents, indices, headers and footers are discarded.
- Images are written to a separate file.
- Text that is connected with copy/paste-link constructs will generate hypertext links.

RTFTOHTM is almost completely customizable. For paragraph and text styles, the rules for translation are contained in a file named *HTML-TRA*. You can teach RTFTOHTM to perform the correct translations for your documents by modifying this file. Your output will be placed in a file named *filename.htm* where *filename* or *filename.rtf* was your input file name.

Images

Images are embedded in RTF in either a binary format or an (ASCII) hex dump of that binary. RTFTOHTM handles the hex format of graphics by converting the hex back into binary and writing the binary to a file. The file extension is chosen by looking at the original image format. The following list shows the image formats understood by RTFTOHTM and their extensions:

pict   Macintosh PICT

wmf   Windows metafiles

bmp   Windows bitmap

RTFTOHTM places a link to the file containing the image in the HTML output file. Since the image formats listed here are not very portable, the filter assumes that you will convert the images to a popular format such as GIF. So the format of the link is:

```
<A HREF="basenameN.ext">anchor text</A>
```

where

basename   The name of the input document (without the .rtf extension)

N   A unique number (starting at 1)

ext   An extension that defaults to GIF, but can be overridden with the -P command line option.

If you prefer, you can have RTFTOHTM use IMG rather than make a link to the images by using the -I command line option. If you choose this option all links to images will be of the form:

```
<IMG src="basenameN.ext">
```

If a graphic is encountered when the filter is in the process of generating a link, the IMG form of the link is used even without the -I command line option.

Making a Named Anchor

To make a named anchor, simply enter the name in the document where you would like the anchor to appear. Then format the text using Outline and Hidden. Be careful in formatting the text that you format *only* the name—be careful not to format leading and trailing spaces or paragraph marks. To change the formatting that produces named anchors, you need to modify the entry in HTML-TRA that specifies "_Name" formatting.

Footnote/Endnote Processing

If your RTF document contains footnotes or endnotes, the filter will place the text of the footnote in a separate HTML document. At the footnote reference mark, the filter will generate a hypertext link to the text of the footnote. This works with either automatically numbered footnotes or user-supplied footnote reference marks.

Discarding Unwanted Text

If you have text that you do not want to appear in the HTML output, simply format the text as Hidden and Plain. If you wish to modify the formatting that discards text, change the entry in HTML-TRA that specifies "_Discard".

Embedding HTML in a Document

Normally, if your RTF document contained the text "<CITE>hello</CITE>", the translator would output this as "<cite>hello</cite>". This would ensure that the text appeared in your HTML output exactly as it appeared in the original RTF document. If, however, you want the <CITE></CITE> to be interpreted as HTML markup, format the tags using Hidden and Shadow. The filter will then send the tags through without translation. If you wish to modify the formatting for embedded HTML, you need to change the entry in html-tra that specifies "_Literal".

Customizing RTFTOHTM

HTML-TRA contains information about the paragraph styles in your document. All paragraph styles used in your document *must* appear in it. This allows you to create a map from any paragraph style to any HTML tag. There are many predefined styles in HTML-TRA, so if you have not defined any special styles in your document, you may not need to modify HTML-TRA. If RTFTOHTM encounters a paragraph style in your document that is not listed in HTML-TRA, a warning will be generated and the text will be written to the HTML file with no special markup.

If you are not sure whether your paragraph styles are already defined, you can easily find out by running RTFTOHTM on your RTF file. Each time it encounters a paragraph style it does not know, it will generate a warning message with the style's name. You can then use the information from the warning messages to update HTML-TRA.

There are four tables in HTML-TRA:

- .PTag
- .TTag
- .PMatch
- .TMatch.

These tables begin with the name (in column one) and continue until the next table starts. All blank lines and lines beginning with "#" are discarded, so if you want to include comments in the file, start the line with #.

The tables themselves are composed of records containing a fixed number of fields which are separated by commas. The fields are either strings (which should be quoted) integers or bitmasks. Entries in the tables are case-sensitive.

.PTag Table

Each entry in the .PTag table describes an HTML paragraph markup. Odds are good that you will not need to update this table since all of the current HTML tags are already defined. Table 10–1 lists the .PTag table variables. The format for entries is:

```
.PTag
"name","starttag","endtag","col2mark","tabmark","parmark",
. allowtext,cannest,DelteCol1,fold,TocStyl
```

TABLE 10–1   .PTag Table Variables

Tag Name	Description
name	A unique name for this entry. These names are referenced in the .PMatch table.
starttag	The string to be output once at the beginning of any text for this markup.
endtag	The string to be output once at the end of any text for this markup.
col2mark	The string to be output in place of the first tab in every paragraph (used for lists).
parmark	The string to be output in place of each paragraph mark (usually or <P>).
allowtext	If 0, no text markup will be allowed within this markup (for example, <PRE> or <H1> don't format well if they contain additional markup).
cannest	If 1, other paragraph markup will be allowed to nest within this markup (used for nesting lists).
DeleteCol1	If 1, all text up to the first tab in a paragraph will be deleted (used to strip out bullets when going to unordered lists, <UL>).
fold	If 1, the filter will add new lines to the HTML output to keep the number of characters in a line to less than 80. For <pre> or <listing> elements, this should be set to 0.
TocStyl	The TOC level. If greater than 0, the filter will create a table of contents entry for every paragraph using this markup.

Sample .PTag Entry

```
"h1","<h1>\n","</h1>\n","\t","\t","<br>\n",0,0,0,1
```

The above entry defines a level 1 heading. The "\n" in the start and end tag fields forces a new line in the HTML output file. Since new lines are ignored in HTML (except in <PRE>), its main purpose is to make the HTML output more readable. There is no difference between the first tab and any other. They both translate to a tab mark. Paragraph marks generate "<BR>" followed by a new line (just for looks). Text markup (like <B>) is not allowed within <H1> text, because we leave that up to the HTML client. No nesting is allowed, and no text is deleted. Every paragraph using this markup will also generate a level 1 table of contents entry.

.TTag Table

Each entry in the .TTag table describes an HTML text markup. Table 10–2 lists the entities in this table. The format is:

```
.TTag
"name","starttag","endtag"
```

TABLE 10–2 .TTag Table Entries

Tag Name	Description
name	A unique name for this entry. These names are referenced in the .PMatch table.
starttag	This string will be output once at the beginning of any text for this markup.
endtag	This string will be output once at the end of any text for this markup.

Unlike the .PTag table, no text markup should appear more than once.

.PMatch Table

Each entry in the .PMatch correlates a paragraph style name to some entry in the .PTag table. These entities are listed in Table 10–3. The format is:

```
.PMatch
"Paragraph Style",nesting_level,"PTagName"
```

TABLE 10–3   .PMatch Table Entries

Tag Name	Description
Paragraph Style	The paragraph style name that appears in the RTF input.
nesting_level	The nesting level. This should be zero except for nested list entries.
PTagName	The name of the .PTag entry that should be used for paragraphs with this paragraph style.

Sample .PMatch Entries

"heading 1",0,"h1"

This is a level 1 heading. Any paragraphs with this paragraph style will be mapped to the entry in the .PTag table named h1.

"numbered list",0,"ol-d"

This is used for numbered lists. Any paragraphs with this paragraph style will be mapped to the entry in the .PTag table named ol-d.

.TMatch Table

Each entry in the .TMatch table describes processing for text styles. Table 10–4 lists these entries. The format is:

```
.TMatch
"Font",FontSize,Match,Mask,"TextStyleName"
```

251

TABLE 10–4 .TMatch Table Entries

Tag Name	Description
Font	The name of a font, or "" if all fonts match this entry.
FontSize	The point size of the font, or 0 if all point sizes match this entry.
Match	A bit mask, where each bit represents a text attribute. These bits are compared to the attributes of the style being output. They must match for this entry to be matched. A 1 in a bit position means that the text style is set, a 0 is not set.
Mask	A bit mask, where each bit represents a text attribute. In comparing the style of the text being processed to the Match bit mask, this field is used to select the bits that matter. If a 0 appears in a bit position, then that style attribute is ignored (for the purpose of matching this entry). Only 1 bits are used in the above comparison.
TextStyleName	This is either the name of an entry in the .TTag table indicating the HTML markup to use, or one of _Discard, _Name, _HRef, _Hot, or _Literal.

RTFTOHTM compares the text style information to see if it matches any entries in the .TMatch table. If there is a match and the entry is for _Discard, _Literal, _Hot, _HRef, _Name, or _Footnote, then the text will be processed accordingly. For example, _Discard text is discarded and _Name text will generate an anchor using the text as a name.

Sample .PTag Entry

```
# Regular matches - You can have multiple of these active
# monospace fonts -> tt
"Courier",0,00000000000000,00000000000000,"tt"
```

This will match any text that uses the Courier font and mark it using the HTML text markup appearing in the .TTag table with the entry.

Adding Paragraph Styles

To add a new paragraph style, go to the .PMatch table and add an entry to the end. Put the name of the paragraph style (quoted), the nesting level (usually 0) and the name of the .PTag entry that should be used. If the paragraph style is not found in the table, it uses the first entry, "Normal".

Command Line Options

The options used in the command line of RTFTOHTM are listed in Table 10–5. The syntax of the rtftohtml command is as follows:

```
C:\> rtftohtm -i -V -o output_filename -P extension -T -G file
```

TABLE 10–5   RTFTOHTM Command Line Options

Option	Description
-i	Indicates that embedded graphics should be linked into the main document using an IMG tag. The default is to use an HREF style link.
-V	Prints the current version.
-o *filename*	Indicates that the output file name should be *filename*. If any other files are created (such as for graphics), the basename of the other files will be *filename* without .rtf if it is present in the name.
-P *extension*	Use *extension* as the extension for any links to graphics files. The default for this is gif.
-T	Indicates that no table of contents file is to be generated.
-G	Indicates that no graphics files should be written. The hypertext links to the graphics files will still be generated. This is a performance feature for re-translating a document in which the graphics have not changed.

TABLE 10–5   RTFTOHTM Command Line Options (Continued)

Option	Description
input_file	The file name to be processed. If no file is given, standard input is used. If standard input is used, the body of the document will be written to standard output (unless overridden by the -o option). If a file name appears, the output is written to *filename* with .htm as an extension. (If .rtf appears as an extension on the original input file, it is stripped before appending the .htm.)

RTFTOHTM Example

Let's look at an example now. We want to include a copy of the table of contents for this book on the CD in HTML format. Our book is in FrameMaker. Since FrameMaker can save files in RTF, we open the file containing our table of contents, and save a copy of the file in HTMLCD.RTF.

Our table of contents does not use any standard paragraph styles, so we will need to edit HTML-TRA to tell it about the paragraph styles in our file. Table 10–6 shows a list of the paragraph styles used in our document along with the corresponding HTML tags to which we want each style to map.

TABLE 10–6   CD Paragraph Styles

Document Paragraph Style	HTML Element
Title	H1
ChapterTitleTOC	H2
AppendixTitleTOC	H2
Heading1TOC	UL
HeadSideTOC	Nested UL

Since we are using standard HTML tags, the only change we need to make is to the .PMatch table in HTML-TRA. We make the following entries to this table:

```
"Title",0,"h1"
"ChapterTitleTOC",0,"h2"
"AppendixTitleTOC",0,"h2"
"Heading1TOC",0,"ul"
"HeadSideTOC",1,"ul"
```

Notice that in our entry for HeadSideTOC, we use a nesting level of 1 rather than 0, since we want a nested list for this paragraph style. Also remember that entries are case-sensitive, so you need to be sure that your tags match the actual tag. For example, "Title" and "title" are not the same. The same rule applies to the PTagName.

Now we are ready to run RTFTOHTM:

```
C:\> rtftohtm htmlcd.rtf
```

This produces a file named htmlcd.htm, which we can then load into a browser to check. RTFTOHTM does not include a title in the HTML output file, so you may wish to manually edit the file and add a title yourself.

HTML to Other Formats

So far we have discussed ways to create HTML files. Now we'll give you some hints about going in the other direction. Many utilities have been written that allow you to convert HTML source into other formats. Unfortunately, most of these utilities were written for UNIX systems. If you have access to a UNIX system, MORETOOL.HTM in the tool chest on the CD has a list of filters that you can get on the Internet.

If all you want to do is remove your HTML markup tags—turn your document into plain text—there is a fairly simple way to do this. Some browsers (NCSA Mosaic is one such browser) allow you to save documents in a number of formats. All you have to do to get a plain-text version of your HTML document is to load it into one such browser and then save it as plain text.

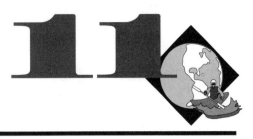

ANNOUNCING YOUR WEB PAGES

What's In This Chapter

Once you have finished authoring documents for your Web site, you naturally want to announce their existence to interested parties. The best method for announcing Web pages depends, of course, on their contents. Before announcing new pages, consider who the best and most appropriate audience might be. Don't announce your pages in an unsolicited way to groups and people who haven't requested the information because, just like unsolicited advertising, you are likely to quickly antagonize them. With this caveat in mind, we mention here some of the most common means for announcing new Web pages and sites.

Personal Home Pages

For personal pages, people are increasingly including the URLs of their home pages in their "signatures" attached to electronic mail. In addition, many people are listing their URLs on their business cards.

Announcing to Newsgroups

A common approach is to advertise your new Web pages in a relevant USENET newsgroup or mailing list. If you choose to do this, you must make sure that the group or list you target is appropriate and that your announcement is directly related to it. Otherwise, your announcement might be treated as "spam," and you risk receiving angry complaints.

In addition, there is a moderated newsgroup for announcing generally interesting and useful Web sites, called comp.info-systems.announce. Before submitting to this group, please read the charter posting and several of the group's postings to get an idea of what is considered appropriate.

Announcing to the Web

Naturally, you can use the Web to announce your new pages or Web server. You can submit your URL to the "What's New Page" at NCSA:

```
http://www.ncsa.uiuc.edu/SDG/Software/Mosaic/Docs/whats-new.html
```

This page will provide you with information on how to send in your listing. However, because of the Web's popularity, it might be a while before your submission appears.

You can also register your pages with sites that are building Web catalogs. These sites collect submitted URLs (and also search the Web itself) in order to generate catalogs of Web documents. These catalogs can then be searched by Web users in order to find documents of interest.

There are many such catalogs, and we provide only the URLs of a few of them here. You can use the listed URLs in order to access the site of each of these catalogs. This will enable you to both search their databases and submit the URLs of your Web pages for inclusion in the catalogs.

The Lycos Database

```
http://www.lycos.com/
```

Yahoo

```
http://www.yahoo.com
```

WWW Virtual Library

```
http://info.cern.ch/hypertext/DataSources/bySubject/Over
view.html
```

ElNet Galaxy

```
http://www.einet.net/
```

ALIWEB index

```
http://web.nexor.co.uk/aliweb/doc/aliweb.html
```

Submit It!

```
http://www.cen.uiuc.edu/~banister/submit-it/
```

This is actually a form that allows you to submit an announcement to many indices at one time.

Announcing a Server

If you are adding a server rather than just a single page or set of pages, you should register in the WWW list of servers maintained at CERN. The URL for this resource is:

```
http://info.cern.ch/hypertext/DataSources/WWW/Geographical
_generation/new-servers.html
```

ISO Latin 1 Entities in HTML

HTML Tag	Character	Description
&AElig;	Æ	capital AE diphthong (ligature)
&Aacute;	Á	capital A, acute accent
&Acirc;	Â	capital A, circumflex accent
&Agrave;	À	capital A, grave accent
&Aring;	Å	capital A, ring
&Atilde;	Ã	capital A, tilde
&Auml;	Ä	capital A, dieresis or umlaut mark
&Ccedil;	Ç	capital C, cedilla
&ETH;	Ð	capital Eth, Icelandic
&Eacute;	É	capital E, acute accent

HTML Tag	Character	Description
Ê	Ê	capital E, circumflex accent
È	È	capital E, grave accent
Ë	Ë	capital E, dieresis or umlaut mark
Í	Í	capital I, acute accent
Î	Î	capital I, circumflex accent
Ì	Ì	capital I, grave accent
Ï	Ï	capital I, dieresis or umlaut mark
Ñ	Ñ	capital N, tilde
Ó	Ó	capital O, acute accent
Ô	Ô	capital O, circumflex accent
Ò	Ò	capital O, grave accent
Ø	Ø	capital O, slash
Õ	Õ	capital O, tilde
Ö	Ö	capital O, dieresis or umlaut mark
Þ	Þ	capital THORN, Icelandic
Ú	Ú	capital U, acute accent
Û	Û	capital U, circumflex accent
Ù	Ù	capital U, grave accent
Ü	Ü	capital U, dieresis or umlaut mark
Ý	Ý	capital Y, acute accent
á	á	small a, acute accent
â	â	small a, circumflex accent
æ	æ	small ae diphthong (ligature)
à	à	small a, grave accent
å	å	small a, ring
ã	ã	small a, tilde
ä	ä	small a, dieresis or umlaut mark
ç	ç	small c, cedilla
é	é	small e, acute accent

HTML Tag	Character	Description
ê	ê	small e, circumflex accent
è	è	small e, grave accent
ð	ð	small eth, Icelandic
ë	ë	small e, dieresis or umlaut mark
í	í	small i, acute accent
î	î	small i, circumflex accent
ì	ì	small i, grave accent
ï	ï	small i, dieresis or umlaut mark
ñ	ñ	small n, tilde
ó	ó	small o, acute accent
ô	ô	small o, circumflex accent
ò	ò	small o, grave accent
ø	ø	small o, slash
õ	õ	small o, tilde
ö	ö	small o, dieresis or umlaut mark
ß	ß	small sharp s, German (sz ligature)
þ	þ	small thorn, Icelandic
ú	ú	small u, acute accent
û	û	small u, circumflex accent
ù	ù	small u, grave accent
ü	ü	small u, dieresis or umlaut mark
ý	ý	small y, acute accent
ÿ	ÿ	small y, dieresis or umlaut mark

ASCII TABLE

00	nul	16	syn	2c	,	42	B	58	X	6e	n
01	soh	17	etb	2d	-	43	C	59	Y	6f	o
02	stx	18	can	2e	.	44	D	5a	Z	70	p
03	etx	19	em	2f	/	45	E	5b	[	71	q
04	eot	1a	sub	30	0	46	F	5c	\	72	r
05	enq	1b	esc	31	1	47	G	5d	]	73	s
06	ack	1c	fs	32	2	48	H	5e	^	74	t
07	bel	1d	gs	33	3	49	I	5f	_	75	u
08	bs	1e	rs	34	4	4a	J	60	`	76	v
09	ht	1f	us	35	5	4b	K	61	a	77	w
0a	nl	20	sp	36	6	4c	L	62	b	78	x
0b	vt	21	!	37	7	4d	M	63	c	79	y
0c	np	22	"	38	8	4e	N	64	d	7a	z
0d	cr	23	#	39	9	4f	O	65	e	7b	{
0e	so	24	$	3a	:	50	P	66	f	7c	|
0f	si	25	%	3b	;	51	Q	67	g	7d	}
10	dle	26	&	3c	<	52	R	68	h	7e	~
11	dc1	27	'	3d	=	53	S	69	i	7f	del
12	dc2	28	(	3e	>	54	T	6a	j		
13	dc3	29	)	3f	?	55	U	6b	k		
14	dc4	2a	*	40	@	56	V	6c	l		
15	nak	2b	+	41	A	57	W	6d	m		

USEFUL URLS

There are many HTML resources for authors available on the Web. Here are some useful links.

General HTML and WWW Information

The World Wide Web Consortium

http://www.w3.org/

WWW Frequently Asked Questions

http://sunsite.unc.edu/boutell/faq/

Introductions to HTML

http://www.ncsa.uiuc.edu/demoweb/html-primer.html

http://www.utirc.utoronto.ca/HTMLdocs/NewHTML/intro.html

HTML Style Guides

http://www.w3.org/hypertext/WWW/Provider/Style/Overview.html

http://info.med.yale.edu/caim/StyleManual_Top.HTML

HTML Working Group Mailing List Archive

http://www.ics.uci.edu/pub/ietf/html/

HTML Bibliographies

http://www.utirc.utoronto.ca/HTMLdocs/NewHTML/bibliography.html

http://info.med.yale.edu/caim/M_Resources.HTML

HTML Elements

Image Map Information

http://hoohoo.ncsa.uiuc.edu/docs/setup/admin/NewImagemap.html

Forms Information

http://www.ncsa.uiuc.edu/SDG/Software/Mosaic/Docs/fill-out-forms/
overview.html

Table Information

http://www.hpl.hp.co.uk/people/dsr/html/tables.html

CGI Information

Documentation

http://hoohoo.ncsa.uiuc.edu/docs/

http://hoohoo.ncsa.uiuc.edu/cgi/overview.html

Default scripts for NCSA httpd: C routines

ftp://ftp.ncsa.uiuc.edu/Web/httpd/Unix/ncsa_httpd/cgi/ncsa-default.tar.Z

Default scripts for NCSA httpd: Perl routines

ftp://ftp.ncsa.uiuc.edu/Web/httpd/Unix/ncsa_httpd/cgi/cgi-lib.pl.Z

CGI Standard

http://hoohoo.ncsa.uiuc.edu/cgi/overview.html

CGI FAQ

http://www.halcyon.com/hedlund/cgi-faq/faq.html

Netscape Extensions

Extensions to the BODY tag:

http://home.netscape.com/assist/net_sites/bg/index.html

Netscape offers a number of GIF-format images suitable for backgrounds on their server. You can find these images at the URL:

http://home.netscape.com/assist/net_sites/bg/backgrounds.html

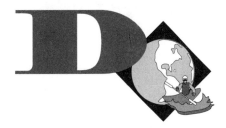

WWW Service Providers

This appendix contains a list of Web service providers. New service providers seem to pop up every day, so if you do not find a service provider that suits your needs listed here, there are a number of places you can check for additional listings on the Internet.

When choosing a Web provider, keep in mind that the Web is a global entity. Your audience may be located anywhere in the world; so as long as *you* have a way to get onto the Internet, your Web provider does not need to be close to you (as opposed to a general Internet service provider, for which you would probably want to have a local access point). Another point to consider while choosing a provider is the provider's focus. Some providers are oriented toward the provision of

Web space for personal use or small business use, while other providers are focused on large business (and the associated big budgets that typically accompany them). In general, the more frills (such as custom page design and high bandwidth connections) a provider has to offer, the greater the cost.

Each provider is listed in the following format:

Provider name
Surface mail address (if available)
Phone number
Fax number
Internet e-mail address
URL

If you are a provider and would like to be added to this list in future editions of this book, please send your update to Vivian@catalog.com.

World Wide Web Service Providers

a2i communications
1211 Park Avenue #202
San Jose, CA 95126–2924
408–293–8078
Fax: 408–263–0461
support@rahul.net

Able Technical Services
ABLECOM.NET
P.O. Box 26530
San Jose, CA 95159
408–441–6000
howard@ablecom.net

Access Nevada, Inc.
702–294–0480
Fax: 702–293–3278
info@accessnv.com

AccuNet
Kansas City, MO
816–246–9094
dwhitten@accunet.com

Achilles Internet Limited
613–723–6624
Fax: 613–723–8583
office@achilles.net

Advanced Network Solutions
http@adnetsol.com
http://www.adnetsol.com/

Berbee Information Networks Corp.

455 Science Drive
Madison, WI 53711–1058
608–233–5222
Fax: 608–233–9795
info@binc.net

Best Internet Communications, Inc.

421 Castro Street
Mountain View, CA 94041
415–964–2378
Fax: 415–691–4195
info@best.com
http://www.best.com

BlueMarble

Bloomington, IN
support@bluemarble.net
http://www.bluemarble.net

BBN Planet Corporation

150 Cambridge Park Drive
Cambridge, MA 02140
800–472–4565
Fax: 617–873–5620
net-info@bbnplanet.com
http://www.near.net/doc/corp.html

Canada Connect Corporation

201 1039 17 Avenue SW
Calgary, Alberta T2T 0B2
Canada
403–777–2025
Fax: 403–777–2026
info@canuck.com
http://www.canuck.com/

Charm.Net

2228 E. Lombard St.
Baltimore, MD 21231
410–558–3900
Fax: 410–558–3901
admin@Charm.Net
http://www.charm.net/

CERFnet

California Education and Research
    Federation Network
P.O. Box 85608
San Diego, CA 92186–9784
800–876–2373
619–455–3900
Fax: 619–455–3990
sales@cerf.net
http://www.cerf.net/

CHANNEL 1 Communications

1030 Massachusetts Avenue
Cambridge, MA 02138
617–864–0100
Fax: 617–354–3100
support@channel1.com
http://www.channel1.com/

CICNet

Committee on Institutional Cooperation
    Network
ITI Building
2901 Hubbard Drive
Ann Arbor, MI 48105
313–998–6703
800–947–4754
info@cic.net
http://www.cic.net/

CityNet

P.O. Box 3235
Charleston, WV 25332
304–342–5700
http://www.citynet.net/

Clarknet

Clark Internet Services, Inc.
10600 Route 108
Ellicott City, MD 21042
800–735–2258
410–254–3900
Fax: 410–730–9765
info@clark.net
http://www.clark.net/

Colorado SuperNet (CSN)

SuperNet Inc.
One Denver Place
999 18th Street
Denver, CO 80202
303–296–8202
Fax: 303–296–8224
help@csn.net
http://www.csn.net/csn/

Computer Service Langenbach GmbH

Germany
http://www.csl-gmbh.net/csl/

Connect.com.au pty ltd

129 Hawthorn Road
Caulfield
Victoria 3161 Australia
61–3–528–2239
1–800–818–262 (Australia-wide)
Fax: 61–3–528–5887
connect@connect.connect.com.au
http://www.connect.com.au/

Crossroads Communications

P.O. Box 30250
Mesa, AZ 85275
602–813–9040
800–892–7040
Fax: 602–545–7470
http://xroads.xroads.com/home.html

CTS Network Services (CTSNET)

Division of Datel Systems Inc.
4444 Convoy Street, Suite 300
San Diego, CA 92111–3761
619–637–3637
Fax: 619–637–3630
info@crash.cts.com (server)
support@crash.cts.com (human)
http://www.cts.com/

CyberGate, Inc.

305–428–4283
Fax: 305–428–7977
info@gate.net
http://www.gate.net/services.html

DASNET

DA Systems, Inc.
1053 East Campbell Avenue
Campbell, CA 95008
408–559–7434

Data Basix

Ray Harwood
P.O. Box 18324
Tucson, AZ 85731
602–721–1988
Fax: 602–721–7240
info@data.basix.com (server)
sales@data.basix.com (human)
http://data.basix.com/

Dayton Internet Services

Dayton Internet Services
3131 South Dixie Drive
Suite 103
Dayton, OH 45439
513–643–0188
Fax: 513–643–0190
http://www.firstnet.net/About.html

Demon

Demon Internet Systems (DIS)
44–081–349–0063
internet@demon.co.uk
http://www.demon.co.uk/

Direct Network Access

2039 Shattuck Avenue, Suite 206
Berkeley, CA 94704
510–649–6110
Fax: 510–649–7130
info@dnai.com (Automated response)
support@dnai.com (User technical
   support)
http://www.dnai.com/

Dreamscape Online

315–446–2626
Fax: 315–446–2626
http://www.dreamscape.com/

EmeraldNet

1718 East Speedway
Suite #315
Tucson, AZ 85719
520–670–1994
Fax: 520–670–1922
INFO@Emerald.NET
http://www.emerald.net/about_eNet.html

EUnet Communications Services BV

Singel 540
1017 AZ Amsterdam
The Netherlands
31–20–623–3803
Fax: 31–20–622–4657
info@EU.net
http://www.eu.net/

Frontier Internet

303–385–4177
jbd@frontier.net
http://www.frontier.net/

Frontier Internet Services

London, UK
01–71–242–3383
Fax: 01–71–242–3384
support@ftech.co.uk
http://www.ftech.co.uk/frontier/frontier.htm

GetNet International, Inc.

7325 North 16th Street, Suite #140
Phoenix, AZ 85020
602–943–3119
info@getnet.com
http://www.getnet.com/about_getnet.html

Global Enterprise Service, Inc.

3 Independence Way
Princeton, NJ 08540
800–358–4437
609–258–2400
Fax: 609–897–7310
market@jvnc.net
http://www.jvnc.net/

Helix Internet

#902–900 West Hastings
Vancouver, B.C., V6C–1E6
Canada
604–689–8544
Fax: 604–685–2554
accounts@helix.net
http://www.helix.net/sub/about.html

HoloNet

Information Access Technologies, Inc.
46 Shattuck Square, Suite 11
Berkeley, CA 94704–1152
510–704–0160
Fax: 510–704–8019
info@holonet.net
http://www.holonet.net/holonet/

HookUp

HookUp Communication Corporation
519–747–4110
Fax: 519–746–3521
info@hookup.net
http://www.hookup.net/

IDS World Network

InteleCom Data Systems
5835 Post Rd., Suite 214
East Greenwich, RI 02818
800–IDS–1680
Fax: 401–886–4050
info@ids.net
http://www.ids.net/idstext.html

IndyNet

5348 N. Tacoma Ave.
Indianapolis, IN 46220
317–251–5208
http://gopher.indy.net/index.html

InfoCom Networks

P.O. Box 590343
Houston, TX 77259–0343
helpdesk@infocom.net
http://www.infocom.net/

Inter'Acces

Montreal, Quebec
Canada
514–367–0002
sales@Interax.net
http://www.interax.net/

InterAcess

3345 Commercial Avenue
Northbrook, IL 60062
800–967–1580
708–498–2542
Fax: 708–671–0113
http://www.interaccess.com/iainfo/Guest.html

Internet Direct, Inc.

800–879–3624
602–274–0100 (Phoenix)
602–324–0100 (Tucson)
Fax: 602–274–8518
sales@direct.net
http://www.indirect.com/

Internet Express

800–592–1240
info@usa.net
http://www.usa.net/

The Internet MainStreet

334 State Street, Suite 106
Los Altos, CA 94022
415–941–1068
info@mainstreet.net
http://www.mainstreet.net/

KAIWAN

Knowledge Added Information Wide Area
   Network Corporation
18001 Sky Park Circle, Suite J
Irvine, CA 92714
714–638–2139
Fax: 714–638–0455
info@kaiwan.com
http://www.kaiwan.com

Klink Net Communications

Gloversville, NY
518–725–3000
800–KLINK–123
admin@klink.net
http://www.klink.net/

Lanka Internet Services, Ltd (LISL)

5th Floor, IBM Building
48 Nawam Mawatha
Colombo 2, Sri Lanka
94–1–342974
Fax: 94–1–343056
info@lanka.net
http://www.lanka.net/lisl.html

LinkAGE Online

webmaster@hk.linkage.net
http://www.hk.linkage.net/

LinkNet

318–442–LINK
Fax: 318–449–9750
support@linknet.net
http://www.linknet.net/

The Little Garden

3004 16th St., #204
San Francisco, CA 94103
415–487–1902
Fax: 415–552–6088
sales@tlg.net
http://tlg.org/

Maestro

Maestro Technologies, Inc.
29 John Street, Suite 1601
New York, NY 10038
212–240–9600
Fax: 212–566–0315
info@maestro.com (server)
staff@maestro.com (human)
http://www.maestro.com

Magic Online Services

1483 Pembina Hwy. #150
Winnipeg, Manitoba R2T 2C6
Canada
204–949–7777
Fax: 204–949–7790
sbrooker@magic.mb.ca
http://www.magic.mb.ca/

MCSNet

1300 West Belmont, Suite 405
Chicago, IL 60657
312–248–8649
Fax: 312–248–8649
support@mcs.com
http://www.mcs.net

Michigan BizServe

Online Technologies Corporation
staff@BizServe.com
http://bizserve.com/

Milwaukee Internet X

Mix Communications
P.O. Box 17166
Milwaukee, WI 53217
414–962–8172
wwwinfo@mixcom.com
http://www.mixcom.com

MindVOX

Phantom Access Technologies, Inc.
175 Fifth Avenue, Suite 2614
New York, NY 10010
800–MindVox
212–989–2418
Fax: 212–989–8648
info@phantom.com
http://www.phantom.com/

MSEN, Inc.

320 Miller Avenue
Ann Arbor, MI 48103
313–998–4562
Fax: 313–998–4563
info@msen.com
http://www.msen.com

MUC.DE e.V.

Muenchner Technologiezentrum
Frankfurter Ring 193 a
80807 Muenchen
Germany
089–324683–0
vorstand@muc.de
http://www/muc.de/

Mundo Internet

Centro de Investigación y de Estudios
    Avanzados del IPN
Unidad Mérida
Sección de Telemática
km 6 Antigua Carretera a Progreso
Apdo. Postal 73 Cordemex Mérida, Yuc. CP
    97310
99–812960, ext. 265
Fax: 99–812923
http://w3mint.cieamer.conacyt.mx/

NeoSoft, Inc.

1770 St. James Place
Suite 500
Houston, TX 77056
800–GET–NEOSOFT
713–968–5800
sales@neosoft.com
http://www.neosoft.com/

Netcom Online Communication Services

P.O. Box 20774
San Jose, CA 95160
408–554–8649
info@netcom.com
http://www.netcom.com/

NETConnect

Cedar City, UT
801–865–7032
http://www.tcd.net/

NetHeaven

518–885–1295
800–910–6671
stpeters@NetHeaven.com
http://www.netheaven.com/

Netrail, Inc.

2007 N. 15 St., Suite 5
Arlington, VA 22201
703–524–4800
Fax: 703–524–5510
sales@netrail.net
http://www.netrail.net/

Network Wizards

PO Box 343
Menlo Park, CA 94026
415–326–2060
Fax: 415–326–4672
info@nw.com
http://catalog.com/

North Shore Access

Eco Software, Inc.
145 Munroe Street, Suite 405
Lynn, MA 01901
617–593–3110
info@northshore.ecosoft.com
http://northshore.ecosoft.com/

NovaLink

Inner Circle Technologies, Inc.
79 Boston Turnpike, Suite 409
Shrewsbury, MA 01545
800–274–2814
508–754–9910
info@novalink.com
http://www.novalink.com/

Nuance Network Services

904 Bob Wallace Avenue, Suite 119
Huntsville, AL 35801
205–533–4296
info@nuance.com
http://www.nuance.com/

OnRamp

1950 Stemmons Freeway
Suite 5061 – INFOMART
Dallas, TX 75207
214–746–4710
Fax: 214–713–5400
Faxback: 214–746–4852
info@onramp.net
http://www.onramp.net/

Open Door Networks, Inc.

110 S. Laurel St.
Ashland, OR 97520
503–488–4127
help@opendoor.com
http://www.opendoor.com/

OuterNet Connections

8235 Shoal Creek, #105
Austin, TX 78758
512–345–3573
info@outer.net
http://www.outer.net/

Panix Public Access Unix

110 Riverside Drive
New York, NY 10024
212–741–4400
infobot@panix.com
http://www.panix.com/

Pavilion Internet

Brighton, Sussex
44–0–1273–607072
Fax: 44–0–1273–607073
info@pavilion.co.uk
http://www.pavilion.co.uk/

Performance Systems International, Inc. (PSI)

510 Huntmar Park Drive
Herndon, VA 22070
800–827–7482
Fax: 800–329–7741
info@psi.com
http://www.psi.net/

Pacific Information eXchange, Inc. NETwork (PIXINET)

1142 Auahi Street, Suite 2788
Honolulu, HI 96814
info@pixi.com
http://www.pixi.com/

Pegasus Networks

PO Box 284
Broadway Q 4006
Australia
61–7–257–1111
Fax: 61–7–257–1087
pegasus@peg.apc.org
http://www.peg.apc.org

PIPEX

Unipalm Ltd.
44–223–424616
Fax: 44–223–426868
pipex@unipalm.co.uk
http://www.pipex.net/

Planet Access Networks

55 Rt. 206 – Suite E
Stanhope, NJ 07874
201–691–4704
info@planet.net
http://www.planet.net/

Portal Communications, Inc.

20863 Stevens Creek Boulevard
Suite 200
Cupertino, CA 95014
408–973–9111
http://www.portal.com/

Power Net

Los Angeles, CA
310–643–4908
sales@power.net
http://www.power.net/

QuakeNet Internet Services

830 Wilmington Road
San Mateo, CA 94402
415–655–6607
Fax: 415–377–0635
info@quake.net
http://www.quake.net/

RainDrop Laboratories

5627 SW 45th
Portland, OR 97221–3505
info@agora.rain.com
http://www.rdrop.com/agora/

Real/Time Communications

6721 N. Lamar, Suite 103
Austin, TX 78752
512–451–0046
Fax: 512–459–3858
sales@realtime.net
http://www.realtime.net/

RedIRIS

Secretaria RedIRIS
Fundesco
Alcala 61
28014 Madrid
Spain
34–1–435–1214
Fax: 34–1–578–1773
secretaria@rediris.es
http://www.rediris.es/

Renaissance Internet Services

Phase IV Systems, Inc.
Huntsville, AL
custsrv@ro.com
http://www.ro.com/

Seanet

OSD, Inc.
Columbia Seafirst Center
701 Fifth Avenue, Suite 6801
Seattle, WA 98104
206–343–7828
Fax: 206–628–0722
seanet@seanet.com
http://www.seanet.com/

Sierra-Net

Lake Tahoe/Northern Nevada
702–832–6911
Fax: 702–831–3970
info@sierra.net
http://www.sierra.net/

South Coast Computing Services, Inc.

713–661–3301
Fax: 713–917–5005
info@sccsi.com
http://www.sccsi.com/

SSNet

302–378–1386
800–331–1386
info@ssnet.com
http://ssnet.com/

Structured Network Systems, Inc.

503–656–3530
800–881–0962
Fax: 503–656–3235
sales@structured.net
http://www.structured.net/

Suburbia PAN

P.O. Box 2031
Barker 3122
Australia
helpdesk@suburbia.apana.org.au
http://suburbia.apana.org.au/

Supernet

800–746–0777
info@supernet.net
http://www.supernet.net/

SWITCH

SWITCH Head Office
Limmatquai 138
CH–8001 Zurich
Switzerland
41–1–268–1515
Fax: 41–1–268–1568
info@switch.ch
http://www.switch.ch/

Systems Solutions Inc.

2108 East Thomas Road, Suite 200
Phoenix, AZ 85016–7758
602–955–5566
Fax: 602–955–0085
webmaster@syspac.com
http://www.syspac.com/

Tachyon Communications Corporation

100 Rialto Place, Suite 747
Melbourne, FL 32901
407–728–8081
Fax: 407–725–6315
sales@tach.net
http://www.tach.net/

TANet

Computer Center, Ministry of Education
12th Floor, Number 106
Sec. 2, Hoping East Road
Taipei, Taiwan
Attn: Chen Wen-Sung
886–2–7377010
Fax: 886–2–7377043
nisc@twnmoe10.edu.tw
http://www.edu.tw/

Teleport

Beaverton, OR
503–223–4245
info@teleport.com
http://www.teleport.com/

TerraNet, Inc.

729 Boylston Street, Floor 5
Boston, MA 02116
617–450–9000
sales@terra.net
http://www.terra.net/

Texas Metronet

1701 W. Euless Blvd.
Metro Center, Suites 130, 131b
Euless, TX 76040–6819
214–705–2900
Fax: 817–267–2400
info@metronet.com
http://www.metronet.com/

UltraNet Communications, Inc.

910 Boston Post Road, Suite 220
Marlboro, MA 01752
508–229–8400
info@ultranet.com
http://www.ultranet.com/

UniComp Technologies International Corporation

15851 Dallas Parkway, Suite 946
Dallas, TX 75248
214–663–3155
Fax: 214–663–3170
info@unicomp.net
http://www.unicomp.net/

UUNET Canada Inc.

1 Yonge Street
Suite 1801
Toronto, Ontario, M5E 1W7
Canada
416–368–6621
Fax: 416–369–0515
info@uunet.ca
http://www.uunet.ca/services/

UUNET Technologies, Inc.

3060 Williams Drive
Fairfax, VA 22031–4648
800–488–6383
703–206–5600
Fax: 703–206–5601
info@uu.net
http://www.alter.net/

Vector Internet Services

12 South 6th Street
Minneapolis, MN 55402
612–288–0880
Fax: 612–288–0889
info@visi.com
http://www.visi.com/

Vnet Internet Access, Inc.

PO Box 31474
Charlotte, NC 28231
800–377–3282
info@vnet.net
http://www.vnet.net

WestNet Internet Services

Westchester County, NY
914–967–7816
chris@WestNet.com
http://www.westnet.com/

Water Wheel Systems

Marlton, NJ
609–596–0032
info@waterw.com
http://www.waterw.com/

Whole Earth 'Lectronic Link (WELL)

27 Gate Five Road
Sausalito, CA 94965
415–332–4335
info@well.sf.ca.us
http://www.well.sf.ca.us/

WIDE

c/o Prof. Jun Murai
KEIO University
5322 Endo, Fujisawa, 252
Japan
81–466–47–5111 ext. 3330
jun@wide.ad.jp
http://www.wide.ad.jp/

Wimsey Information Services Inc.

8523 Commerce Court
Burnaby, BC V5N 4A3
Canada
604–257–1111
Fax: 604–257–1110
info@wimsey.com
http://www.wimsey.com/wimsey/

@wizard.com

Las Vegas, NV
702–871–4461
Fax: 702–871–4249
gajake@wizard.com
http://www.wizard.com/

WombatNet

236 Hamilton Avenue
Palo Alto, CA 94301
415–462–8800
Fax: 415–462–8804
info@batnet.com
http://www.batnet.com/

The World

Software Tool & Die
1330 Beacon Street
Brookline, MA 02146
617–739–0202
office@world.std.com
http://world.std.com/

World Web Limited

906 King Street
Alexandria, VA 22314
support@worldweb.net
http://www.worldweb.net/

WorldWide Access

P.O. Box 285
Vernon Hills, IL 60061–0285
708–367–1870
Fax: 708–367–1872
http://www.wwa.com/

The Xensei Corporation

Boston South Shore area
617–376–6342
info@xensei.com
http://www.xensei.com/

XNet Information Systems

3080 E. Ogden Ave. , #202
Lisle, IL 60532
708–983–6064
Fax: 708–983–6879
info@xnet.com
http://www.xnet.com/

Zilker Internet Park

1106 Clayton Lane, Suite 500W
Austin, TX 78723
512–206–3850
Fax: 512–206–3852
support@zilker.net
http://www.zilker.net

zNET

777 South Pacific Coast Highway
Suite 204
Solana Beach, CA 92075
619–755–7772
Fax: 619–755–8149
info@znet.com
http://www.znet.com/

GLOSSARY

ACK

Acknowledgment. A message sent to indicate that data has been received.

anchor

One of the ends of a hypertext link.

anonymous FTP

A mechanism that allows public files to be copied from systems on the Internet without having a login account on the system. It uses the login name "anonymous" with a password of "guest" or the e-mail address of the person using anonymous login. Browsers use anonymous FTP when an FTP URL is chosen.

ASCII

American Standard Code for Information Interchange. It is a 7-bit code that can represent up to 128 characters. Appendix B contains a list of ASCII characters.

attribute

An optional indicator that can be added to markup tags in order to specify a specific variation in the way the tag is displayed.

browser

An application used to display HTML documents. Browsers may be used to display local HTML documents or to retrieve documents across the Internet. Some popular browsers are Netscape Navigator and NCSA Mosaic.

cello

Along with NCSA Mosaic, one of the first graphical browsers available for Windows. It was created at the Cornell Legal Information Institute (LII).

CERN

European Center for Particle Physics, located in Geneva, Switzerland. Birthplace of the Web.

CGI

Common Gateway Interface. An interface for running external programs or scripts under an information server, such as a Web server. A common use of a CGI script is handling data from HTML forms.

clickable image

See Imagemap.

client

A general term for a computer or application that can access and retrieve information from a server computer. A Web client is usually called a Web browser.

container

See Markup Tag.

CSLIP

Compressed SLIP. See the entry for SLIP.

dial-up

A connection made between machines using phone lines and modems.

DTD

Data Type Definition for the HyperText Markup Language; provides a formal description of HTML with respect to SGML.

element

A portion of an HTML document delineated by markup tags.

entity

An HTML symbol representing a special character. A list of ISO character entities may be found in Appendix B.

e-mail address

The address that is used to send electronic mail to a specified destination. For example, Vivian's e-mail address is "vivian@catalog.com".

FAQ

Frequently Asked Questions. List of frequently asked questions and their answers.

finger

An application that shows information about all of the users logged on to a system. It can also display information about a particular user. It typically shows full name, last login time, idle time, terminal line, and terminal location (where applicable). It may also display plan and project files left by the user.

form

Fill-out forms are HTML tags that were added to HTML 2.0, which enable documents to display interactive elements used on forms, such as radio buttons, checkboxes, and text-entry boxes.

FTP

File Transfer Protocol. The protocol that defines the way in which files are exchanged around the Internet. FTP also refers to the name of the application that uses the FTP protocol.

FYI

For Your Information. FYI also represents a series of informational documents about the Internet published by the Internet Engineering Task Force (IETF).

gateway

A program or device that passes information between networks or applications.

GIF

Graphic Interchange Format. An image storage format developed by Compuserve. It is the most widely supported image format on the Web.

Gopher

A menu-driven information service developed at the University of Minnesota that makes information across the Internet available through a single application. Gopher clients can get information from any accessible Gopher server, providing the user with a single "Gopher space" of information.

head

The beginning of an HTML document. The head portion of an HTML document should contain the document's title.

host

A computer; usually one that is connected to a network.

home page

A browser's home page refers to the first document that is loaded when the browser is started up. A user's personal home page refers to a Web page that describes and introduces that individual. A company or organization home page is its top-level or starting Web page.

hostname

The name given to a computer.

HTML

HyperText Markup Language. The language in which Web documents are written; what this book is about.

HTTP

HyperText Transfer Protocol. The protocol used to transfer HTML documents on the Web.

hotlist

The term used in Mosaic to describe the list of URLs that it remembers; also known as a bookmark list.

hypermedia

Hypermedia is hypertext which may include nontext elements such as images, video and sound. The Web is a hypermedia system.

hypertext

A hypertext document is a document that contains links to other parts of the document or to other documents. Users can select hypertext links in order to view documents in a nonlinear and individual way. The term was coined by Ted Nelson in 1965.

IETF

Internet Engineering Task Force. The technical group that works on protocol standards used on the Internet.

image map

An image map is a graphical image containing "hot spots." When a hot spot is clicked on by a user, the browser loads the corresponding document.

Interlaced GIF

The scanlines in an interlaced GIF have been rearranged so that when it is viewed in a browser with appropriate support, it will first appear with poor resolution and then, over time, improves in resolution until the entire image is loaded. This is a useful technique for giving users a quick impression of the image, without having to wait for it to be entirely loaded.

inline image

Inline images in HTML documents are images that appear as part of the document rather than shown by an external viewer.

internet

While an internet is a network, the term "internet" is usually used to refer to a collection of networks interconnected with routers.

Internet

(Note the capital "I.") The Internet is the largest internet in the world.

internet address

An IP address that uniquely identifies a node on an internet. An Internet address (capital "I") uniquely identifies a node on the Internet.

Internet Relay Chat (IRC)

A worldwide "party line" protocol that allows one to converse with other people on the Internet in real time via typed comments.

IP address

The 32-bit address defined by the Internet Protocol in STD 5, RFC 791. It is usually represented in dotted decimal notation; for example, 10.0.0.51.

ISO

International Organization for Standardization. An international standards body that defines many technical standards.

JPEG

Joint Photographic Experts Group. A standard format for image storage created by this group. It is a popular image storage format on the Web.

knowbot

A knowbot (or softbot) are programs that wander the Web collecting document titles and URLs. These are then indexed and can be searched by users.

line-mode browser

A nongraphical Web browser. These browsers may be used on dumb terminals. Although they cannot display graphics, most of the other features in a graphics-based browser may still be accessed with this type of browser. Lynx is one of the most popular browsers of this type.

link

A link (or hyperlink) is the pointer in a hypertext document that points to another location or another document.

Lynx

A line-mode browser developed at the University of Kansas. Versions are available for many platforms, including DOS.

mail gateway

A computer that connects two or more electronic mail systems (including dissimilar mail systems) and transfers messages between them.

mail server

A software program that distributes files or information in response to requests sent via e-mail. Internet examples include Almanac and netlib. Mail servers have also been used in Bitnet to provide FTP-like services.

mailing list

A list of e-mail addresses used to send e-mail messages to groups of people. Generally, a special-interest group mailing list is used to discuss a specific topic.

markup language

A language that is used to specify document formats by embedding tags within the document. These tags are then interpreted by browsers in order to properly display the document.

MIME

Multipurpose Internet Mail Extensions. An extension to Internet e-mail which provides the ability to transfer nontextual data, such as graphics, audio and fax. It is defined in RFC 1341.

Mosaic

One of the most popular Web browsers. The first widely used graphical browser. See also NCSA.

MPEG

Motion Picture Experts Group. One of the most widely used formats for storing video on the Internet.

NCSA

National Center for Supercomputing Applications based at the University of Illinois. This is where NCSA Mosaic was developed.

netiquette

A pun on "etiquette" referring to proper behavior on a network.

Netnews

A bulletin board system.

NNTP

Network News Transfer Protocol. The protocol used to transfer network news. It is defined in RFC 977.

OS

Operating System. The program that controls a computer's hardware. Operating systems typically control the use of the CPU (through a scheduler), memory, and peripheral devices (through device drivers). User applications send requests to the operating system to access the computer.

Perl

Practical Extraction and Report Language. It is an interpreted language created by Larry Wall. Originally based on UNIX systems, it is now available on other platforms, including DOS. A number of useful HTML filters have been written in Perl.

PPP

Point-to-Point Protocol—defined in RFC 1171. It provides a method for transmitting packets over serial point-to-point links.

POP

Post Office Protocol. A protocol designed to allow single user hosts to read mail from a server. There are three versions: POP, POP2 and POP3. Later versions are not compatible with earlier versions.

post

To send a message to a newsgroup or e-mail list. Also, a method for accessing a CGI application.

protocol

A standard communication format allowing networked computers to exchange information. Protocols are developed for each kind of information exchange; for example, electronic mail uses the SMTP protocol, and the Web uses, among others, the HTTP protocol.

proxy server

A proxy server acts by keeping local copies of documents requested by users. When a local user requests a document, the proxy server is first consulted to see if a copy is held there. If it is, the user receives the document much more quickly than were it remotely retrieved.

Quicktime

A digital video and audio standard developed by Apple Computer.

RFC

Request For Comments. A document series, begun in 1969, which describes the Internet suite of protocols and related experiments. Not all (in fact, very few) RFCs describe Internet standards, but all Internet standards are written up as RFCs.

RFC 822

The Internet standard format for electronic mail message. headers. Mail experts often refer to "822 messages." The name comes from "RFC 822," which contains the specification (STD 11, RFC 822). 822 format was previously known as 733 format.

RFC 1392

Internet Glossary. If you run across an Internet-related term that isn't defined here, check the Internet Glossary. It is available on internic.net in /pub/rfc/rfc1392.txt

robot

See knowbot.

server

A program that handles certain types of requests on a continuous basis. For example, a mailing list server handles requests for list subscriptions and may also handle archive file requests from list members.

SGML

Standard Generalized Markup Language. SGML is a broad language used to define specific markup languages. HTML is a particular application of SGML.

signature

The three- or four-line message at the bottom of a piece of e-mail or a Usenet article which identifies the sender. Many mail programs allow you to setup a signature and automatically attach it to all the messages that you send. Long signatures (over five lines) are generally frowned upon.

SLIP

Serial Line IP. A protocol used to run IP over serial lines, such as telephone circuits or RS-232 cables, interconnecting two systems. SLIP is defined in RFC 1055.

SMTP

Simple Mail Transfer Protocol. A protocol defined in STD 10, RFC 821, used to transfer electronic mail between computers. It is a server-to-server protocol, so other protocols are used to access the messages.

spider

See knowbot.

tag

See markup language.

TCP/IP Protocol Suite

Transmission Control Protocol over Internet Protocol. This is a common shorthand which refers to the suite of transport and application protocols which runs over IP.

Telnet

Telnet is the Internet standard protocol for remote terminal connection service. It is defined in STD 8, RFC 854, and extended with options by many other RFCs.

UNIX

One of the most popular operating systems in use on the Internet today.

URL

Uniform Resource Locator. The address for a document on the Web. The format for a URL is

```
protocol://pathname
```

URN

Uniform Resource Name.

Usenet

A collection of thousands of topically named newsgroups, the computers which run the protocols, and the people who read and submit Usenet news. Not all Internet hosts subscribe to Usenet, and not all Usenet hosts are on the Internet.

viewer

A special-purpose application program for displaying data in specific formats. For example, a GIF viewer is used to display GIF images.

WAIS

Wide Area Information Servers. A distributed information service which offers simple natural language input, indexed searching for fast retrieval, and a "relevance feedback" mechanism which allows the results of initial searches to influence future searches.

whois

An Internet program which allows users to query databases of people and other Internet entities, such as domains, networks, and hosts. The original whois databases are kept at the Internet Network Information Center (NIC) or Data Defense Network (NIC) depending on what you need, but many companies and educational institutions also make whois databases available now. The information for people shows a person's company name, address, phone number and e-mail address.

WWW

World Wide Web (W3). A hypertext-based, distributed information system created by researchers at CERN in Switzerland. Users may create, edit or browse hypertext documents.

Zine

On-line magazine.

INDEX

F

G

H

Ozone Books:
 company overview, 178, 180
 company summary, 179
 contact information, 179-80
 logo, 178, 180
 order form, 181-88
 page divisions, 180
 top-level page design, 178, 180-81

P

P and /P tags, 21-22
Pacific Information eXchange, Inc. NETwork (PIXINET), 280
Page design/layout, 151-52
 footer elements, 152
 header elements, 151
Panix Public Access Unix, 279
Paragraph styles, 254
 RTFTOHTM, 253
Paragraph tags (<P> and </P>), 21-22
parmark, .PTag table, 249
Password fields, 94-95
Pavillion Internet, 279
PBMPLUS'PBM format, 69
PCX image, 69
Pegasus Networks, 280
Performance Systems International, Inc. (PSI), 279
Period (.), in URLs, 49
Perl (Practical Extraction and Report Language), 294
Personal home pages, 163-77
 announcing, 258
 Kelly Kayaker's home page, 166-69
  document, 169-73
  guest book, 173-74
 Mimi's home page, 175-77
-P extension, RTFTOHTM, 253
PGM format, 69
Physical style tags, 37-40
PICT image, file extension, 61
PIPEX, 280
Planet Access Networks, 280
Plus (+), in URLs, 49
.PMatch table, 248, 251, 252
 sample entries, 251
Pointers, 82
Point-to-Point Protocol (PPP), 291
PolyForm, xxxvii, 109-21, 204-5
 Beeper22, 117
 errors, 120-21
 example, 117-20

existing form, linking to, 116
features of, 109
form, creating, 115-16
icon, 110
installing, 110
online help system, 117
PolyForm Window, 112
registering, 121
scripts, 112-16
 creating, 115-16
 mail options, 114-15
 object returned to client, 114
 output file, 113
 script name, 113
setup, 111-12
 E-mail Return Address, 111
 HTML Editor, 112
 Logs Directory, 112
 Mail Server Address or Name, 111
 Server Domain Name, 111
 Text Editor, 111-12
WGGSETUP, 110
 files installed by, 110
POP (Post Office Protocol), 294
Portal Communications, Inc., 280
Post, defined, 294
POST method, 107
 forms, 88
PostScript file, file extension, 61
Power Net, 280
PPM format, 69
PPP (Point-to-Point Protocol), 291
P and /P tags, future versions of, 22
Preformatted text, markup tag, 31-33
PRE tag, 31-33, 61, 128
"Previous" button, 158
Price, HTML editors, 218
Protocols, 6, 50, 295
Proxy server, 295
PTagName, .PMatch table, 251
.PTag table, 248, 249-50, 252
 sample entry, 250, 252

Q

QuakeNet Internet Services, 280
Quarterdeck Mosaic, 11
QUERY_STRING environment variable, 107
QuickCam, 82

LICENSE AGREEMENT AND LIMITED WARRANTY

READ THE FOLLOWING TERMS AND CONDITIONS CAREFULLY BEFORE OPENING THIS CD PACKAGE. THIS LEGAL DOCUMENT IS AN AGREEMENT BETWEEN YOU AND PRENTICE-HALL, INC. (THE "COMPANY"). BY OPENING THIS SEALED CD PACKAGE, YOU ARE AGREEING TO BE BOUND BY THESE TERMS AND CONDITIONS. IF YOU DO NOT AGREE WITH THESE TERMS AND CONDITIONS, DO NOT OPEN THE CD PACKAGE. PROMPTLY RETURN THE UNOPENED CD PACKAGE AND ALL ACCOMPANYING ITEMS TO THE PLACE YOU OBTAINED THEM FOR A FULL REFUND OF ANY SUMS YOU HAVE PAID.

1.   **GRANT OF LICENSE:** In consideration of your purchase of this book, and your agreement to abide by the terms and conditions of this Agreement, the Company grants to you a nonexclusive right to use and display the copy of the enclosed software program (hereinafter the "SOFTWARE") on a single computer (i.e., with a single CPU) at a single location so long as you comply with the terms of this Agreement. The Company reserves all rights not expressly granted to you under this Agreement.

2.   **OWNERSHIP OF SOFTWARE:** You own only the magnetic or physical media (the enclosed CD) on which the SOFTWARE is recorded or fixed, but the Company and the software developers retain all the rights, title, and ownership to the SOFTWARE recorded on the original CD copy(ies) and all subsequent copies of the SOFTWARE, regardless of the form or media on which the original or other copies may exist. This license is not a sale of the original SOFTWARE or any copy to you.

3.   **COPY RESTRICTIONS:** This SOFTWARE and the accompanying printed materials and user manual (the "Documentation") are the subject of copyright. The individual programs on the CD are copyrighted by the authors of each program. Some of the programs on the CD include separate licensing agreements. If you intend to use one of these programs, you must read and follow its accompanying license agreement. If you intend to use the trial version of Internet Chameleon, you must read and agree to the terms of the notice regarding fees on the back cover of this book. You may not copy the Documentation or the SOFTWARE, except that you may make a single copy of the SOFTWARE for backup or archival purposes only. You may be held legally responsible for any copying or copyright infringement which is caused or encouraged by your failure to abide by the terms of this restriction.

4.   **USE RESTRICTIONS:** You may not network the SOFTWARE or otherwise use it on more than one computer or computer terminal at the same time. You may physically transfer the SOFTWARE from one computer to another provided that the SOFTWARE is used on only one computer at a time. You may not distribute copies of the SOFTWARE or Documentation to others. You may not reverse engineer, disassemble, decompile, modify, adapt, translate, or create derivative works based on the SOFTWARE or the Documentation without the prior written consent of the Company.

5.   **TRANSFER RESTRICTIONS:** The enclosed SOFTWARE is licensed only to you and may not be transferred to any one else without the prior written consent of the Company. Any unauthorized transfer of the SOFTWARE shall result in the immediate termination of this Agreement.

6.   **TERMINATION:** This license is effective until terminated. This license will terminate automatically without notice from the Company and become null and void if you fail to comply with any provisions or limitations of this license. Upon termination, you shall destroy the Documentation and all copies of the SOFTWARE. All provisions of this Agreement as to warranties, limitation of liability, remedies or damages, and our ownership rights shall survive termination.

7.   **MISCELLANEOUS:** This Agreement shall be construed in accordance with the laws of the United States of America and the State of New York and shall benefit the Company, its affiliates, and assignees.

8.   **LIMITED WARRANTY AND DISCLAIMER OF WARRANTY:** The Company warrants that the SOFTWARE, when properly used in accordance with the Documentation, will operate in substantial con-

formity with the description of the SOFTWARE set forth in the Documentation. The Company does not warrant that the SOFTWARE will meet your requirements or that the operation of the SOFTWARE will be uninterrupted or error-free. The Company warrants that the media on which the SOFTWARE is delivered shall be free from defects in materials and workmanship under normal use for a period of thirty (30) days from the date of your purchase. Your only remedy and the Company's only obligation under these limited warranties is, at the Company's option, return of the warranted item for a refund of any amounts paid by you or replacement of the item. Any replacement of SOFTWARE or media under the warranties shall not extend the original warranty period. The limited warranty set forth above shall not apply to any SOFTWARE which the Company determines in good faith has been subject to misuse, neglect, improper installation, repair, alteration, or damage by you. EXCEPT FOR THE EXPRESSED WARRANTIES SET FORTH ABOVE, THE COMPANY DISCLAIMS ALL WARRANTIES, EXPRESS OR IMPLIED, INCLUDING WITHOUT LIMITATION, THE IMPLIED WARRANTIES OF MERCHANTABILITY AND FITNESS FOR A PARTICULAR PURPOSE. EXCEPT FOR THE EXPRESS WARRANTY SET FORTH ABOVE, THE COMPANY DOES NOT WARRANT, GUARANTEE, OR MAKE ANY REPRESENTATION REGARDING THE USE OR THE RESULTS OF THE USE OF THE SOFTWARE IN TERMS OF ITS CORRECTNESS, ACCURACY, RELIABILITY, CURRENTNESS, OR OTHERWISE.

IN NO EVENT, SHALL THE COMPANY OR ITS EMPLOYEES, AGENTS, SUPPLIERS, OR CONTRACTORS BE LIABLE FOR ANY INCIDENTAL, INDIRECT, SPECIAL, OR CONSEQUENTIAL DAMAGES ARISING OUT OF OR IN CONNECTION WITH THE LICENSE GRANTED UNDER THIS AGREEMENT, OR FOR LOSS OF USE, LOSS OF DATA, LOSS OF INCOME OR PROFIT, OR OTHER LOSSES, SUSTAINED AS A RESULT OF INJURY TO ANY PERSON, OR LOSS OF OR DAMAGE TO PROPERTY, OR CLAIMS OF THIRD PARTIES, EVEN IF THE COMPANY OR AN AUTHORIZED REPRESENTATIVE OF THE COMPANY HAS BEEN ADVISED OF THE POSSIBILITY OF SUCH DAMAGES. IN NO EVENT SHALL LIABILITY OF THE COMPANY FOR DAMAGES WITH RESPECT TO THE SOFTWARE EXCEED THE AMOUNTS ACTUALLY PAID BY YOU, IF ANY, FOR THE SOFTWARE.

SOME JURISDICTIONS DO NOT ALLOW THE LIMITATION OF IMPLIED WARRANTIES OR LIABILITY FOR INCIDENTAL, INDIRECT, SPECIAL, OR CONSEQUENTIAL DAMAGES, SO THE ABOVE LIMITATIONS MAY NOT ALWAYS APPLY. THE WARRANTIES IN THIS AGREEMENT GIVE YOU SPECIFIC LEGAL RIGHTS AND YOU MAY ALSO HAVE OTHER RIGHTS WHICH VARY IN ACCORDANCE WITH LOCAL LAW.

ACKNOWLEDGMENT

YOU ACKNOWLEDGE THAT YOU HAVE READ THIS AGREEMENT, UNDERSTAND IT, AND AGREE TO BE BOUND BY ITS TERMS AND CONDITIONS. YOU ALSO AGREE THAT THIS AGREEMENT IS THE COMPLETE AND EXCLUSIVE STATEMENT OF THE AGREEMENT BETWEEN YOU AND THE COMPANY AND SUPERSEDES ALL PROPOSALS OR PRIOR AGREEMENTS, ORAL, OR WRITTEN, AND ANY OTHER COMMUNICATIONS BETWEEN YOU AND THE COMPANY OR ANY REPRESENTATIVE OF THE COMPANY RELATING TO THE SUBJECT MATTER OF THIS AGREEMENT.

Should you have any questions concerning this Agreement or if you wish to contact the Company for any reason, please contact in writing at the address below.

Robin Short
Prentice Hall PTR
One Lake Street
Upper Saddle River, New Jersey 07458

SOFTWARE LICENSE for Microsoft® Internet Assistant for Word for Windows®

1. GRANT OF LICENSE. Prentice Hall PTR (COMPANY) grants to you a nonexclusive, royalty-free right to make and use an unlimited number of copies of the software provided with this Agreement ("Software"), provided that each copy shall be a true and complete copy, including all copyright and trademark notices.

2. COPYRIGHT. The SOFTWARE is owned by COMPANY or its suppliers and is protected by United States copyright laws and international treaty provisions. Therefore, you must treat the SOFTWARE like any other copyrighted material (e.g., a book or musical recording) *except* that you may either (a) make one copy of the SOFTWARE solely for backup or archival purposes, or (b) transfer the SOFTWARE to a single hard disk provided you keep the original solely for backup or archival purposes.

3. OTHER RESTRICTIONS. This License is your proof of license to exercise the rights granted herein and must be retained by you. You may not reverse engineer, decompile, or disassemble the SOFTWARE, except to the extent the foregoing restriction is expressly prohibited by applicable law.

LIMITED WARRANTY

NO WARRANTIES. COMPANY expressly disclaims any warranty for the SOFTWARE. The SOFTWARE and any related documentation is provided "as is" without warranty of any kind, either express or implied, including, without limitation, the implied warranties of merchantability, fitness for a particular purpose, or noninfringement. The entire risk rising out of the use or performance of the SOFTWARE remains with you.

NO LIABILITY FOR CONSEQUENTIAL DAMAGES. In no event shall COMPANY or its suppliers be liable for any damages whatsoever (including, without limitation, damages for loss of business profits, business interruption, loss of business information, or any other pecuniary loss) arising out of the use of or inability to use this COMPANY product, even if COMPANY has been advised of the possibility of such damages. Because some states/jurisdictions do not allow the exclusion or limitation of liability for consequential or incidental damages, the above limitation may not apply to you.

U.S. GOVERNMENT RESTRICTED RIGHTS

The SOFTWARE and documentation are provided with RESTRICTED RIGHTS. Use, duplication, or disclosure by the Government is subject to restrictions as set forth in subparagraph (c)(1)(ii) of The Rights in Technical Data and Computer Software clause at DFARS 252.227-7013 or subparagraphs (c)(1) and (2) of the Commercial Computer Software-Restricted Rights at 48 CFR 52.227-19, as applicable.

EXHIBIT C

Notice regarding Microsoft® Internet Assistant for Word for Windows®

This program was reproduced by Prentice Hall PTR [COMPANY] under a special arrangement with Microsoft Corporation. For this reason, [COMPANY] is responsible for the product warranty and for support. If your CD is defective, please return it to [COMPANY], which will arrange for its replacement. PLEASE DO NOT RETURN IT TO MICROSOFT CORPORATION. Any product support will be provided, if at all, by [COMPANY]. PLEASE DO NOT CONTACT MICROSOFT CORPORATION FOR PRODUCT SUPPORT. End users of this Microsoft program shall not be considered "registered owners" of a Microsoft product and therefore shall not be eligible for upgrades, promotions or other benefits available to "registered owners" of Microsoft products.